Decision Making, Assessment and Risk in Social Work

Sara Miller McCune founded SAGE Publishing in 1965 to support the dissemination of usable knowledge and educate a global community. SAGE publishes more than 1000 journals and over 800 new books each year, spanning a wide range of subject areas. Our growing selection of library products includes archives, data, case studies and video. SAGE remains majority owned by our founder and after her lifetime will become owned by a charitable trust that secures the company's continued independence.

Los Angeles | London | New Delhi | Singapore | Washington DC | Melbourne

Decision Making, Assessment and Risk in Social Work

BRIAN J. TAYLOR

3rd Edition

⊙SAGE | *m* LearningMatters

Learning Matters
An imprint of SAGE Publications Ltd
1 Oliver's Yard
55 City Road
London EC1Y 1SP

SAGE Publications Inc.
2455 Teller Road
Thousand Oaks, California 91320

SAGE Publications India Pvt Ltd
B 1/I 1 Mohan Cooperative Industrial Area
Mathura Road
New Delhi 110 044

SAGE Asia-Pacific Pte Ltd
3 Church Street
#10-04 Samsung Hub
Singapore 049483

© Brian J. Taylor 2017

First published as Professional Decision Making in
Social Work in 2010
Second edition published as Professional Decision
Making and Risk in Social Work in 2013
Third edition published in 2017

Editor: Kate Keers
Production controller: Chris Marke
Project management: Swales & Willis Ltd, Exeter,
Devon
Marketing manager: Camille Richmond
Cover design: Wendy Scott
Typeset by: C&M Digitals (P) Ltd, Chennai, India
Printed by CPI Group (UK) Ltd, Croydon, CR0 4YY

Library of Congress Control Number: 2017931588

British Library Cataloguing in Publication Data

A catalogue record for this book is available from the
British Library

ISBN: 978-1-5264-0104-5
ISBN: 978-1-5264-0105-2 (pbk)

At SAGE we take sustainability seriously. Most of our products are printed in the UK using FSC papers and boards.
When we print overseas we ensure sustainable papers are used as measured by PREPS grading system.
We undertake an annual audit to monitor our sustainability.

Contents

Foreword   vii

About the author   ix

Preface to the third edition   xi

Acknowledgements   xiii

Introduction   1

1 A framework for decisions,
  assessment and risk   9

2 Client decisions, perspectives,
  emotions and crises   26

3 Legal aspects of decisions,
  assessment and risk   48

4 Assessment, risk assessment and
  decision support systems   70

5 Professional judgement, bias and
  using knowledge in assessment
  and decisions   91

6 Judgements about safeguarding
  and service eligibility, and
  predicting harm   111

7 Risk-taking care choices: values,
  gains and hazards   137

8 Collaboration, communication and contest in assessment, risk and decision processes 159

9 Dynamics of practice: managing risk, re-assessing and changing your mind 178

10 Managing decisions, assessment and risk: support, blame and learning 194

Conclusion 213

Appendix 1 Pointers in designing or completing an assessment to inform a decision in uncertainty 221

Appendix 2 Supported decision tool 223

Appendix 3 Professional Capabilities Framework 225

Glossary of terms 226

References 232

Index 248

Foreword

All the texts in the post-qualifying social work practice series have been written by people with passion for excellence in social work practice. They are written primarily for social workers who are undertaking post-qualifying social work awards but will also be useful to any social worker who wants to consider up-to-date practice issues.

Brian Taylor has made an enormous contribution to the social work profession over the years and this third edition of his text is another excellent example of his contribution. Fundamentally, social work practice is all about making decisions, assessment and managing risk and this text is a gold mine of advice and support to all social work professionals who seek to serve their clients in the very best way possible. Brian's passion for research and practice excellence is so evident through this text and I warmly commend it to all.

The books in this series are also of value to social work students as they are written to inform, inspire and develop social work practice.

Professor Keith Brown
Series Editor
Director of the National Centre for
Post-Qualifying Social Work and Professional Practice
Bournemouth University

About the author

Brian Taylor is Professor of Social Work at Ulster University, where he has a lead role in post-qualifying education and training. His research and teaching interests are in decision making, assessment, risk and evidence-based practice, and he leads a research cluster focusing on this area (**www.ulster.ac.uk/dare**). He previously spent 12 years as a practitioner and manager in social work, residential care, primary school teaching and youth work. He worked for 15 years in social work training, and organisation development in health and social care, including three years as a project manager implementing new children's legislation. His doctorate was on risk and decision making in community care and he had a lead role in developing the Northern Ireland Single Assessment Tool for the health and social care of older people. Brian has undertaken research and teaching for over 20 years on the related topics of assessment, risk and decision making. His is an author of *Understanding and Using Research in Social Work* and editor of *Working with Aggression and Risk in Social Work*, both published by Sage. **www.ulster.ac.uk/staff/bj.taylor.html**

Preface to the third edition

No writer writes out of his having found the answer to the problem; he writes rather out of his having the problem and wanting a solution.

(May, 1969, p170)

Four years have passed since the second edition of this book and it seems timely to undertake a revision. The context of social work is ever-evolving, particularly in relation to the challenges of risk; our understanding of professional judgement and decision making; the development of assessment processes; and gradually increasing respect for social workers as expert witnesses in court proceedings. A recent UK government report highlighted the need for the profession to focus on professional judgement (Kirkman and Melrose, 2014). This is a timely contribution to stimulate our research and teaching on this topic, and a valuable complement to our stronger engagement with issues of assessment, risk and decision processes.

This third edition brings these three elements together more cohesively than the previous editions. New material has been added on assessment tools and analysis in assessment; use of knowledge in decisions in the context of professional working relationships; client involvement in assessment, risk-taking and decision making including 'problem solving'; impact of the Human Rights Act on decisions by public sector social workers; continuing developments in our limited knowledge of risk factors, and the inclusion of mitigating and desistance factors; the distinction between risk and uncertainty; decision trees; web-based knowledge supports; emerging conceptualisations of *risk* relevant to how we communicate about risk with clients, families and other professionals; supervision as a process for managing risks and decisions; connecting the time process in managing risks, decisions and re-assessment; skills in leading multi-professional decision-making processes; and principles for organisations in carrying out their responsibilities for managing risk and decisions.

In particular, this edition includes some preliminary comments on the emerging concept of *psycho-social rationality* to encompass the middle ground for conceptualising professional judgement between comprehensive actuarial (statistical prediction) models and purely narrative (descriptive) approaches. This encapsulates the variety of emerging *heuristic* (rule-of-thumb, shortcut) models as well as the well-known example of a *fuzzy logic* model developed by Paul Brearley (1982). Most of the material on legal aspects has been brought together into one chapter, and this now includes a section on legal aspects of risk communication. In response to reader comments there is now more visual material, particularly in the first chapter.

The content has been developed in relation to assessment as it relates to risk and decision making, and including strengths as well as needs and context dimensions. 'Assessment' is a common way in which social workers conceptualise some key activities, normally for the overarching purpose of making a professional judgement leading to a decision; and the context is often risk, or uncertainty. The title of the book has been adapted from *Professional Decision Making and Risk in Social Work* to *Decision Making, Assessment and Risk in Social Work*, to make these connections more explicit. This connection reflects the focus of the Decisions, Assessment and Risk Special Interest Group of the European Social Work Research Association. It also reflects the focus of the biennial international symposium in Belfast, Northern Ireland, on *Decisions, Assessment, Risk and Evidence in Social Work* (**www.ulster.ac.uk/ dare**), which has been gathering momentum since 2010. Some chapter titles have been modified to reflect the expanded content, and the sequence of some material has been amended to what I hope is a clearer *framework for risk, assessment and decisions*. The overall balance has been retained, with one chapter (Chapter 10) devoted to professional management of decisions, assessment and risk, and the main focus in the other nine chapters being on practice.

As in the previous editions, the aim has been to keep the text generalisable across countries, jurisdictions and organisational contexts whilst learning the lessons from recent research, theoretical insights, practice developments and tragedies. Care has been taken to ensure that the language is applicable across the wide range of social work client groups, and will prompt reflective practice in different contexts. The examples have been selected to reflect a diversity of practice but essentially to illustrate underlying principles that are applicable across client groups and settings. The book has now been used on post-qualifying courses at a higher specialist level that focused on one particular client group and on qualifying social work courses, as well as in generic post-qualifying courses for newly qualified social workers from which it grew. The aim, as before, is to focus on professional knowledge that can usefully inform practice. I hope that this third edition will support knowledge and skills development in decision making, assessment and risk in the challenging situations in which we operate as social workers for the ultimate benefit of the clients and families who we serve.

Brian Taylor
24 January 2017

Acknowledgements

First, I would like to thank my father, Bernard Taylor, for his example of integrity in every decision that I ever saw him make, and my mother, Lorna Taylor, for her example of creative, purposeful risk-taking in her everyday faith-journey through life. I am grateful to all the clients, teachers, managers and other colleagues from whom I learned the practice of social work. Many thanks to my family, friends and colleagues – too many to mention – for their support and encouragement during the writing of this book.

I am indebted to Professor Michael Donnelly, Centre for Public Health, Queen's University Belfast, for his inspiring encouragement of my research on risk and decision making and to Mr David Carson, Associate, Ulster University and previously Reader in Law and Behavioural Sciences at the University of Portsmouth, for his invigorating enthusiasm in his work on the interface between law and professional risk-taking. I would like to thank Professor Dr Gerd Gigerenzer and his colleagues at the Adaptive Behaviour and Cognition Research Group and the Harding Centre for Risk Literacy at the Max Planck Institute for Human Development in Berlin for their warm welcome and sharing of ideas during my visits. Grateful thanks are due to the *Deutscher Akademischer Austausch Dienst* (German Academic Exchange Service) for the Senior Scholarship which made my first visit possible.

I would like to thank the social workers on post-qualifying courses and other colleagues in practice who shared examples of their judgements, decision making and dilemmas with me. I am grateful for the comments from the two anonymous Sage reviewers and from readers. Their ideas were added into the 'Notes for changes' from my teaching and research (coming to over 60 pages over the years since the second edition!) and have been taken into account in this revision. I am very grateful to a member of the general public who has used services, and colleagues who assisted with the first edition with comments on draft chapters, exercises, bullet lists of pointers and questions, etc., from the perspectives of clients, education and training, information technology, law, management, regulation and research, as well as professional practice. I would particularly like to thank Garth Agnew, Taralisa Allen, Patricia Casey, Eithne Darragh, Helen Gault, Marc Harvey, Jan Houston, Campbell Killick, Marie McCann, Oonagh McGivern, Eileen McKay, Rita McKelvey, Helen McVicker, Jacinta Miller, Stephen Russell, Debbie Stringer and Richard Taylor. Any errors or omissions are, of course, the responsibility of the author.

Very many thanks to Miss Janice McQuilkin, Assistant Subject Librarian at Ulster University, for her help and patience in accessing and referencing legal documents, and to Miss Mabel Stevenson, Research Assistant, for assistance with some graphics. Sincere thanks to Mrs Siobhan Irwin, Mrs Sharon Lucas, Mrs Sue Gamble and Mrs Janice Clayton for loyal administrative support over the years.

I apologise for any omissions to these acknowledgements.

Last, but not least, heartfelt thanks to my wife Mary for her unfailing support, not least during the busy months of pulling together a decade of teaching, research, writing and reflection for the first edition of this book.

Introduction

Much of what social workers do concerns decisions about future courses of action, which puts decision making at the heart of social work as a core professional activity.

(Banks, 2001, p9)

The place of decision making in social work

You are probably in social work – or training for social work – because you want to help people with psycho-social needs. You are probably finding out – rather rapidly – that the job entails a substantial component of assessing situations, weighing up risks and engaging in decision-making processes. Social work intrinsically involves making decisions that impact on the lives of vulnerable people. These decisions have traditionally been about whom amongst so many fellow citizens in need should receive scarce resources, whether these have come from charitable or government sources. As social work has developed an increasing role in protecting the most vulnerable on behalf of society, we have become involved in crucial decisions hinging on the role of the state in intervening in the lives of families to protect individuals. Such decisions may involve high risks, such as continued abuse or the death of a child or a vulnerable adult. These decisions are never easy and there are no simple solutions! Some of the media in some countries are quick to highlight instances where it seems in hindsight that social workers or other professionals might have prevented some harm inflicted by one person on another. There are also lower profile decisions, such as where social workers are supporting someone with a disability, or on hospital discharge, to take steps towards more independent living. Social work decisions span a wide range, from safeguarding through to allocating services and advising clients and families on courses of action to improve their lives.

This book aims to address this central practice issue, namely to improve social work decisions in the context of risk, utilising effective assessment. This is particularly timely as there is now a growing, though still small, body of research developing on risk and decision making in social work, and the work on developing assessment tools continues to grow steadily. The focus of this book reflects the focus of the Decisions, Assessment and Risk Special Interest Group of the European Social Work Research Association. It also reflects the focus of the biennial international symposium in Belfast, Northern Ireland, on *Decisions, Assessment, Risk and Evidence in Social Work* (**www.ulster.ac.uk/dare**), which has been gathering momentum since 2010.

This book responds to the need for greater professionalism in social work, by which we mean a clearer evidence base for the judgements being made in complex, 'risky' situations. In the words of Sir James Munby, President of the Family Division (2013), *Social workers are experts ... Social workers may not be experts for the purposes of FPR Part 25, but that does not mean that they are not experts in every other sense of the word. They are, and we must recognise them and treat them as such* (p3). This sentiment needs to be taken to heart in relation to practice with all client groups, particularly in countries where the profession feels under attack from some of the media and politicians. We are charged with undertaking complex judgement processes – sometimes in situations of high risk, intense emotion and heart-rending moral dilemmas – with limited investment in research and training to support the profession. I hope that this book will help to build confidence that – given the complexity of the work and the limited research base – we are doing a good job in the circumstances. We do, however, need to develop a more cohesive knowledge base founded on robust research and theoretical insights, and building on practice wisdom, in order to improve our knowledge and skills.

This book is about the art and the science of professional judgement. We advocate the use of the most reliable information about the problem, strengths and situation of the client (and, where appropriate, family); the use of the best evidence of the effectiveness of possible interventions and helping processes; a sound knowledge of legislation, regulations, guidance, standards, policies, procedures and the services and mandate of your organisation. Yet there always remains the unknown and unknowable about the client and family dynamics; the as-yet unexplored domains of professional knowledge beyond our current research and theory; the client whose circumstances provoke the journey towards fresh insights that inform future practice. This book draws together ideas from a range of research and theory of decision making, assessment and risk to develop an evidence base to guide professional practice. As a practitioner, you will need to draw upon various sources of professional knowledge – such as law, policy, research, theory, standards, principles and practice wisdom – to inform complex and sensitive judgements and decisions in uncertain ('risky') situations where harm may ensue. Values of the client, our profession, your organisation and society are an intrinsic part of decision making and must be related to these other aspects in decision-making processes. These various strands must be brought together as we participate in organisational and societal decision-making systems, including child protection case conferences, decisions about capacity to consent to care and treatment, panels within organisations to allocate care resources and court hearings. The types of risks and professional dilemmas that are being considered in the writing of this book include:

- **Family and Child Care** – conflict between respect for family life under the Human Rights Act versus the child protection role; families 'dumping' feelings on the social worker because of their protective role;

- **Residential Child Care** – challenge in engaging young people in good decision making and minimising risks such as absconding, drugs, promiscuity, etc.;

- **Child Care Aftercare** – clarifying roles and responsibilities as children reach the age where there are reducing state responsibilities for their care;

- **Children with Disability** – maintaining a good working relationship despite lack of resources that could reduce risks;

- **Mental Health** – making 'best interests' judgements where person lacks capacity, safety planning, seeking to develop recovery models with intrinsic risk-taking; linking risk assessment to care (safety) planning;

- **Learning Disability** – challenge of risks in personal relationships and defining professional responsibilities regarding this;

- **Physical Disability and Sensory Impairment** – balancing aspirations for independence with professional responsibility and expectations of society;

- **Hospital Social Work** – pressures to discharge people despite risks in returning home; and

- **Older People** – judging risks and defining what is 'exceptional' in relation to eligibility criteria for services; making decisions in crisis.

This textbook is written to provide a consolidated framework of knowledge and skills relevant to assessment, professional judgement, decision making and managing risk with diverse client groups. The text is illustrated with examples from family and child care, older people, mental health, disability and criminal justice. The focus is on concepts, principles and processes that are transferable across jurisdictions and organisational arrangements, so specific legislative and government policy references for particular client groups have been kept to a minimum. All chapters are applicable to all client groups, and are intended to help the reader apply the concepts to their own context. The focus is on empowering front-line professionals – through reflective practice – to integrate multiple factors and perspectives into sound problem-solving judgements to support client decision making, safeguarding and gate-keeping decisions. It is increasingly important for social workers to be able to articulate the rationale for their judgements and decisions, drawing on research evidence, theory and the use of robust assessment tools, and relating these to relevant parameters of law, policy and principles. This book assists in that process. Whilst the book cannot provide all the supporting knowledge necessary for any specific decision, it aims to provide a framework for the practitioner to use sound evidence and approaches to inform decision making.

Knowledge and skills for professional practice

This book is written primarily for newly qualified social workers and those in the final stages of qualifying training. It is assumed that the reader has a foundation in the roles and tasks of social work in a democratic society, and knowledge and skills in basic social work helping processes (Taylor and Devine, 1993; Shulman, 2011) applied in contexts including counselling and care planning roles. This book has been written specifically to support social workers undertaking awards within the post-qualifying frameworks for social work in the UK. For Scotland, Wales and Northern Ireland, this book addresses the following post-qualifying requirements:

- competence in working effectively in complex situations (Post-Qualifying Award, Requirement PQ2, *Scotland & Wales (= UK Framework 1990–2007)*);

- competence in exercising the powers and responsibilities of a professional social worker, including the appropriate use of discretion and the management of risk (Post-Qualifying Award, Requirement PQ3, *Scotland & Wales (= UK Framework 1990–2007)*);

- ability to make informed decisions (Post-Qualifying Award, Requirement PQ4, *Scotland & Wales (= UK Framework 1990–2007)*);

- demonstrate consistent and sustained sound judgement and decision making in the context of complexity, risk, uncertainty, conflict and contradiction (*Consolidation Award Requirement 3, Northern Ireland Social Care Council, 2016*);

- use a range of skills and methods of intervention, work effectively and creatively and with initiative in a context of risk, uncertainty, conflict and contradiction where there are complex challenges. Make informed and balanced judgements in the context of relevant policy and legislation (*Specialist Award Requirement 5, Northern Ireland Social Care Council, 2016*);

- work creatively, innovatively and effectively, taking a leading role in the context of risk, uncertainty, conflict and contradiction or where there are complex challenges and a need to make informed, independent and balanced judgements (*Leadership and Strategic Award Requirement 5, Northern Ireland Social Care Council, 2016*).

In terms of the Professional Capabilities Framework (College of Social Work, 2012; see Appendix 3) this will in particular support social workers in their early career after qualifying, including during the Assessed and Supported Year in Employment (undertaken immediately after qualifying in England). In Northern Ireland, this corresponds to the Assessed Year in Employment and the Initial Professional Development Programme which is the first stage of post-qualifying, post-graduate study. Within the Professional Capabilities Framework, during the early stage of their career, social workers are expected particularly to: grow in confidence and independence of judgement; work effectively as an equal with other professionals; take account of risk factors; and make higher quality judgements in situations of increasing complexity, risk, uncertainty and challenge. This text is closely matched to these expectations. This book will assist social workers to demonstrate consistent and sustained sound judgement and decision making in the context of complexity, risk, uncertainty and conflicts of interest. It will assist particularly in:

- reflecting on, and analysis of, practice to inform and provide a rationale for professional decision making (PCF Area 6);

- use of professional judgement and authority to intervene with individuals and families to promote independence, provide support and prevent harm, neglect and abuse (PCF Area 7); and

- applying the range of professional knowledge including social sciences, law and social work practice theory (PCF Area 5).

The final chapter will also contribute particularly to aspects of Area 9 of the Professional Capabilities Framework: to take responsibility for the professional learning and development of others through supervision, leadership and management.

This book addresses skills specified in the National Occupational Standards for Social Work (TOPSS, 2005), in particular Key Role 4: Manage risk to individuals, families, carers, groups, communities, self and colleagues – although this book addresses aspects of Units within all of the Key Roles.

Although written primarily in relation to social work in the UK – and recognising the separate organisation arrangements in England now existing for family and child care social work as distinct from social work with adult client groups – this book takes account of the international perspective on the role of social workers (IASSW and IFSW, 2001). This seems prudent in this age of international mobility, and in order to strengthen the profession in terms of its knowledge base so that it may better serve clients and families. Reference to statutes, national policy and organisational arrangements has been kept to a minimum so that the fundamental principles and core knowledge may be applied in a wide variety of countries and contexts. For other professions, parallels may be drawn as there are many similar issues and areas of knowledge and skill even though some aspects (such as the active interface with the law and engaging family and community resources) may have a higher profile in social work. The main focus of the book is on knowledge and skills for practice. However, all social workers at some stage of their career should engage in teaching, research and leadership of others in some way, as well as in practice. Hence the text has occasional words of encouragement addressed to the practitioner to extend their horizons in the best interests of the profession and of our clients.

Structure of this book

There is a challenge in writing a book (which has a linear sequence of chapters) on this topic, where many dimensions and aspects influence each other in complex ways. The chapters have been sequenced in what seems to be the most logical order, but each chapter might be viewed as illuminating a different aspect rather than as strictly sequential steps in a process. The book begins with an overview of concepts and terminology, and outlines a *decision, assessment and risk model* (Chapter 1) to give a framework for practice. Chapter 2 focuses on the client perspective on care decisions, including crises and emotions, with Chapter 3 outlining legal aspects of decisions, assessment and risk. Chapter 4 highlights the common social worker–client activity of assessment, focusing particularly on assessing risk and its function in relation to professional judgement. Chapter 5 then examines the central activity of professional judgement. Two key types of judgements and decisions in social work are the focus for the following two chapters. Making a safeguarding or service eligibility judgement against threshold criteria is the focus of Chapter 6; making care planning choices where risk-taking is a consideration is the focus of Chapter 7. Social workers often contribute their judgements about risks to collaborative assessment and decision processes with others, and this is the theme in Chapter 8. The book concludes with a chapter on time dimensions of risk and decision making (including re-assessment or 'review') (Chapter 9) and a chapter on managing these various processes of risk, assessment and decisions (Chapter 10). From the perspective of research on human judgement, the material in Chapter 6 is newer and perhaps more complex than that in Chapter 7. As this is essentially a textbook to support professional practice, rather than a text on decision science itself, these chapters have been ordered thus because this sequence reflects the typical flow of the social work process, from assessment against thresholds to care planning choices.

Topics are included where they seem most appropriate, but the reader needs to be aware that there are many interconnections between chapters and it would be tedious if I attempted to highlight them all. As an example, the issue of making a decision on limited information relates to legal aspects of standards of care in emergencies (Chapter 3), the suitability of assessment tools and processes (Chapter 4) and a satisficing decision model about the 'cost' of gathering more information for a fuller assessment on which to base a more robust decision (Chapter 6). Ethical issues are incorporated into all chapters as appropriate. For example, client values and perspectives are central to Chapter 2; avoiding bias is a professional value issue as explored in Chapter 5; and weighing up options in making choices involves values placed on outcomes as discussed in Chapter 7.

By its nature this topic has many interconnections with other sources of knowledge, such as about the needs, social welfare statutes, standards and services for each client group. The reader will need to draw on these as appropriate for their own setting for practice. In particular, there are connections with engaging resistant clients for which the reader is referred to *Working with Aggression and Resistance in Social Work* (Taylor, 2011) and the use of knowledge to inform decisions for which the reader is referred to *Understanding and Using Research in Social Work* (Taylor *et al.*, 2015).

Reflective practice and continuing professional development

This book has been written to support professional social workers in making the best judgements and decisions possible in the light of the knowledge available at the time when carrying out their roles in relation to clients, families and society. The aim is to support the reader in a process of learning by doing, by providing concepts and examples that enable and prompt reflection on your practice. Case studies, research summaries and activities are included to illustrate and support the application of concepts. You will gain more from the book if you take the time to apply the concepts and principles to your own experience. Reflection on practice – informed by insights derived from research, theory, models, statutes, case law, standards, values, guidelines, inquiries, policy and principles – is a key tool for continuing professional development (Brown and Rutter, 2006).

This book provides conceptual models to assist the professional to integrate the multiple complex strands inherent in making decisions. This involves both re-conceptualising tasks that have always been carried out by social workers and also seeking to learn from, and apply, more recent research and theorising. When I first felt the urge to write this book (more than ten years before the first edition appeared!), I hoped that I would be able to present a unified model for decision making in social work, parallel to that which I presented on assessment and care planning in an earlier book with a colleague (Taylor and Devine, 1993). No such unified theory of decision making exists in social work or in the wider world of research and theorising on decisions. So, a range of concepts, tools and insights from research to aid reflection on practice are presented here, drawn from wider decision research and applied to social work. Part of professional knowledge and skill is in selecting an appropriate model for a specific practice situation. This is a source book of key ideas for a creative journey, involving contributing to developing our professional knowledge base as well as creativity in finding ways to engage with and help clients.

It is not possible to be prescriptive about the level of autonomy with which a social worker may make a decision as this varies across jurisdictions, states, cultures and organisations. For example, in parts of the USA it is possible for a social worker to admit a child to care in an emergency on his or her own authority, whereas in the UK a more complex process is followed requiring authorisation by a magistrate or judge, who must be available out-of-hours if necessary. Wise use of supervision (and corresponding levels of autonomy) in relation to decision making and managing risk should also vary with the level of experience of the worker. It is highly desirable that newly qualified social workers have closer supervision of their decision making as they grow during their first year or two to the level of handling more complex work with 'normal' levels of supervision (Taylor *et al.*, 2010). If concepts raised here suggest modifications to the normal levels of delegation of decision making and risk-taking within your organisation, you should discuss the matter with appropriate senior professionals responsible for these systems (through your line manager or professional supervisor) rather than try to change systems unilaterally.

Caveat

This book is for general education, not to provide guidance in specific cases. The purpose of this book is to provide a framework for reflecting on professional practice that will support you in purposefully integrating the diverse aspects of making judgements, managing risk and participating in decision-making processes. Any change in practice that you intend to implement cannot be undertaken in isolation. You need support to implement a new approach, and an organisation requires a degree of uniformity to fulfil its duty to ensure quality of decisions and resource allocation that is appropriate to needs and risks. Ensure that you make good use of professional and line management supervision, and use the policies and procedures of your organisation. References to legal aspects in this book are for general education on principles only, written by a non-lawyer for non-lawyers. In any situation where legal action might be a consideration (of your client or of your organisation), you should consult with your line management and professional supervisor and seek legal advice through appropriate channels.

Terminology

Key terms are discussed in the text at appropriate places; a list is included in the Glossary.

Some social workers in the UK prefer the term *service user* to *client*. Looking at the best evidence I have been able to find, research suggests that this is not a preference of people who come to social workers (Lloyd *et al.*, 2001; Keaney *et al.*, 2004; Covell *et al.*, 2007; Taylor and McKeown, 2013). It may be that the current vogue for the term *service user* in the UK is driven by politicians rather than by people who come into contact with social workers (Heffernan, 2006). The traditional and international term *client* seems to convey better the professional responsibility of the social worker for his or her actions (Seal, 2008, page ix), which is a key focus of this text. On a more personal note, my internet service provider refers to me as a *service user* and for me the term has connotations of a faceless organisation to which I am known primarily by a 30-digit number! To get my needs met, I have to struggle through a fog of jargon and alien procedures. By contrast, the aromatherapist and solicitor that I see on occasion refer to me as their *client*. They have helped me through various stresses and crises of life, and within their own discipline they are each competent and caring about my welfare. I still make the ultimate decision about treatment or action, but as the client I have the support of a confidential professional relationship with each of them. The professional relationship, where the social worker contributes a particular area of knowledge and skills within an ethical framework, remains at the heart of effective social work practice. I would argue that this is better conveyed by the term *client* so that is normally used here, although *patient, survivor, tenant, resident, service user* and *customer* may be used occasionally.

Concluding comments

A short book can give only an overview of this vast and exciting topic. The references to material have been limited to readily available texts and articles that are likely to be of interest to a wide range of social workers. For further study consider also related topics such as those that apply these principles to your own client group; clinical and social care governance; evidence-based practice; social welfare legislation and the statutory duties and powers of social care organisations; standards of central and local government, service commissioning bodies, employers of health and social care staff and professional bodies; health and safety legislation, policy and procedures; decision-making processes, including case conferences, panels, courts, the legal system and legal processes; inter-professional working as it relates to decision making; and decision aids, including assessment tools and computerised systems. This book is designed to support you in that crucial process of conceptualising your professional role and task in making judgements and decisions, so as to continually improve the service we offer for the benefit of clients, families and society.

Chapter 1
A framework for decisions, assessment and risk

Good judgement and quality decisions are two of the marks of the competent professional in any field.

(Simmonds, 1998, p175)

Introduction

This first chapter introduces concepts of *judgement, risk* and *decision making* in both everyday life and social work practice. A framework for assessment, professional judgement, decision making and managing risk is outlined, drawing on a range of models. Key terms are discussed and defined. The theoretical material in this chapter provides a framework for understanding situations and a foundation for later chapters by introducing concepts about judgement, risk, assessment and decision making that are then expanded in later chapters where they are applied to practice.

Everyday decisions and risk

How do you make your everyday decisions such as what to eat, what to wear and how to spend your time? We make judgements every day, for example about the anticipated tastiness of some food in a shop, about the likely weather today, and about the value or pleasure that we expect if we use our time in a particular way. We also take risks every day, such as the risk of food poisoning, the risk of embarrassment or getting wet because of choosing the 'wrong' clothes to wear or of feeling we have wasted our time on an activity. Decisions, judgements and risk-taking in the face of uncertainty are everyday activities of life. Life without risk would be dull, and lacking in the stimuli that lead to learning and growth. Making choices in the face of uncertainty is part of the challenge and joy of being human; it is part of normal development for children as they grow in knowledge, skill and confidence in dealing with the world.

As social workers, we make many judgements and decisions daily. Our judgements cover diverse domains, such as whether a child should be regarded as in need of protection, assessing the risks inherent in a proposed care arrangement following hospital discharge or selecting a practice method for work with a particular family. Some decision making (generally where consequences are more serious) is formalised into group or organisational processes, such as court hearings, strategic planning meetings, case discussions, family meetings and reviews. Some collaborative decisions are more informal, for instance a practitioner checking a decision with the team leader as he or she is dashing down the corridor to a meeting!

Decision making in situations of uncertainty is a central professional activity in health and social care services. We are making decisions in uncertainty, or *taking risks*, every time we support a person with a disability to achieve greater independence, plan the discharge of an older person or psychiatric patient from hospital, support a family in a state of dysfunction or intervene to protect an individual from abuse. The fundamental professional task of assessing needs and planning care (including psycho-social interventions such as counselling or group work) is given added complexity by our pivotal decision-making role as social workers in assessing risk as well as needs (Taylor and Devine, 1993; Parton *et al.*, 1997) and the professional judgement that is required.

Our professional judgement and decision making takes place in a variety of contexts including the client, family and wider society; the professional task and role; and the organisation within which the professional is employed. We consider these in turn as we build up a map of concepts to guide our journey through the rest of the book, at the same time defining key terms and integrating these considerations with the social work helping process. The frame of reference by which we conceptualise and articulate a problem situation is crucial to turning need, distress or chaos into a manageable decision process where we can help clients and families to change and where we can undertake safeguarding and service gate-keeping functions on behalf of society. We draw upon research to inform our understanding and our practice.

There is growing interest in moving beyond simplistic laboratory-type research on decisions and a dominant focus on probabilities (of harm) in the conceptualisation of risk to engage with the concepts of complexity and chaos theory (Haynes, 2003). These have an obvious attraction in the complex world of social care delivered within the multiple dimensions of family and social life. This focus opens up consideration of critical incidents and interactions within systems with relevance to social work (Bostock *et al.*, 2005; Fish *et al.*, 2008). Perhaps one contribution of complexity theory may be to dispel the notion that risk could be eliminated if we had sufficient knowledge or control mechanisms. Rather, the more helpful perspective may be to seek to identify those aspects (including interactions) of the care system that are most likely to experience highly undesirable events, and to address those through parts of the organisation that are suitably amenable to change (Taylor and Campbell, 2011). Although complexity and chaos theory seem to have little in the way of principles or tools that are readily applicable in practice, these approaches may lend support to the proposition that the development of expertise amongst social workers in exercising professional judgement (and using knowledge in doing so) is at least as important as developing regulatory systems in ensuring quality decisions (Stacey, 2000). Our overarching model of assessment incorporating risk and problem solving, and leading to decisions informed by evidence (knowledge), is illustrated in Figure 1.1.

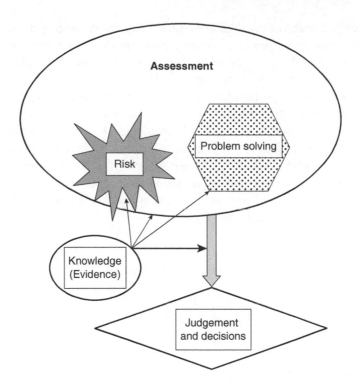

Figure 1.1   Overall schema of decisions in the context assessment, risk and evidence

Engaging clients, families and other stakeholders in assessment and decision processes

Social work practice has learned the lesson over the decades that effective practice needs to engage clients and families as far as possible. Chapter 2 focuses on engaging clients effectively in risk and decision making. Client engagement has particular challenges where – for example – there are issues of addiction and in those countries where the mass media creates a hostility towards social workers. These issues are complex enough to merit the focus of a whole book such as Taylor (2011), to which the reader is referred for further discussion.

Professional social work practice normally takes place within an organisation, whether statutory or voluntary, although a few social workers provide counselling to individuals, family work and expert witness services to courts as self-employed practitioners. The most important decision making will not be left to the individual but will be part of a process within the organisation. By *important decisions*, we mean those with the most impact on people's lives (such as taking a child into care) or those with the greatest resource implications. Thus, the most important social work decisions will not be made unilaterally, but will be subject to various checks and balances involving other people. Your line manager or professional supervisor will be involved in these decisions; the most serious decisions will go further up the line management. Other professionals should be involved as and when appropriate in accordance with their area of knowledge and skill in relation to the needs of the client or family. It frequently falls to the social worker to co-ordinate the multi-professional process. In terms of our training this seems appropriate, as the profession with the most holistic, user-centred view of the needs, risks, resources and options. The knowledge, skills and tools of assessment are discussed further in Chapter 4. The contributions of different professions need to be co-ordinated effectively and efficiently, and this is discussed more fully in Chapter 8. Issues of working effectively within professional supervision and management arrangements are discussed in Chapter 10. Key elements of the decision process might be conceptualised as

- involving:

    o clients, children, families, other carers (see Chapter 2);

    o other professionals and organisations (see Chapter 8);

    o professional supervision (see Chapter 10);

- and using knowledge of:

    o family, community (see Chapter 2);

    o law, policies, procedures, standards (see Chapter 3);

    o services and eligibility criteria (see Chapters 6, 7);

    o research, theory (see Chapter 5).

These decision-making processes (which often take place as part of 'assessment' and 'review' – see Chapters 4 and 9) feed into and are fed by the individual cognitive judgement of the social worker in order to gather and order appropriate information, 'frame' the decision and analyse options.

ACTIVITY *1.1*

Meanings of words where outcomes are unknown

What do these words mean to you in the context of your work?

How does their usage differ among your peers at work and in the wider society?

- *Dangerousness*

- *Fate*

- *Risky*

- *Risk-taking*

- *Vulnerable*
- *Gamble*
- *God's will*
- *Harm*
- *Hazard*
- *Judgement*

Conceptualising risk, risk-taking and risk communication

Our judgements and decisions are made in situations where the outcome is uncertain. As the outcome is uncertain, there is always the possibility that a less desirable outcome will ensue, possibly some harm or loss. Such losses or harms are sometimes referred to as *risks*, such as in phrases like *the risk of further abuse* or *the risk of falling*. Where the term *risk* means simply *the likelihood of* or *the probability of*, we shall use here these phrases instead as they are more precise. Hence we would refer to *the likelihood of further abuse* or *the probability of falling* rather than *the risk of falling*. For rational human behaviour, we assume that the decision is made in order to achieve some sort of *benefit*, interpreted broadly to include not only good health or financial gain but also such qualities as social independence or moral integrity. Taking risk is intrinsic to human decision making, and hence to social work practice in advising and supporting clients to make decisions. Thus, we use the term *risk* to mean *a decision-making situation where the outcomes are uncertain and where benefits are sought but undesirable outcomes are possible.*

In general, the term *risk* can lead to unnecessary confusion as it has so many meanings (Dowie, 1999), so we will normally use alternative expressions. It is often better to use a term such as *probability* (when referring to the likelihood of something undesirable happening), *harm* to refer to the undesirable consequence of an event, and *hazard* or *danger* to refer to the foreseen circumstance or object that may lead to harm. Undesirable events are not equally undesirable and in this respect the term *risk* relates closely to values. Just as values vary between individuals – whether service users or service providers – so concepts of risk vary (Killick *et al.*, 2015; Taylor, 2006b). This is discussed more fully in Chapters 2 and 8. The contexts where the term *risk* seems most useful are in *risk-taking*, and in organisational *risk management*. The term *risk factor* (common shorthand where we are considering factors that influence the likelihood of something undesirable occurring) is so well established that we have retained it here. Note, however, that in common usage the term *risk* may refer to an undesirable outcome or may refer to a factor that leads to an undesirable outcome.

It is becoming common to distinguish between *risk* and *uncertainty*, where *risk* is used to connote a calculable probability of a decision outcome (usually an undesirable outcome) and *uncertainty* is used where the probability of outcomes cannot be calculated. For many social work decisions, there is insufficient information available from research at the present time to give us data from which to calculate the probabilities of harmful outcomes. The term *risk* is retained in this book on the basis that in principle risk factors could be calculated for many health and social care decisions if suitable research were undertaken. Issues of risk and uncertainty will be revisited in later chapters, particularly in Chapter 3 on legal aspects; Chapter 6 on safeguarding decisions; and Chapter 7 on choosing between courses of action where the outcomes are uncertain.

ACTIVITY 1.2

Reflections on risk and uncertainty

- *What are the risks in your own life at present? Consider domains such as relationships; finances; sports; use of the internet; driving, cycling, walking and using public transport.*

- *Do you feel differently about risks and risk-taking in different domains?*

- *What do you do practically to manage risks and risk-taking?*

- *What factors lead you to be more risk-averse?*

- *What supports you to take risks in a domain such as relationships?*

- *To what extent do you try to calculate risks?*

- *In what ways do you try to manage risks?*

Communication about possible adverse consequences of a course of action is increasingly referred to as *risk communication* (Taylor and Moorhead, in press). *Risk communication* and *risk-benefit communication* can be conceptualised as involving a sender of information; a receiver; the content of the communication; and the format of the communication (Stevenson *et al.*, in press). The reader interested in a fuller discussion of the theory of risk is recommended to look at Reason (1991) and, in relation to the ways that people may be misled by risk communications, see Gigerenzer (2014) on being 'risk savvy'.

The social work role in assessment, risk and decisions

The protective role of social workers acting on behalf of society now extends beyond seeking to protect children from abuse to include protecting vulnerable adults from others and themselves. The task has become more complex as more knowledgeable and skilled approaches are demanded. Social workers in most countries have the lead role in relation to child protection and are often blamed by the media if a tragedy occurs (Pascoe-Watson and Wilson, 2008), despite the multi-professional nature of the work and the impossibility of predicting harm by a particular individual with any great degree of accuracy. Do we make rational decisions based on objective facts? If our decision making is *rational*, on what facts is it based? If it is not rational, how are our activities justified to society, the taxpayer or the contributor to the employing charity? How do value issues, legal parameters and political pressures fit into the decision-making process?

- Do we consider the situation *in the past*, as in the traditional social work emphasis on taking a social history in such fields as child protection, mental health and criminal justice?

- Do we consider the situation *now*, as in functional assessment of older people and those with complex health and social care needs?

- Do we consider predictions about *the future*, as in recommendations about returning home a child who has been abused in the past, or the discharge of a person who has been violent or suicidal from psychiatric hospital?

- Do we consider the likely *impact* of an intervention, as in using evidence of the effectiveness of specific health and social care interventions in a situation with particular features?

A key issue is *who is at risk* and *who is taking the risk* in decisions about care planning, such as safeguarding a vulnerable person, seeking greater independence and choosing to take the risks that enable rehabilitation and recovery from mental and physical illnesses. We can consider major categories of possible harm as being:

- by others, e.g. abuse, whether physical, sexual, emotional, neglect or financial;

- to others, e.g. violence, aggression, accidentally setting fire to housing, etc.;

- to self, e.g. self-harm, suicide, self-neglect, etc.

It is very important in working through the material in this book to consider your role as a social worker. You need to bear in mind continually what areas you are deemed to be competent in by virtue of your professional qualification, irrespective of other knowledge acquired, for example, from working with members of other professions.

The law and protecting people's health and safety

Within the UK there is legislation regarding health and safety at work that embodies stringent protective measures introduced across the European Union. The statutes (Health and Safety at Work [etc.] Act 1974; Health and Safety at Work (NI) Order 1978, both as subsequently amended) deal with responsibilities of employers and employees, and provide protection towards employees and visitors to employer premises including public buildings such as hospitals and social work offices. This legislation requires employers and employees to take reasonable steps to protect others from harm. There are tensions in that this legislation does not embody any concept of *risk-taking* such as we are discussing here, even though it is intrinsic to the professional role of health and social care staff. This is discussed further in Chapter 3 in the context of the law relating to *reasonable decisions*, and in Chapter 7 in the context of balancing possible gains against possible harm or loss.

CASE STUDY **1.1**

Clarifying your role

A key part of my social work role is to enable any vulnerable adult to access support to enable him or her to live a life free from abuse, exploitation or neglect. My work entails investigating alleged or suspected situations of abuse, exploitation or neglect; assessing and managing the risk to the higher-risk vulnerable adults within the multi-professional team; working with individuals and families to seek to resolve issues underlying the abuse or neglect, and put in place safeguarding measures; fulfilling statutory functions; and working with the police and other agencies as appropriate particularly where criminal prosecution is a consideration.

- *Do you have a clear statement of the scope of the work undertaken by your team or unit or department?*

- *If you have a particular role within the team or section, do you have a clear statement of your role?*

The assessment-risk-decision helping process

We consider the professional helping process to have four main aspects: *assess – plan – implement – evaluate*, as conceptualised in Taylor and Devine (1993). This professional practice process of assessing needs and planning care is defined broadly to include the functions of assessment and planning inherent in any psycho-social intervention (such as varieties of counselling, family work and group work) as well as co-ordination of a range of health and social care services, now generally known as *case management* or *care management*. Despite the complexities of social work professional practice and the immensely varied situations of individuals, it is important to have some robust yet flexible framework to shape practice. That is the focus of the chapter. The traditional basic framework is expanded here to give particular attention to risk and decision-making aspects of assessment and care planning.

In terms of the helping process, *judgement* focuses on the stages of assessing and planning an intervention. *Decision making* might be regarded as following on from a judgement (Figure 1.1) or might be viewed as encapsulating all of the stages, including the evaluation of the effectiveness of the decision.

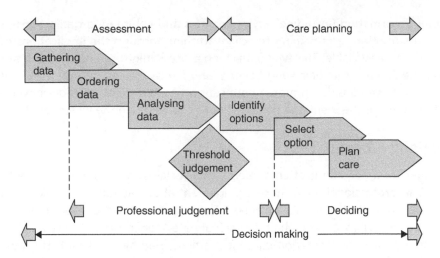

Figure 1.2   Judgement, decisions and the assessment and care planning cycle

Assessment is considered here in terms of three key functions: gathering, ordering and analysing information. These three aspects are considered in greater detail in Chapter 4, which considers the use of assessment tools to support professional judgement and decision-making processes. The assessment stage leads on to the planning stage, which includes identifying options, selecting an option and care planning, which are discussed in greater depth in Chapter 7.

Assessment takes place at a critical point where knowledge derived from research, theory, law, standards and policy are brought to bear on the facts of the client situation. A professional has a body of knowledge, skills and values that a typical member of society will not have. However, this does not mean that we *know it all*, even in relation to our own domain of expertise. We all have blind spots, particular enthusiasms and a perspective that reflects our professional journey to date. There is a long history of research in psychology on potential bias in decision making (Beach and Connolly, 1997; Hardman, 2009); we consider this further in Chapter 5 in relation to reflective practice, the professional judgement process and the task of using knowledge to inform judgements.

Types of social work decisions

Social workers make many judgements and decisions and these may be analysed using models developed in other fields of study such as psychology (Taylor, 2012c). We consider four major types of decisions here: enabling client decisions; eligibility for services; safeguarding decisions; and care planning decisions.

1. Enabling client decisions

Our starting point is the client and family with their hopes and fears, their relationships and the crisis or need that has brought them to the attention of a social worker. *Normally* clients should be supported to make their own decisions (DH, 2007) in accord with their own values. The professional role in this case might focus on providing information (including service contacts and voluntary organisations), challenging assumptions and helping the client to think through the implications of the choices that are available. This type of decision process might be characterised as *envisioning the future* or as *balancing benefits and harms* (Taylor, 2006b). In Chapter 2 (in particular) we consider in more depth supporting the client decision-making process, the values of the client and the *risk culture* and values in the wider society.

2. Eligibility for services

The trigger for a decision is often a referral to a social worker by whatever route this comes. The professional must make a judgement about action to be taken, even if the decision is ultimately to take no action. The referral may be to a social care service for which the social worker is the professional gate-keeper. We characterise this type of decision process as a *criterion-based judgement* (Hammond, 1996). The situation of the client and family are being judged in relation to the criteria for eligibility for a particular service at this point in time, however these are determined. We consider this type of decision further in Chapters 2 and 6. Judging a service (such as the Early Years service) against a standard might also be considered as similar in terms of the model of judgement required.

3. Safeguarding decisions

In some situations – such as where the client lacks capacity to decide or where there is a mandate from society to protect a child or vulnerable adult from abuse – the professional may have to act to safeguard an individual, often in opposition to the views of some family members or others. This type of decision process might be characterised as a *criterion-based judgement* and as an *ethical decision-making process*. In essence the client or family situation is being judged against criteria or thresholds at which the organisation should intervene on behalf of society to protect an individual. Such decisions often carry with them an expectation of predicting possible harm, such as in the questions: *Is it safe to return this child home?* and *How safe is it for this patient to be discharged from the psychiatric hospital?* Emergency out-of-hours decisions are a particular type of safeguarding judgement, as are judgements about whether service quality (such as in homecare or Early Years services) meets stated standards. We discuss these types of safeguarding decisions in Chapter 6.

4. Care planning decisions

The assessment phase is not an end in itself, but is normally the starting point for planning an intervention, whether care service provision or some form of counselling or other psycho-social intervention (Taylor and Devine, 1993). Even where there has been a *criterion-based judgement* regarding eligibility for a service, or in relation to a threshold for implementing compulsory safeguarding measures, there then follows a decision about planning the next step. The *balancing benefits and harms* model may be helpful at this stage of the process, as the professional seeks to weigh up the possible alternative courses of action. We consider this type of decision further particularly in Chapters 7 and 9. These four types of decision are illustrated in Figure 1.3.

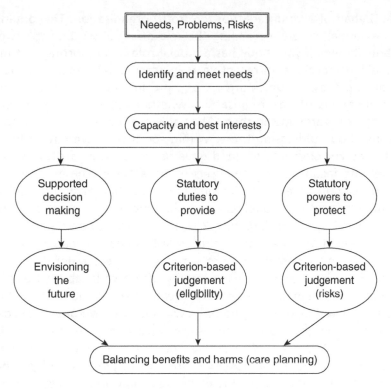

Figure 1.3   Common decision types in social work practice

Managing risks and decisions over time

Within the basic model of the helping process – *assess, plan, implement, evaluate* – referred to above the stage of *implementation* requires the professional to manage the risks inherent in the provision of care or intervention, whatever form that takes. Key aspects of managing risks are to have (1) systems to monitor welfare (and risk); and (2) systems for action in response to critical points or issues which become evident through monitoring. Effective management of risks to individual clients and families requires clear objectives for care (and protection, if appropriate) and contingency ('what if?') planning in advance. Over time risks need to be monitored and reappraised; assessments need to be repeated (often called 'review'); and decisions need to be reviewed and sometimes changed. These aspects relating to changes over time are discussed further in Chapter 9.

Risks and decisions in their organisational context

The main focus of this book is on the activities of the professional social worker with his or her client and colleagues. However, the duties carried out by social workers are normally on behalf of an employing organisation, whether they are statutory functions carried out by a publicly funded body, or aspects of social helping on behalf of a voluntary (not-for-profit) organisation. This organisational context is essential for understanding the role of social work in the twenty-first century, and the employing body has a crucial role in supporting and managing decision-making processes. In recent years increasing investment has been made in governance processes, which are systems put in place so that the senior staff and board members of an organisation (whether public, private or charitable) know the major hazards facing them. They are thus more readily held to account for decisions about addressing these. Within social work we have a long history of many of the key elements of good governance, such as professional supervision and seeking feedback from the users of our services. These various activities, and some new approaches to addressing risk issues and ensuring quality of services, are now being drawn together under the umbrella of social care governance (Simmons, 2007; Taylor and Campbell, 2011). The focus to date has tended to be on risk management activities, such as risk registers and the management of complaints. However, managers need a broad focus to reflect wider developments in terms of decision management. Each inquiry into a child abuse tragedy brings increased pressure on senior managers and greater clarity about roles and responsibilities. The focus will increasingly be on how resources have been managed, what policies, support and governance systems are in place, and what training has been provided for staff. *Defensive beliefs and reactive approaches to risk (managing the harm once it has occurred) will increasingly be challenged by developments in risk assessment and risk management. The emphasis is moving to decision-making processes and their management* (Carson, 1996, p4).

The activities of the individual social worker are illustrated in their broader organisational context in Figure 1.4. The main contributions to the judgement, risk and

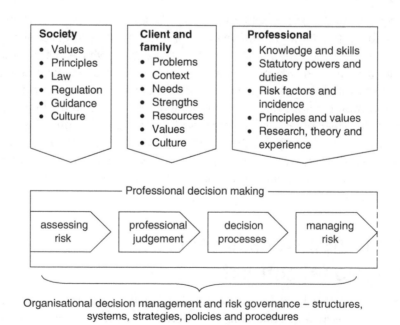

Figure 1.4   Risk, assessment and decisions in their organisational context

decision process regarding individual care are identified under the headings of *client*, *professional* and *society*. An alternative way to conceptualise these is in terms of the 'decision-making ecology' of organisational, case, decision-making and external factors (Baumann *et al.*, 2011). The assessment, judgement, decision-making and care planning process is underpinned by the policies, systems and procedures of the employing organisation. These latter aspects are discussed more fully in Chapter 10.

Conceptualising 'judgement' and 'decision making'

The terms *judgement* and *decision making* are often used interchangeably. In this book, where they are to be distinguished, the term *judgement* focuses on an individual *assessing alternatives* and the term *decision making* focuses on an individual or group *choosing between alternatives* (Dowie, 1993, p8). We define a *professional judgement* to be *when a professional considers the evidence about a client or family situation in the light of professional knowledge to reach a conclusion or recommendation.* There is a usage of the term *professional judgement* to refer to the discretionary space within which the professional operates. This, however, omits the more common – and probably more important – role of the professional using his judgement to make a recommendation (such as to a supervisor or multi-professional group) about a decision. We use the term *evidence* rather than *information* to highlight the fact that the range of data that we have about a client, family and situation has varying degrees of reliability, just as our professional knowledge has varying degrees of reliability. The number of days of school attendance may be reasonably factual; the *reasons* why the young person has missed so many days of schooling may be a rather less reliable composite picture put together from perceptions gathered through interviews with the child, parents and school teacher. In this definition, we use the term *professional knowledge* to include all varieties of sources of knowledge that we rely on in our work, such as statutes, case law, policy, theory, research, standards, principles, protocols, procedures, values and experience.

We define a *decision* to be *the selection of a course of action as a result of a deliberate process by one or more people.* Sometimes, judgements and decisions merge into each other; in other situations they are more distinct. A decision may be made by one person, or it may be the result of a *decision process* involving a number of people.

The study of individual human judgement can be conceptualised into three domains:

- **normative approaches** – starting from a model of how people ought to make judgements if they are 'rational' and then study ways in which they follow or deviate from this model;

- **descriptive approaches** – studying how people make judgements in the 'real world', without assuming any prior model of how decisions would be made if 'rational';

- **prescriptive approaches** – exploring ways to improve decision making without seeking to use any particular model or understand how the decisions are made.

Normative approaches normally start from an assumption that a rational approach to human judgement is to balance the options against each other in terms of the benefit that is expected from each outcome. This is known as *subjective expected utility*, the word 'subjective' recognising that different people may accord different value to particular outcomes. If outcomes are uncertain, the probability of each outcome is calculated and multiplied by the value ascribed to that outcome. The calculation of such values and probabilities can seem unrealistic in practice. A *balancing benefits and harms* model is used as a basis in Chapter 7 in relation to choices between care (risk) plan options.

Descriptive approaches to studying human judgement have traditionally focused on biases that can be demonstrated through research. Some of these are discussed in Chapter 5. A weakness of this approach is that research findings tend to be piecemeal and do not build readily into a cohesive understanding (model) of judgements. More recently there has been increased interest in *heuristic* models as a way to describe how people use short-cut approaches to effective judgements using limited amounts of information. These approaches are discussed in Chapter 6 particularly in relation to safeguarding judgements and judgements about eligibility for a service against some threshold of need.

Prescriptive approaches might be typified by prescribed assessment tools that are intended to standardise the collection of information about clients and families but without any underlying model of how the judgement is to be formed. Although some assessments are linked to specific interventions (such as family therapy, for example), many social work assessments are holistic rather than built on a specific theory of need or helping process. The development of assessment tools is a topic in its own right, and is beyond the scope of this book. There is further discussion of this approach in Chapter 4 on assessment.

An emerging approach to modelling professional judgement in social work is termed *psycho-social rationality* (Taylor, in press). This fits within the *descriptive* approaches outlined above, and is an approach that is premised on human judgements being rational, even if they do not weigh up the (positive and negative) values and likelihood of every factor or every option. Instead, it is posited that humans use simple rules to make decisions selecting appropriate rules, each of which is applicable to a limited domain (Gigerenzer and Gaissmaier, 2015). The term *psycho-social rationality model* is used here to incorporate both:

- *risk cluster* models such as those considering risks in terms of *risk clusters* reflecting the relationship between predisposing factors (vulnerabilities), precipitating factors (triggers) and strengths (mitigating factors); and

- *heuristic* models derived from concepts of *bounded rationality,* including *satisficing* and *fast and frugal decision trees.*

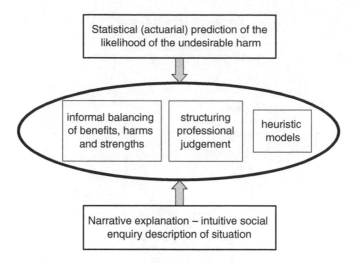

Figure 1.5   Scope of psycho-social rationality models of professional judgement

Heuristic models of human judgement are at an early stage of development, and are not yet established as tools for professional judgement. They are included here because they are being discussed publicly (Kirkman and Melrose, 2014), and to give inspiration and indicate areas for further research.

Psycho-social rationality models of professional judgement may be another way of conceptualising what is sometimes described as *structured professional judgement* (Bouch and Marshall, 2005), combining the expertise of the professional that is not yet articulated (and primarily learned from experience) with a knowledge base of risk factors (see Figure 1.5). We consider this further in Chapter 6.

A framework for risk, assessment and decisions

The chapters in this book are framed around the *framework for risk, assessment and decisions,* which is illustrated in Figure 1.6, and which provides a summary of the chapters in this book. Two foundational elements are client context, emotion, crisis and choice (Chapter 2) and the legal framework for decisions, assessment and risk (Chapter 3). These both feed into assessment (Chapter 4), the forming of a professional judgement (Chapter 5) and engagement in risk and decision processes with others (Chapter 8). The assessment, professional judgement and decision processes are to be informed by two strands of understanding risk and decision making: *threshold judgements* such as safeguarding and service eligibility (Chapter 6) and *choice judgements* such as risk-taking care planning (Chapter 7). Risks must be monitored, assessments revisited (review) and care plans adapted; these three time dimensions are considered in Chapter 9. Organisational considerations such as support, allocating blame and learning from adverse events are discussed in Chapter 10.

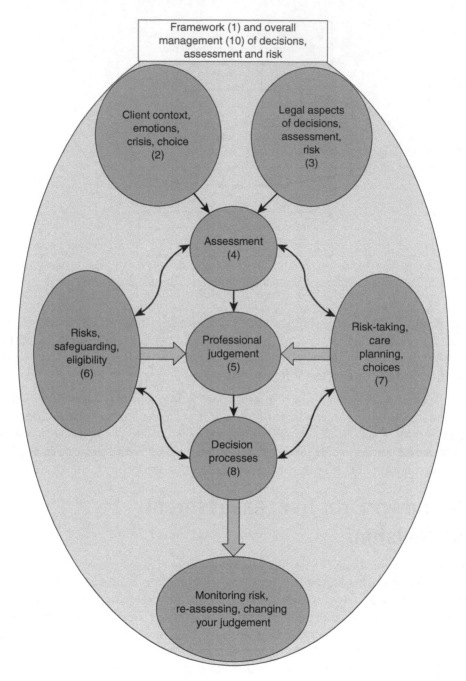

Figure 1.6   Schema of book illustrating framework for decisions, assessment and risk

Chapter summary

- This chapter has introduced and clarified concepts of decision making and risk in both everyday life and social work practice, linking these to assessment, professional judgement and planning care.

- As social workers, we support clients in assessing needs, risks and strengths; in problem solving; and in decision making, as well as having to make professional judgements ourselves in roles such as safeguarding and gate-keeping access to publicly or charitably funded social care services.

- Several decision models have been outlined, including: envisioning the future; balancing benefits and harms; fuzzy set theory; heuristic models; and making a criterion-based judgement. A general framework of *psycho-social rationality* has been delineated.

- The chapter presents an overarching model of professional judgement and decision making in a context of risk or uncertainty, and linked to social work processes of assessment and planning care.

- Key concepts have been discussed and defined in this chapter, and these are listed in the Glossary.

FURTHER READING

Beach, L.R. and Connolly, T. (1997) *The Psychology of Decision Making: People in Organisations.* Thousand Oaks, CA: Sage.

This is a very readable book giving a balanced overview of theories of decision making including: (1) those beginning from an assumption of rational decisions and then considering how true to life these are (normative models); (2) those beginning from studies of real-life decisions (descriptive); and (3) more recent attempts to integrate these through naturalistic decision-making models.

Hardman, D. (2009) *Judgement and Decision Making.* Oxford: Oxford University Press.

This is a well-written, detailed textbook outlining major theories and models of decision making and giving references to underpinning research.

Taylor, B.J. and Devine, T. (1993) *Assessing Needs and Planning Care in Social Work.* Aldershot: Ashgate.

This very readable classic outlines the basic social work helping process – assessing, planning, intervening, evaluating – and is a widely used textbook on qualifying social work courses. The present book builds on this basic model by considering in more detail the risk, judgement and decision-making aspects.

Chapter 2
Client decisions, perspectives, emotions and crises

And those who try to avoid all risk, those who would try to guarantee that their hearts will not be broken, end up in a self-created hell.

(Nouwen, 2001, p26)

Introduction

If you have engaged with a social worker as a client – or were to consider doing so – how would you expect the discussion to proceed about developing a common understanding of the issues (*assessment*) and agreeing what to do about them? This chapter starts from the needs and crises that bring clients to social workers. We consider the position of a client or family making sometimes difficult choices, their values and how they might engage with information about hazards they face and options they have. We consider client perspectives of risk; the place of emotion in decision making; confidentiality; and resilience. We discuss the professional engaging with clients and other family stakeholders in decisions; *game theory* to help us understand the dynamics of the decision-making process between professional and client; and the role of the social worker in (normally) supporting informed, reasonable and reasoned client decisions. We utilise UK guidance on *supported decision making* as a tool to support shared decision making, and *image theory* as a model for understanding how clients and families might make decisions about their own care issues. Engagement of clients in assessment processes is discussed in Chapter 4; risk communication and wider decision processes are discussed in Chapter 6. Legal aspects of client consent are discussed in Chapter 3.

Needs and decisions in crisis

How do clients perceive the risks and decisions that must be made in terms of care for themselves or their family member? Voluntary clients generally come to social workers because of a sense of *need*. Theories of need usually begin by considering basic biological drives, such as for food, clothing, shelter and a safe environment (Doyal and Gough, 1991). Maslow's hierarchy (1943) suggests that these more basic needs must be satisfied before we can strive to meet higher order needs, such as for emotional, sexual and intellectual fulfilment. Other approaches focus on moral imperatives and the rights of individuals to the basic essentials required for a reason-able life, such as the right to family life, to be free from persecution or torture and to hold your own beliefs provided they do not actually harm others. Such rights depend on another person or group of people (usually a society) accepting that they have the corresponding duties to allow or provide these rights. In social work a combination of these approaches seems to be common. *Needs* are distinguished from *wants* by some consideration of their universal nature and the seriousness of the harm to the well-being of the person if they are not met. *Needs* are often considered to be those which might reasonably be met, subject to available resources, by the public purse or the charitable giving to the organisation (Taylor and Devine, 1993). We often make judgements about the eligibility of the presenting needs for the provision of publicly funded services.

Some of the situations where needs are presented and judgements have to be made are situations of crisis for clients and their families. The decisions that they might make may not be their *normal* decisions. They may be willing to share their feelings more and welcome a trusted professional who understands their sense of panic, dread or pressure. The client and family may be more open to change than normal and thereby open to the possibility of supportive professional help to make changes to such major issues as lifestyle and relationships (Roberts, 2000; O'Hagan, 1991). We may help by partialising the problem-solving and decision-making processes into manageable steps. This may be an opportune time to offer to support family problem-solving interaction. Depending on the degree of urgency, a *holding decision* may be made while further assessment is undertaken.

Risks may be seen as part of the change process for the client. The client may have sought help in order to explore risks, e.g. of self-harm or the more vague feeling that their life is chaotic. The client may be seeking stability and some direction. The social work task is to give space to allow an exploration of risk and decisions that must be made whilst offering sufficient stability and sense of boundary so that these are not experienced as overwhelming – for the client or the worker. A respectful space is needed to engage with painful feelings whilst being emotionally secure within the supportive bounds of the helping relationship. For the reader interested in exploring communicating risk in crisis further, Sellnow (2015) may be of interest.

RESEARCH SUMMARY 2.1

Older people entering long-term care

With the increasing pressure on social and health care resources, professionals have to be more explicit in their decision making regarding the long-term care of older people. This grounded theory study used 19 focus groups and nine semi-structured interviews (99 staff in total) to explore professional perspectives on this decision making. Focus group partici-pants and interviewees comprised care managers, social workers, consultant geriatricians, general medical practitioners, community nurses, home care managers and occupational

(Continued)

(Continued)

therapists. The emerging themes spanned context, clients, families and services. Decisions were often prompted by a crisis, hindering professionals seeking to make a measured assessment. Fear of burglary and assault, and the willingness and availability of family to help were major factors in decisions about living at home. Service availability in terms of public funding for community care, the availability of home care workers and workload pressures on primary care services influenced decision 'thresholds' regarding admission to institutional care. Assessment tools designed to assist decision making about the long-term care of older people need to take into account the critical aspects of individual fears and motivation, family support, and the availability of publicly funded services as well as functional and medical needs.

(Taylor and Donnelly, 2006b)

Confidentiality, values and resilience

There are many challenges to supporting client decision making. Some client values are different from those of society in general, as well as from those of the profession. Much careful discussion is required to ensure a common understanding in decision processes with clients, taking account of varying socio-cultural and ethnic perceptions.

As well as changing the ways in which people create their social networks (Best *et al.*, 2015), the development of the internet is opening up many possibilities for service provision (Best *et al.*, 2013) that were not available a generation ago. Even simple communications with clients are greatly facilitated by mobile phones and text messages. However in this 'digital age', you need to reflect carefully on your use of information that relates to your work in relation to sharing material through social media, for example if it might possibly be identifiable in relation to a particular family or if it might bring your employer into disrepute. The 'digital revolution' also requires that you are sensitive to likely differences in expectations about communication patterns and sharing of information depending on age as well as culture (Best *et al.*, 2014). Consider what actions you need to take to safeguard your integrity and that of your profession and organisation within decision-making processes with clients. How will issues of confidentiality be handled? How will you ensure that the copy of the child protection case conference minutes that turns up on a bus or a rubbish dump is identifiable as the copy that was given to the client so that a professional will not be blamed wrongly? Tensions can sometimes arise when there are conflicting imperatives, such as protecting another worker by sharing information about threats of violence versus respecting the client's right to confidentiality. Similarly, dilemmas arise with anonymous allegations or where we are told something *in confidence.* How will you establish and clarify the boundaries of confidentiality? What support from your line manager or professional supervisor do you need in order to justify the contexts (such as violence towards staff and alleged abuse) where protecting another person overrides the right to confidentiality? For some further consideration of legal aspects of overriding the normal standards for respecting confidentiality see Chapter 3.

RESEARCH SUMMARY *2.2*

Understanding client values and preferences

Objective

To test the effects of providing non-professional case managers with a tool to assess and respond to client values on their knowledge of clients' preferences and their practice in arranging community services.

Method

A quasi-experimental design with newly enrolled, cognitively intact older people being assessed for home care and day care services. Case managers, clients and care plans at the experimental and control agency were compared. Each agency covered ten counties and a total of 313 clients participated in the study. The experimental group included 18 case managers, the control group 21. The intervention for the experimental group included: (1) participation by case managers in developing a values assessment tool; (2) training in using the tool involving role play; (3) case managers administered the tool routinely to all new clients; (4) clients left with a large-print brochure encouraging them to consider their own values and preferences, and the implications for their care; (5) research team analysed the early values assessments completed and gave the case managers feedback; (6) staff development sessions focusing on ways to make care plans more responsive to client values; and (7) a series of case conferences to consider the values information in the light of other information about those particular clients. One-way ANOVA was used to test for statistical significance between the experimental and control groups after the intervention.

Results

Three weeks after enrolment, clients of case managers in the experimental group were significantly more likely to report that the case manager had asked them about their own preferences and offered them choices about services. At the three-month follow-up, the case managers in the experimental group reported more case activity tailoring plans to client preferences, a finding confirmed by a review of records. The intervention was found to improve the awareness of client values, but a key finding was that case managers were generally inaccurate in predicting how their clients would state their values three months after referral. In general, the case managers: (1) greatly underestimated the importance of religious activity to clients; (2) underestimated their desire to be protected; (3) overestimated their desire to take risks; and (4) underestimated their willingness to forgo help in order to maintain privacy in financial affairs.

Conclusion

It is possible to improve the sensitivity of case managers to the importance of assessing and acting on client values, but greater understanding of this aspect of practice is required.

(Kane et al., 1999)

As well as not underestimating the powerful emotions with which clients may be contending, it is important also not to underestimate the resilience of many clients in the face of adversity. Strengths-based approaches to practice are a growing interest across all client groups (Graybeal and Konrad, 2008). Judgements about risk-taking decision making may depend on considerations of the resilience of the client and hence their capacity to cope with greater trust or independence (Hackett, 1999).

Emotion in assessment and decisions

The context for social work involvement in client decision making may be emotional, involving crisis, stress, tension, and sometimes a lack of understanding, effective problem-solving skills or capacity for action. Clients and their families may have a variety of emotions because of their life situation, because of the crisis that has brought them to our attention, and in relation to accessing help. Clients may overreact to circumstances. They may hope for help but may also feel fear, anxiety, hostility or concerns about what sort of person they will be dealing with and their values and manner. Clients may have a wide variety of emotion as we engage with them in decision making, such as panic, anger, blame, frustration, regret, over-confidence or resentment at being obliged to do certain things or at needing to ask for help. *We arrive at some of the greatest decisions of our lives based not so much on reason or logic but on what is going on deep within us – in our hearts – and then we look for logical reasons to support our feelings* (Hughes, 2005, p33).

When we make decisions, we may (with varying degrees of consciousness) get in touch with deeper feelings and perhaps share them with others before making the decision. We may be reluctant decision makers, *beset by conflict, doubts and worry, struggling with incongruous longings, antipathies and loyalties, and seeking relief by procrastinating, rationalising or denying responsibility for [our] own choices* (Janis and Mann, 1977, p15). Decision making can be tough; emotions and avoidance behaviours are to be expected. The emotional challenge of decisions needs to be recognised. Otherwise we may fall into the bias of being reluctant to make appropriate decisions, leading to results such as children in care being allowed to 'drift' rather than having robust decisions made about their future. We discuss bias in decision making further in Chapter 5.

> *It is as if each human person constitutes a committee constantly sitting to decide life's questions and the behaviour desired in a given situation. This committee has many members within, each voicing a particular slant – our fears, feelings, dreams and hopes, our history and relationships, our memory, our various sub-personalities and our reason. Hopefully the chairperson of that committee is reason, deeply influenced and guided by affectivity. Descriptively the task of a human person appears to become more and more integrated, whole, 'together' within that on-going meeting. All the voices need to be heard and listened to. Ultimately, at their best, people make choices that chart the direction and, over time, develop the person.*
>
> (Dyckman and Carroll, 1981, p33)

People seeking social work help may have a sense of losing control of the decision and the management of the risks that they face. An individual or family crisis, whether abuse, illness or a crucial decision about greater independence, may be the emotional context for approaching a social services department. Knowledge and skills drawn from crisis theory (Roberts, 2000) may be appropriate in responding to an emotional decision situation. They may come with a sense of unfairness (such as the stigma of disability) or a feeling that their choices are limited (such as by illness or compulsory safeguarding measures). Emotion in decisions should not be seen as entirely negative. On the positive side, people in crisis may be more open to the possibilities for change. This is particularly relevant to considering the client contact as a decision point for the client. Further consideration of resistance among clients is in Taylor (2011). For research and discussion on deception by clients see Reinhard *et al.* (2014).

ACTIVITY 2.1

Spirituality in personal decision making

The experience of sadness, anxiety can prompt us to reflect on our life situation and what needs to be changed. People may turn to their religious beliefs to help in dealing with distressing emotions, not to find a fool-proof method for making the decision, but rather to find pointers to growing more perceptive and responsive to the action of God in their lives.

(Hughes, 2008, Chapter 12)

- *What place does spirituality or deep personal beliefs have in your personal decisions, particularly where the decisions are about your well-being?*

- *How can you best engage some of the strength of a client in terms of personal beliefs or spirituality that they have in managing risks and making decisions about care?*

The reader interested in further exploration of beliefs and spirituality in relation to social work is referred to Matthews (2009).

RESEARCH SUMMARY 2.3

Enabling discussion of risk issues with clients

Context

Assessing risk with adults with physical disabilities who receive social care services is a task at the confluence of three perspectives on risk: the rights and choices of clients, the role

(Continued)

(Continued)

and task of the social worker, and the responsibilities of the employing body in managing risk as a dimension of social care governance.

Purpose

This article describes a project to engage clients in jointly assessing their risks with social workers, undertaken with teams in the Physical Health and Disability Programme of Care in a Health and Social Care Trust in Northern Ireland.

Method

A Project Group comprising a social worker from each physical disability team, together with an occupational therapist, met monthly over five months to develop a risk assessment tool, later named a Safety Checklist. Between sessions participants used drafts of the tool with clients and discussed its merits with them and with their own team colleagues. Twenty clients completed a qualitative questionnaire evaluating the use of the tool.

Results

The Safety Checklist that was developed covered domains such as vulnerabilities, awareness of personal safety, ability to summon help if required and mental well-being (broadly interpreted) including mood and aggressive behaviour. The Safety Checklist tool facilitated discussion between client and social worker of sensitive topics, such as financial abuse (involving the possibility of police prosecution of a family member), addictions, aggressive behaviour and adherence to the agreed care (risk) plan. The tool simultaneously improved the involvement of social work practitioners with risk management systems within the organisation. An interesting incidental finding was that participants generally preferred the term client to service user.

Conclusion

A tool such as a Safety Checklist can be used effectively to facilitate both engagement of clients in managing risks with professionals, and engagement of professionals in organisational risk management systems.

(Taylor and McKeown, 2013)

CASE STUDY **2.1**

Client emotion in decision making

Mr Doherty is a 90-year-old man who was referred to the community social work team for older people following a fall and a period of rehabilitation in a residential home.

> *Mrs Doherty has mental health problems and did not think that a care package was necessary for her husband, and was refusing to follow the safety recommendations of the multi-professional team. It was only through building a good working relationship with Mrs Doherty that I was able to understand her own physical and mental health issues, and hence to encourage them both to engage with a care plan for the benefit of both of them.*
>
> * *Consider a recent case in which the emotions of a client have blocked a decision that otherwise seemed sound and sensible?*
>
> * *What unanticipated factors might have been at work in the situation?*

Emotion may enhance or inhibit decision making (Pfister and Bohm, 2008). In their conflict theory of decision making, Janis and Mann (1977) pose four basic questions that the decision maker may be asking if emotional conflict is playing an important role in the decision:

* Are the risks serious if I do not change?

* Are the risks serious if I do change?

* Is it realistic to hope to find a better solution?

* Is there time to search and deliberate?

CASE STUDY *2.2*

Conflicting emotions in decision situations

Lucy Brown (aged 4 years) was referred to our team by the playgroup because of a number of concerns that might indicate neglect. I visited her mother Sabrina, a single parent aged 23 years, because of these concerns and to explore what support we might offer. As I spent time with Sabrina it was apparent that she had many conflicting emotions, not least wanting to care well for her daughter but struggling in her relationship with her partner and with the threat of redundancy from her work at the local supermarket. I was also aware of my own feelings of inner conflict, not least as a mother myself.

* *Identify the emotions underpinning a recent decision situation for the client, other family members and for you as the social worker.*

Our own emotions may detract from our decision making and helping. Too little emotion may be inhuman, suggesting a lack of engagement with the client and limited ownership of the problem or its solution. Too much emotion may suggest being overwhelmed with stress, the bias of over-identifying with a client's problem or the confusion of excessive fear or anger from personal issues that are not sufficiently resolved. We should also consider whether and how our own emotion, such as fear, relates to emotions experienced by the family members of this person (see Cocker and Allain, 2011, Chapter 3). One way in which emotion is conceptualised in relation to decision making is in terms of how much regret the person might have if a particular outcome ensued. The interested reader is referred to sources such as Byrne (2005).

ACTIVITY 2.2

Emotion in professional decision making

- *What types of decisions in your role affect you emotionally?*

- *Why do you think these decisions particularly affect you emotionally?*

- *What emotions do you have when engaging with clients in situations such as:*

    o *supporting clients and families in making their own decisions?*

    o *deciding on eligibility for publicly funded or charitably funded services?*

    o *making safeguarding decisions to protect an individual from harm?*

- *What impact might your feelings have on you and on the decision?*

Framing the assessment, risks and decision

One task of the social worker is to 'frame the decision' (Kühlberger, 2017). In part this means understanding the 'world' of the client, including community (such as neighbour support, poverty, criminal pressures), social (such as family support) and psychological (such as emotions and ability to address problems) dimensions. In part the social work task also includes working with the client to create a frame for the risks and decisions that enable the constructive steps towards resolving issues to be taken. The *decision frame* is the range of psycho-social contextual factors and events that give the decision and risk situation its meaning, limitations and possibilities.

One way of structuring the decision process with a client might be conceptualised as:

1. **Goals** – clarify the decision to be made and convey value of client opinion;

2. **Options** – clarify the possible options and contribute knowledge to discuss the pros and cons of these;

3. **Choices** – clarify client preference and the client knowledge and values supporting this, ensuring that consequences of the choice are understood; and

4. **Decision** – establish client wish to make the decision and discuss realistic next steps.

This is a simple framework based on the *subjective expected utility* model of individual judgement which is explained further in Chapter 7. An alternative model based on *image theory* is discussed later in this chapter.

ACTIVITY **2.3**

Professional knowledge and skills in client decision steps

- *Take a client scenario from your practice or from elsewhere in this book, and for each of the four items in the list above:*

  o *Identify the knowledge base that you might inform a good decision outcome;*

  o *Consider (and discuss with colleagues) how you might best contribute this to the discussion with the client;*

  o *Analyse the interpersonal skills required using your training and experience in social work or a text such as Shulman (2011).*

Relationships and risk in engaging with clients

In some respects, care aims to minimise risk to individuals, families and society. But how does this fit with clients choosing to *take risks*, not only in morally contentious areas such as drug misuse, but also in everyday matters such as an older person in a home choosing to go for a walk alone contrary to the advice of the staff (Brearley, 1982)? What is the professional role in encouraging, discouraging, preventing or condoning such varieties of risk-taking? How do we best incorporate knowledge about risks in our working relationships with clients?

As in other aspects of social work, the words and timing of discussing what may be difficult risk issues and decisions facing a family need careful attention (Stevenson and Taylor, in press; Taylor and McKeown, 2013). People's concepts of risk may vary (Taylor *et al.*, 2014). As an example, the word 'harm' may be more acceptable – and effective enough – than 'abuse' in some discussions with older people (Montgomery *et al.*, 2016). The conceptualisation of risk is something that you can develop with the client as part of your helping process (Best *et al.*, in press). For a more detailed consideration of young people's conceptualisation of risk, see Green *et al.* (2000).

The social work principle of empowerment involves seeking to maximise the power of clients and give them as much control as possible over their circumstances (Banks, 2001). In the context of decisions, empowerment might be viewed as *the entitlement to take risks and to exercise choice* (Ross and Waterson, 1996). Our social work role includes such dimensions as engaging clients in understanding and assessing risks to their health and well-being, helping them to clarify their values regarding options and helping communication and negotiation between family members where values and opinions differ. Does the client welcome or resent the choices available with their inherent dangers? It is important to recognise that values and perceptions of risk are likely to vary considerably between one individual and another, and between clients, professionals and society at large.

Engaging clients: using an interpreter

I am a hospital social worker. I am working with Mr Cheng, who is terminally ill with nasal cancer, towards discharge. Mr Cheng and his family are from the Chinese community. Communication with Mr Cheng has been difficult due to fluctuating confusion; Mrs Cheng has limited English. They were reluctant to involve an interpreter due to the nature of the issues to be discussed, preferring instead to involve their son, aged 11 years. However, as Mr Cheng's illness progressed and the nature of the issues became more personal I thought that it was not appropriate for their son to be involved. I carefully explained this to Mr and Mrs Cheng as well as I could. I tried to get an interpreter for the next meeting but none was available at short notice, but Mrs Cheng brought along a trusted friend who could interpret. The meeting went well, even though the use of an interpreter presented a challenge for me in discussing sensitive issues.

- *What are your employer's arrangements for when you need an interpreter?*
- *What knowledge, skills and practical arrangements do you need in order to use an interpreter most effectively?*

We have a key role in helping clients to verbalise potential gains in possible courses of action (such as quality of life, normalisation, independence, etc.) as well as possible harms in decisions as a rationale for taking risks. In responding to clients, we need to try to assess severity and complexity of problems and their intent and motivation to change. We may need to promote an awareness of dangers, to help clients consider the long-term effects (health, relationships, financial, etc.) of a decision, to address risk issues including conflict with social norms, to consider the responsibility of roles that they have (e.g. as a parent or employee), and to help them reflect on the appropriateness of spontaneous decisions in terms of the implications for themselves and others. *To make good choices people need to understand the consequences and take some responsibility for them. So we want to promote a culture of choice that entails responsible, supported decision making* (DH, 2007, p1).

As social workers, our task is not only to carry out safeguarding tasks, to undertake therapeutic work or to be a gate-keeper for publicly funded or charitably funded services. We also try to facilitate clients and families in good decision making, perhaps by clarifying and strengthening their own powers of will and decision. Part of the assessment process (see Chapter 3) is the social worker helping the client towards a greater self-consciousness and a broader perspective on the issues he or she is experiencing. There are many schemas that might be used depending on the client and the issue, including the Janis and Mann model cited above or the following:

- What are the main issues and responsibilities in this decision?
- What are the principles and values informing the decision?

- What are the consequences (impact) of the available options?

- Who would be a good person to ask for advice, and why?

- What do your conscience and intuition suggest?

- What is the reasoning process, and is it logical?

A key skill in avoiding bias (see Chapter 4) is to 'keep close' to the information provided by the referral source(s) and the client. Assessment involves a process of exploring the problem step by step, at the client's pace, informed by professional knowledge but avoiding making assumptions or foreclosing options by precipitate words or actions.

CASE STUDY **2.4**

Client capacity to choose

Brendan (aged 27 years) has a learning disability and lives in a supported housing scheme. He decided that he wanted to buy some brightly coloured shorts. The care worker did not think that they suited him and said that he should not buy them. She later discussed this with me in supervision as the social worker managing the scheme. The care worker came to recognise that Brendan had capacity to make this decision. At the end of the day there was no substantive reason why he should not buy these shorts, such as, for example, a level of immodesty that might cause offence to others. Brendan lives in a holiday town and this style of shorts was being worn by other young men.

Person-centred approaches are central to social work (Taylor and Devine, 1993; DH, 2001 and 2009). However, our values as individuals or as a profession may not concur with those of our clients. We have responsibilities as a profession to make judgements about the provision of appropriate services, to be able to stand over any decision to support risk taking by an individual client, to undertake statutory safeguarding responsibilities, and to prioritise services across clients as public and charitable resources are not sufficient to meet the needs of all those seeking them. These various dimensions, and their interplay with any particular client and family, require knowledgeable and skilled professional approaches.

Collaborative decisions and games people play

In common with other citizens, our clients may be more sceptical than in previous generations about the expertise of professionals (Slovic, 1999). With the ever-expanding volume of potentially useful knowledge, it is important not only that professionals keep up to date but also that we recognise our limitations. With our consistent approach to being person focused and listening to the client, social work does not lag behind other professions in this regard. Social workers have a key role in helping to provide security and protection for individuals in society, even though it is impossible to predict or prevent all harm. Making effective decisions that minimise the probability of unwanted harm is most effective as a collaborative exercise between professional and client wherever this is possible. Measures to promote respect and effective communication are central to our professional task of creating trusting relationships where dangers can be discussed openly and honestly, and decisions made that are most helpful in enabling, safeguarding and advising clients.

As social workers we sometimes make judgements about the most desirable course of action in the best interests of the client and family. We then try to bring clients and families along with these proposals. There may be varying levels of support from different family members. In the study of decision making, such situations are called *game theory*. This does not imply that the consequences do not matter or that the content is purely recreational. Game theory is essentially about power, relationships and interactions that occur in decision making. *Game theory attempts to mathematically capture behavior in strategic situations, in which an individual's success in making choices depends on the choices of others* (Wikipedia, 2009, **http:// en.wikipedia.org/wiki/Game_theory**). There may be active competition to *win* this serious *game*, with very different views of what is a desirable outcome! Other *players* in the decision (clients, family, other professionals and organisations) may be seeking their own concept of a fair outcome (which may be different from your own) or may deliberately sabotage your attempts at *reasonable* decision making (Beach and Connolly, 1997).

Clients may be less familiar with the *rules* of *the game* particularly if they are complex, such as in child protection court hearings. On the other hand, some clients are rather more streetwise than professionals, and can readily find out about and use (or misuse) legitimate or illegitimate loopholes that they perceive in order to thwart safeguarding plans. As another example, it is well known that some clients will create a commotion to get their own way, perhaps utilising the media or a sympathetic politician. They know that most organisations and managers have little stomach for a fight and are likely to give in to their demands, even though this almost always means that other clients (normally not so visible, on a waiting list) will receive less or no service (Taylor, 2006b). The reader interested in the victim-persecutor-rescuer 'game that (some) people play' is referred to Karpman (1968).

Client problem solving and collaborative assessment

Supporting clients in their own problem solving is a key social work task (Best *et al.*, 2016). This should not be forgotten even though this book is written from a frame of reference that focuses on risks, assessment and decision making. Some people can have distorted views about the causes of harmful outcomes or unrealistic expectations of positive outcomes. Part of the social work task is to understand a person's strengths (both psychological and social) and find creative ways to enable people to feel the satisfaction of using their strengths to address the issues. Part of the social work role may equally be to challenge the person to reflect on their own knowledge and values in the light of more objective evidence and the values of the wider society. Sometimes it may be necessary to tolerate minor short-term risks for long-term gains; clients may be more willing to engage, even if they do not agree with the outcome, if the process is skilful. A *problem-solving* approach emphasises the creativity in finding solutions aspect of decision making more than the choice aspect. The time aspect – such as monitoring developments and reviewing progress – as discussed in Chapter 9, will be particularly relevant. The reader interested in problem-solving approaches to helping is referred to Egan (2010). Further material on assessment can be found in Chapter 4.

ACTIVITY **2.4**

A checklist for managing personal problems

1. *Am I engaging in the steps of effective problem management?*

2. *Am I owning responsibility for the authorship of my life?*

3. *Am I in touch with my underlying feelings?*

4. *Am I using self-talk constructively?*

5. *Are my personal rules and directives helping rather than harming me?*

6. *Are my perceptions accurate regarding myself and others?*

7. *Are my attributions of cause accurate?*

8. *Are my predictions realistic?*

9. *Am I articulating my goals clearly and do they reflect my values?*

10. *Am I using visualizing to best effect?*

(Nelson-Jones, 1989, Table 11.1, p180)

Supporting client decision making

Supporting clients in making choices to achieve increased independence may involve risk-taking in situations where clients, professionals and organisations are aware of exposure to potential loss and have to accept that in the hope of potentially greater gains. Supporting clients and families in these complex decision-making processes requires a person-centred approach to practice. Clients need information upon which to base their choices and a key role for social workers is to inform clients with reliable information based on sound sources of knowledge.

The reader interested in supporting clients through structuring decision making is referred to the literature review in Davidson *et al.* (2015).

CASE STUDY 2.5

Engaging clients in decisions and risk taking

Mr Smith, 89 years old, had a prolonged hospital admission caused by a fractured neck of femur, and complications caused by heart failure. When referral was made to me to make plans for appropriate discharge, assessments had already been undertaken by a range of professionals who had reached a consensus that Mr Smith's physical health and care needs had changed significantly enough during hospital placement that he would require long-term nursing home care.

An important part of my task involved exploring Mr Smith's perception of the benefits of taking the risks involved in his wish to be at home. These could be recognised as his sense of emotional well-being, sense of independence and control of his life. Mr Smith said that he placed greater importance and value on the independence of living alone in his own home above more support with his physical needs which he recognised that he may receive in a care home setting.

The outcome was that Mr Smith was fully aware and understood the impact of the changes in his health and the limitations that this placed on his ability to be fully independent at home. He openly acknowledged and accepted that he would have to change his routine and lifestyle at home to reduce risks. Mr Smith and his family were taking responsibility for the risks and their decisions. The strengths in this situation were that Mr Smith's family fully supported his decision to take the risk and at least have a trial period at home. This was completely successful; Mr Smith continues to live in his own home with a mixture of support from statutory services, family and voluntary agency. Part of the social work role in this case was also bringing along others in the multi-disciplinary team with the outcome and helping them understand the reason for Mr Smith's decision.

As an adult with full capacity to make decisions, Mr Smith always had the ultimate decision about his discharge plan. However, engaging in the risk assessment process not only fulfilled agency requirements and ensured that risks were not ignored, but it also enabled Mr Smith to make an informed decision. The involvement of his family in the risk assessment process led to them being committed and involved in the risk management plan, which included:

- *a care package with four structured daily calls by a home care worker;*

- *a daily visit by a family member (which was taken in turn);*

- *a fortnightly visit by a district nurse;*

- *use of an aid call button which would be worn at all times by Mr Smith (to be used in the event that he fell or was unwell); and*

- *regular review and monitoring by the community social worker.*

Taylor (2006b) suggests that health and safety legislation (see Chapter 8) and fear of litigation is pushing professionals to be less willing to take risks in their recommendations. The effect may be lost opportunities to promote client health and well-being. The complex issue of client choice versus the responsibility of professionals and organisations if some harm should ensue to someone with whom they have had dealings has led to a welcome publication by the UK Department of Health (DH, 2007) on professionals supporting decision making by adult clients. This provides a helpful framework of common principles to underpin good practice. The starting point is the right of clients to make choices unless they are not capable or this would cause harm to others or would otherwise break the law. *The governing principle behind good approaches to choice and risk is that people have the right to live their lives to the full as long as that does not stop others from doing the same. Fear of supporting people to take reasonable risks in their daily lives can prevent them from doing the things that most people take for granted* (DH, 2007, p3, para. 5). A number of key principles are outlined in this UK government document for social workers supporting adult client decision making.

To put this principle into practice, people supporting users of services have to:

- *help people to have choice and control over their lives;*

- *recognise that making a choice can involve some risk;*

- *respect people's rights and those of their family carers;*

- *help people understand their responsibilities and the implications of their choices, including any risks;*

- *acknowledge that there will always be some risk, and that trying to remove it altogether can outweigh the quality of life benefits for the person; and*

- *continue existing arrangements for safeguarding people.*

(DH, 2007, pp12–13, para. 1.7)

The Department of Health has made available a supported decision tool (see Appendix 2) as an aid to standardising basic best practice. While this does not go into the complexities that are frequently involved in social work decisions with clients, it does provide a sound starting point in terms of supporting clients' decisions as a basic normal approach where possible. The very use of such a structured tool should assist in developing consistent, robust decision making, not least by promoting thorough record-keeping on decision processes.

This supported decision tool highlights the role of the professional in providing information to assist in client decision making. Too often this role is not noticed because it is not recorded. The provision of timely and appropriate information is a practical way in which social workers empower clients to make decisions. It is beyond the scope of this book to consider the legal and communication issues where an individual lacks capacity to make a decision. The interested reader is referred to Godefroy (2015).

RESEARCH SUMMARY 2.4

Older people's concept of elder abuse and access to services

Purpose

This study focused on older people's concept of elder abuse and their perspectives on access to services.

Method

Fifty-eight people aged 65 years and over participated in focus groups across the island of Ireland, including both urban and rural settings. Four peer-researchers were trained to assist in recruitment, data collection, analysis and dissemination. This qualitative study used elements of a grounded theory approach.

Findings and conclusion (1)

Increasing lack of respect within society was experienced as abusive, and as under-pinning the growing problem of abuse. The vulnerability of older people to abuse was perceived as relating to the need for help and support, where standing up for themselves might have repercussions for the person's health or safety. Emotional (psychological) abusiveness was viewed as underpinning all forms of abuse, and as influencing its experienced severity. Determining whether an action was abusive required an understanding of intent; actions that an outsider (such as a professional) might view as abusive may be acceptable to enable the older person to continue living at home. Preventing abuse requires a wide-ranging approach including re-building respect for older people within society. Procedures to prevent elder abuse need to take into account the emotional impact of family relationships and the intent of the alleged perpetrator, rather than focusing on a description of behaviours that have occurred (reported in O'Brien et al., 2011).

Findings and conclusion (2)

Participants identified community-based schemes and peer support as important mechanisms to support people experiencing, and being at risk of, elder abuse. Choices regarding care provision and housing, as well as opportunities for engagement in community activities where they can discuss issues with their peers, were identified as ways to prevent abuse. Enhanced attention and resources should be directed to community activities that enable older people to share their concerns informally, thereby gaining confidence to seek more formal interventions when necessary (Begley et al., 2012; Taylor et al., 2014).

Client engagement in decision outcomes

Co-operation is often required in order to achieve the goals that the client and you (on behalf of your profession and organisation) desire. Negotiation and collaboration are essential in order that each person plays their part. Careful thought may need to be given to the best strategy to *win* the desired outcome – particularly in a safeguarding situation – to the ultimate benefit of the vulnerable client, even if other family members may not be seeking the same solution. Aspects such as building trust and encouraging client motivation through approaches designed to elicit co-operation are an important part of the professional task. We will return to this theme in Chapter 8 in terms of justifying risk-taking decision making and in Chapter 9 in terms of the goals of care planning. The results of various experiments suggest that generosity and openness pay off best in eliciting co-operative behaviour (Hardman, 2009, p167), confirming basic social work values. Efforts to engage clients in evaluating meaningful outcomes are becoming increasingly a focus in social work (see Case Study 2.6), and there is increasing attention on developing effective approaches to shared decision making, including provision of information (Turnpenny and Beadle-Brown, 2015) and facilitating more explicit discussion of risk issues (Stevenson *et al.*, in press). For fuller discussion of outcomes and their evaluation – for both clients and organisations – the reader is referred to Taylor *et al.* (2015).

CASE STUDY 2.6

Questions to appraise parental engagement when a child is admitted to care

- *Did you read the assessment of your child's needs before it was presented at the review?*

- *Were you satisfied with your level of involvement in your child's care plan?*

- *Were you satisfied with the level of communication with the key worker during the placement?*

Envisioning the future in decision making

One of the tasks for the social worker may be to help the client and family to *envision the future*. This concept is adapted from more recent approaches to conceptualising decision-making processes known as *image theory*, which is part of a broader framework known as *naturalistic decision making* (Beach and Connolly, 1997). Being able to visualise the consequences (both positive and negative) can be particularly difficult when in a state of crisis or at a critical decision point. The multiple, conflicting pressures may make it difficult to hope sufficiently to believe in a positive outcome; earnest aspirations for a life with greater independence may cloud judgement about the real hazards ahead. This might be viewed as a decision-making parallel to solution-focused brief therapy methods of helping clients.

Image theory suggests three key main categories of images that people use to guide their decision making. Each image category is used in turn to provide standards that are used to screen out unacceptable options.

1.   **Values image**

     Image theory gives a primary place to the values of the decision maker, reflecting the way that they think things should be and the principles that underpin their own and others' behaviour. The starting point in a decision situation is to consider the basic values, principles, conscience and beliefs of the individual. This may be sufficient to address a dilemma and clarify how the presenting situation fits with the rest of the individual's life and purposes.

2.   **Life goals image** (also called 'Trajectory image')

     Decision makers have a vision or goal of the situation they want to be in, the way they want their life to be. This constitutes a vision that shapes the decision-making process. If a person's basic values and principles (as in 1) do not clarify the choice to be made, an exploration of their life goals or vision may clarify the choice between alternatives. This ensures that this decision fits within a broader meaningful framework for the individual.

3.   **Tactics image** (also called 'Strategic image')

     Decision makers have operational tactics for engaging in decision-making and problem-solving processes, and ways in which they attempt to forecast the outcomes in turn guide how they behave in making or influencing decisions. If the consideration of fundamental values and life goals (as in 1 and 2) does not

Table 2.1   Supporting the client in envisioning the future

---

1. Values image
- o   What are the relevant values of the decision maker?
- o   How do they think things should be?
- o   What beliefs and principles should underpin their own and others' behaviour?
- o   What impact do these have on the decision?

2. Life goals image

   If the values image in stage 1 does not resolve the decision dilemma:
- o   What vision does the decision maker have of the situation they want to be in?
- o   How do they want their life to be?
- o   What goals are most important?
- o   Which option fits best within the life goals for the decision maker?

3. Tactics image

   If neither the values image in stage 1 nor the life goals image in stage 2 fully resolve the decision dilemma:
- o   What are the decision-making processes for the individual regarding this issue?
- o   What options are available for engaging in the problem-solving process?
- o   What outcomes are likely for each option?
- o   What tactics are likely to be most effective to achieve the desired goals?

(Adapted from image theory of decision making; see Beach and Connolly, 1997)

resolve the dilemma, this consideration of the approach to engaging in a more detailed decision process may be required.

To illustrate this model in practice, a decision may be made on the basis of your beliefs and values (stage 1). For example, if you do not agree morally with gambling you will use this first category of images to decide to ignore an invitation to buy a lottery ticket. If you are facing a decision where either option is acceptable in terms of your values, this model suggests that you then decide in terms of life goals (stage 2). As an example, you make a career choice on the basis of the job you would like to be doing in ten years' time, although your present job and the one advertised are both morally acceptable (i.e. both meet the standard of the first values image). If you do not eliminate the options through either the first or second option you may make the decision on the basis of the third category of images, tactics or processes to achieve what you want. For example, you want your children returned home from state care (on the basis of your values, image category 1), you want a family lifestyle that includes the children (on the basis of your life goals, image category 2), so the decision is about the tactics of how to engage with the child protection case conference to which you have been invited (see Table 2.1). If there is still more than one option remaining after reaching this third category of images, you may find it helpful to consider the decision model of *balancing benefits and harms* which is considered in Chapter 8.

Managing risk: client ownership of the decision

Engaging clients in assessment and decisions is particularly pertinent in terms of care (risk, safeguarding) planning, in other words, how the decision will be implemented. We have already considered some issues in engaging clients in the decision process; consent as a mechanism to manage risk in supporting clients in reasoned, reasonable risk-taking is discussed further in Chapter 3. Where there are multiple challenges facing clients, we need to partialise and prioritise in deciding about services and support for change (Doel and Marsh, 1992).

Although the main factors to be taken into account in considering the likelihood of harm are those (*actuarial*) factors that are tested through research, the less tangible *clinical* factors take on greater importance in implementing the decision through a care plan. Those less tangible factors about the client, family and their situation need to be considered more fully at this stage to:

- seek maximum ownership of the implementation of the decision;

- maximise motivation to improve adherence to the plan;

- take into account cultural, religious and ethnic aspects of regular routines of living;

- ensure that the care plan is workable; and

- tailor the plan to the unique needs of this client and family within the framework of an intervention that is proven to be effective in situations that are somewhat similar.

For those working in the mental health field there will be guidance, and often statute and regulation, about ascertaining client capacity to consent. The general principles can be applied to client consent to decisions and risk-taking in various practice settings. The rationale for a risk-taking decision may require you to articulate why client engagement and motivation is important for this helping relationship and for the eventual care outcomes.

CASE STUDY **2.7**

Mental capacity legislation

Mental capacity legislation in England and Wales (Mental Capacity Act 2005) indicates the following considerations in ascertaining capacity to consent.

Is the client able to:

11. *understand the relevant information? (information given in a simple appropriate way is sufficient)*

12. *retain that information? (retaining the information for a short period only is sufficient)*

13. *use that information in making the decision? (the information relevant to a decision includes information about the reasonably foreseeable consequences of deciding one way or another, or failing to make the decision)*

14. *communicate his decision? (by any means)*

This is a brief summary of essential points for a general audience; for detailed guidance and application to any particular case where this is mandatory see the mental capacity legislation in your jurisdiction.

Chapter summary

- People who come in contact with social workers – whether voluntarily or involuntarily – are often at a point of crisis and facing difficult decisions; the security of the relationship may be a key to doing the work around risk and decisions.

- The decisions of clients and families involve emotions, their values, their spirituality, and their understanding of information relevant to the decision such as the likelihood of harm, the options that they have and possible benefits in the alternative courses of action.

- Trust, resilience and confidentiality are often key issues for clients as they face difficult choices. Inappropriate use of social media can undermine the public credibility of professionals.

- The way that the problem and risks are framed, and the engagement of the client and family in the assessment process, can be crucial for subsequent decision processes.

- *Game theory* can help us to understand the dynamics of decision-making processes with clients and families.

- As a social worker, you have a role in supporting reasonable and informed client decisions in accord with professional guidance, values and standards, and the legal and policy frameworks for your practice.

- The decision model known as *image theory* can help us to conceptualise the professional role in supporting clients in decision making in some circumstances.

FURTHER READING

Department of Health (2007) *Independence, Choice and Risk: A Guide to Best Practice in Supported Decision Making.* London: Department of Health. **www.thinklocalactpersonal.org.uk/_assets/Resources/Personalisation/Direct_Payments/Risk_Management/DH_074775.pdf**

This best practice guide by the UK Department of Health is for the use of everyone involved in supporting adults using health and social care within any setting, whether community or residential, in the public, private and voluntary sectors. This is a key text giving principles for supporting client decision making, and recognising that caring for people involves supporting them in reasonable risk-taking.

Department of Health (2010) *Practical Approaches to Safeguarding and Personalisation.* London: Department of Health.

This guide provides useful pointers to reconciling a responsibility to promote the choice of service users with a responsibility to safeguard the vulnerable from harm.

Shulman, L. (2011) *The Skills of Helping Individuals, Families, Groups and Communities.* Itasca, IL: F.E. Peacock.

This is an excellent text for social work practice skills, which are an essential underpinning for working with individuals and families in decision-making processes.

Taylor, B.J. (ed.) (2011) *Working with Aggression and Resistance in Social Work.* London: Sage.

This readable textbook contains general chapters on topics such as understanding resistance and defusing aggression as well as chapters about working more effectively with each major client group.

Thom, B., Sales, R. and Pearce, J.J. (eds) (2007) *Growing Up with Risk.* Bristol: Policy Press.

This book summarises research regarding children and a wide range of risk issues in growing up. It is useful for helping to understand the world of children and risk.

Chapter 3

Legal aspects of decisions, assessment and risk

Give your decisions, never your reasons; your decisions may be right, your reasons are sure to be wrong.

(Earl of Mansfield (1705–1793) quoted in Peter, 1980, p273)

Introduction

This chapter considers legal aspects of assessment, risk and judgement which are common across client groups. Legal aspects of collaborative decision making, including the social work role in formal settings such as a court, are discussed further in Chapter 8. We consider the principles underlying consent and negligence as a benchmark for good decision making in legal and, by extension, other contexts where decisions are challenged also. We outline in lay terms the principles underpinning the law relating to the tort of negligence as it relates to the duty of care of professionals, highlighting the need to seek legal advice through organisational arrangements as appropriate. The law is viewed as supporting reasoned, reasonable risk-taking as something inherent in the professional task. The case law developments are put in the context of the more recent codification of some relevant principles in the Human Rights Act 1998. We discuss liability for multi-professional 'decision making' and legal aspects of decisions under time pressure. We mention briefly capacity to make decisions; for a fuller discussion of mental capacity the reader is referred to Brown *et al*. (2015). Our basic approach is to help you to be a competent, confident, caring professional through a fuller appreciation of how the law supports reasonable, reasoned decision making.

This chapter is intended only as an introductory guide to legal aspects of professional decision making. Do not rely upon this book as a substitute for legal advice on any individual set of circumstances. This chapter aims to inform you about general principles and issues so that you are more able to identify when legal advice needs to be sought, and enable you to better understand and discuss the issues. This book does not purport to address the detailed legal requirements in any particular jurisdiction, but to educate on general principles that are common in democratic countries for 'defensible' (rather than 'defensive') professional practice.

The basis of law

What avenues for redress do you think that you should have as a citizen if you think that a public body or licensed professional has made a wrong decision relating to some service that you want to receive? Conversely, what protections do you think that you as a professional should have from complaints about your decisions, complaints which may be malicious or ill-informed? There are various remedies in democratic societies for those who are aggrieved, and for applying sanctions, pressure or penalties to those who make decisions that are not regarded as sufficiently robust. In our society these include inquiries, serious case reviews, inspections, reports by commissions and actions by politicians and the media to name and shame public bodies and individual employees. The law is a primary mechanism for accountability and that is our focus here, although the principles apply in other contexts where professional decisions are challenged.

There are two main branches to the law in the democratic world: criminal law and civil law. Criminal law relates to conduct deemed so undesirable that it is prohibited and made a criminal offence. Civil law provides a forum for an individual to argue the case for compensation or other civil remedy when he feels wronged by another citizen or an organisation. In the UK there are two main sources of law: legislation and common law.

Legislation may place specified responsibilities on government departments and public bodies that employ social workers, such as local authorities and Health and Social Care Trusts in Northern Ireland (where statutory functions are vested in the Health and Social Care Board which then delegates powers and duties to the Trusts). Such statutory functions include both powers and duties. Duties are things that the authority *shall* do; powers are things that it *may* do. An organisation or individual may only exercise powers or duties that are prescribed for that organisation or individual.

Common law is formed by the decisions of courts in decided cases. Through an appeal to a higher court the principles on which a judgement has been made will be clarified and the judgement may be upheld or overturned. A precedent is the judgement in a legal case which will then be used in future by courts in decisions regarding similar cases. Higher court judgements become binding on all lower courts (see, for example, the case of Diane Pretty in relation to her attempt to seek permission from the courts for her husband to assist her to end her own life: **http://en.wikipedia.org/wiki/Diane_Pretty**). Case law precedent is the basis for most of our consideration of professional negligence and standards of care, although increasingly the Human Rights Act 1998 is being used in this context.

Regulation of professionals

One of the mechanisms in democratic societies for ensuring high quality work (including assessments and decisions) is to require registration of major professions and employment groups. This includes a diverse range including accountants, electricians, engineers, medical doctors, and the whole range of health and social care professions – including social work in most developed countries. Registration normally requires the attainment of qualifying training that meets specified standards (at graduate level for a profession); a register from which individuals can be struck off for bad practice; and some provision for making it a crime for someone to pass themselves off as a qualified worker if they are not appropriately qualified. In the European Union, these three standards apply to registration of professions, and social work in all parts of the UK now meets the EU standards. Such regulatory bodies have quasi-legal mechanisms to determine whether a professional is fit to continue practising. The main focus of this chapter is on the interface between the law and professional practice as it applies to client situations, including the general standards of practice that are required of professionals making decisions and managing risk. The law in the UK expects professionals to exercise professional discretion that is reasoned and reasonable.

CASE STUDY 3.1

Expectations of professional judgement

A profoundly disabled young man was living with his mother and two siblings. He was considered under the relevant social welfare statute (the Chronically Sick and Disabled Persons Act 1970 and the direct payments for care regulations in England) for publicly funded services. The court criticised a social worker for reporting that a certain level of care was needed whilst failing to indicate that he or she thought that this level of care was required and for failing to explain why such a level of care might be required. It was not acceptable for a professional simply to reiterate the family views.

R (on the application of KM) (by his mother and litigation friend JM) v Cambridgeshire County Council *[2012] UKSC 23 (also at: 1218-1236 All England Law Reports [2012] 3 All ER).*

The law and reasonable decision making

The main aim of this chapter is to reduce anxiety about legal aspects of decision making so as to support confident, sound professional practice. A key concept is that of *reasonable* decision making. Lord Diplock, summing up the court judgement in *Council of Civil Service Unions v Minister for the Civil Service* [1985] AC 374, identified three grounds of review of administrative decisions (illegality, irrationality and procedural impropriety) and suggested that a fourth ground (proportionality – a European Law concept) might also be adopted in the future.

- Legality involves the appropriate interpretation of statutes for their intended purpose, so decisions must take into account relevant criteria and not take into account irrelevant considerations.

- Rationality means not deliberately evading the purpose of legislation by making an obscure, irrational decision that takes advantage of a loophole. It applies to a decision that is *so unreasonable that no reasonable authority could ever have come to it* in the words of Lord Greene (*Associated Provincial Picture Houses v Wednesbury Corporation* [1948] 1 KB 223).

- Procedural propriety means observing the rules of natural justice and giving a fair hearing to the issues, and also observing statutory requirements.

- Proportionality (as a result of the Human Rights Act 1998) has become an increasingly important ground of review and means asking whether it is necessary to act in a way which will result in the limitation of an individual right and whether the action is the least necessary to achieve the aim being pursued (*R (Daly) v Home Secretary* [2001] UKHL 26).

Decisions about individual clients cannot be made with disregard to the issue of overall resources for services, and the courts generally recognise this. The general requirement is that where resources for a service are being reduced, it is not acceptable simply to reduce the service for individual clients without a re-assessment of their needs. For the chief officer of a public health and social care organisation there may also be a statutory duty to stay within budget.

Decisions themselves must not only be fair but also the manner in which a decision is made must also be fair. Reasonable processes in terms of decision making also include dimensions such as participation, information-sharing, timeliness and consideration of relevant factors.

Decision policies along the lines that we discuss in Chapter 6 may be useful to promote consistency of decision making by individuals. However, in terms of decision policies to promote consistency across an organisation, case law seems to indicate that 'decision makers' must not fetter their own discretion through having over-rigid policies. In other words, a decision policy *assists good administration by promoting consistency and indicating to applicants how discretion might be exercised. However, a policy must not be mechanically applied and must not be so rigid that it prevents the decision maker from exercising discretion in any given case* (White et al., 2009, p98). Case law precedents seem to indicate that organisations can be obliged to make exceptions for situations that otherwise might not seem exceptional in relation to the purpose of the decision policy (see, for example, *Eisai Limited v the National Institute for Health and Clinical Excellence (NICE)* [2007] EWHC 1941 (Admin) QBD (Admin)). This makes the development of policies to promote consistent judgement more difficult. The word *normally* might usefully be included in such decision policies! In exercising discretion, professionals and managers must consider the matter at issue and not just say *no*. The following points may be useful to help you make reasoned, reasonable ('defensible' rather than 'defensive') decisions.

You should:

- identify the correct basis in law, regulations, guidance, standards, policy and procedures;

- and follow any statutory criteria (e.g. in the application of terms used in an Act or in any procedural requirements);

- make sure you know what your powers are; do not go beyond them and use them for the powers for which they are intended (the spirit as well as the letter of the law);

- take into account relevant considerations and do not take into account irrelevant considerations (including avoiding discrimination);

- follow the requirements of natural justice (for example: letting people have their say; not making up rules after the event; hearing 'both sides'; avoiding bias);

- use mandated assessment processes and any relevant employer procedures to gather appropriate information;

- reach decisions based on the evidence;

- be able to demonstrate the basis for your views and the communication with the client before reaching conclusions (see Baker J in *CC v KK and another* [2012] EWHC 2136(COP));

- act in good faith and with fairness;

- apply appropriate statutory safeguards (such as the Human Rights Act 1998, which is now relevant to all decisions of 'public authorities' in the UK); and

- act reasonably: there should be some rational line of argument that you can adduce to support your decision.

(Cf. Bingham, 2011)

The last bullet above about a professional having a rational line of argument in order for the decision to be considered reasonable provides the legal imperative for evidence-based practice in social work, including knowledge from research and theory as well as up-to-date information about the client and family context. The reader interested in more on the use of knowledge within professional decision making is referred to Taylor *et al.* (2015).

It should be noted that courts in the UK seem to draw a distinction between the liability of professionals and organisations in relation to children who are in the care of the state and situations of investigating (assessing) situations of alleged abuse (where sufficient powers and freedom from impediment are required in order that the task may be carried out effectively). For example in *S v Gloucestershire County Council* [2000] 3 CCLR 294, a child was placed with foster parents who sexually abused the child. The court found the local authority which provided these social services as liable for damages. Conversely in *D v Bury Metropolitan Borough Council* [2006] EWCA Civ 1, a four-month-old baby was found to have fractured ribs and it was thought that these had been caused by a non-accidental injury. The local authority social services department obtained an Interim Care Order which permitted it to remove the baby from the parents. It was later discovered that the baby had, in fact, suffered from brittle bone disease and the injuries were indeed accidental. The baby was returned to the parents and care proceedings against the parents terminated. The parents then sued the local authority in negligence for the psychological harm that they had suffered as a result of the unsubstantiated allegations against them and the removal of their baby. Despite acknowledgement by the court that the parents were entirely innocent of committing any abuse and had indeed suffered psychological harm as a consequence of the allegations, the case was held to be not actionable in negligence. In other words, social workers were held not to owe a duty of care to the parents and therefore could not be sued. It would not be possible for professionals such as social workers to carry out their responsibilities effectively in areas such as protecting children from abuse if they were liable for decisions that had been carried out in good faith, using appropriate processes and using the best knowledge available at the time.

Gross negligence in criminal law

Our main focus is on negligence in civil law. We should mention briefly that there is the possibility in the most serious cases of an individual being prosecuted for the crime of gross negligence (see, for example, *Prentice* [1993] 3 WLR 927 approved by House of Lords in *Regina Respondent v Adomako Appellant* [1994] 3 WLR 288 and [1995] 1 AC 171). As there is no known case at present of a social worker being convicted of gross negligence manslaughter, we will not consider the matter further here and the interested reader is referred to a more detailed text such as Carson and Bain (2008).

Human Rights Act

The European Convention on Human Rights (1950) (ECHR) was ratified by the UK in 1951. This international treaty focuses on identifying and protecting certain fundamental rights and freedoms such as the right to life; the right to a fair trial; freedom of thought, conscience and religion; and freedom of expression. The Human Rights Act 1998 (HRA) came into force in the UK in October 2000, requiring all courts to take into account the European Convention on Human Rights. Some rights relate to actions of public authorities; others relate to the broader culture which governments have agreed should be created within society. Actions or inactions of public sector social workers and their employers, and failure to comply with these 'human rights', may be and are subject to challenge in court.

A key issue for social work practice in signatory countries is Article 8 of the European Convention on Human Rights (Council of Europe 1953), whereby everyone has the right to *respect for his private and family life, home and correspondence*. This right is a qualified right; that is, it is subject to restriction clauses that enable a consideration of the balance between the rights of the individual and the public interest. This article states: *There shall be no interference by a public authority with the exercise of this right except such as in accordance with the law and is necessary in a democratic society in the interests of … public safety, … for the prevention of crime and disorder, for the protection of health or morals, or for the protection of the rights and freedoms of others.*

Articles 2 and 3 of the ECHR are also relevant to practice decisions. The Convention rights impose positive obligations to promote and protect, such as responding to alleged abuse (see for example *Osman v UK* (23452/94) [1998] 29 EHRR 245 and *Z v UK* [2002] 34 EHRR 3), as well as negative obligations not to interfere. Article 5 and the *Bournewood* case (*HL v UK* [2004] 40 EHRR) influenced the development of the Mental Capacity Act 2005.

Other potential areas of impact of the Human Rights Act relevant to the focus of this book are:

- delays in assessment of individuals for domiciliary care services;

- retraction of services already being provided;

- failure to take account of the client's views;

- failure to respect confidentiality; and

- failure to meet an assessed need, and within a reasonable time.

Public sector employers of social workers need to demonstrate in formal decision pro-cesses that clients' rights under this legislation have been considered and taken into account. It should be noted that the last of these bullets requires a different interpre-tation of the task of 'assessing needs' than in many textbooks, including Taylor and Devine (1993). Rather than assessing needs in a holistic fashion (as broadly as seems appropriate) and then selecting those relevant to the purpose and services of the organisation, professionals now need to be careful to describe needs being assessed in relation to relevant services being considered. It was recognised in subsequent case law (*Re JC; D v JC* [2012] MHLO 35 (COP)) that a public service provider may be compelled by resources available to it to adopt a system which seeks to balance the fulfilment of those needs with the needs of others. Commonly this may be a waiting list system. This is not regarded as the organisation refusing to meet the applicant's assessed needs.

Human rights principles should inform and be an explicit part of the thinking and records in the professional decision-making processes. The following pointers may be useful.

- Involve those affected in the decision-making process, including family members, as far as is reasonable and practicable (see Chapter 2).

  - Note that this does not give clients or others a veto over a decision that is a responsibility of the organisation (see later in this chapter).

- Expressly consider the individual rights of each person involved.

- Consider the risks (to the vulnerable person) of any proposed measure (see Chapter 6).

- Consider the least intrusive measure that would achieve the desired objective.

- Consider the options available and the risks inherent in each (see Chapter 7).

- Balance the rights and freedoms of affected parties with the risks to the vulnerable person.

Contravention of an ECHR right may be made on the basis of a *legitimate aim*, such as when a social worker acting on behalf of a public body brings a court action to protect a child from abuse. Interference with a Convention right must be proportionate, i.e. the interference must be proportionate to the harm that it is intended to prevent, and must be carried out appropriately. For social workers, the core practice issue is that where there is a relevant right under the HRA, *interference* with that right must be explicitly justified when undertaking compulsory safeguarding actions both in the decision processes and in the decision outcomes.

The tort of negligence

An individual can take proceedings against another in the civil courts for compensation for loss or personal injury, usually on the basis of negligence or breach of statutory duties. The law in relation to negligence is largely determined by case law rather than by statutes. A liability in tort is conduct (other than in relation to a contract), which gives the victim a right to sue for compensation. Our focus is on the tort of negligence, which may be considered as *failure to take such care as the law requires*.

An individual may sue an organisation that employs a social worker, as well as the individual social worker, because they deem the social worker to have acted negligently. They are able to sue an employer as the employer may be liable for the acts of an employee. This is known as vicarious liability. However, if you are deemed to have acted outside of the scope of your authority then the employer will not be liable for the acts of the employee. In this situation only the employee, that is the social worker, will be liable for the payment of compensation. In the tort of negligence, the plaintiff must prove that:

- the defendant owed the plaintiff a legal duty of care;
- the legal duty of care was breached; and
- damage was suffered as a consequence.

This suggests five key questions for a professional defending a claim for negligence.

- Was there a duty of care?
- Did I breach the (relevant) standard of care?
- Did my breach of the standards of care cause the losses?
- Are those losses recognised by the law for compensation purposes?
- Were those losses reasonably foreseeable?

(Marsh and Soulsby, 1994; Carson and Bain, 2008; White, 2008)

We will consider these five questions in turn.

Who has a duty of care?

In *Pippin and Wife v Sheppard* [1822] 147 Eng. Rep. 512, the court found that *a medical practitioner has a duty to exercise reasonable skill and care*. This judgement would apply in principle to other professions. This common law principle was developed in *Donoghue v Stevenson* [1932] AC 562 12, identifying that a duty of care might be owed when any person is taking an action and where injury might be foreseen.

The first question is whether social work is a profession, which was addressed in 1994:

> *Those who engage professionally in social work bring to their task skill and exper-*
> *tise, the product partly of training and partly of experience, which ordinary,*
> *uninstructed members of the public are bound to lack. I have no doubt that they*
> *should be regarded as members of a skilled profession.*

(Sir Thomas Bingham in *M (Minor) v Newham London Borough Council; X v Bedfordshire County Council* [1994] WLR 554)

Since that time, social work in the UK has become a profession recognised across the European Union as it now meets the requirements of having a protected title; a register of those permitted to practise; and a requirement of three years of relevant study in higher education to qualify to practise.

One question that courts consider is: *Is it fair, just and reasonable to impose a duty of care on professionals carrying out a public service role* (cf. Carson and Bain, 2008)? Would imposing a duty of care deter or prevent social workers from carrying out essential public functions effectively? This is akin to the debates about the level of criminal activity (for example drug-taking) which a professional, such as a social worker, nurse or youth worker, should be obliged to disclose to the police in order to avoid committing an offence themselves. Would imposing a duty of care make the professional task of trying to help people in these situations impossible or ineffective?

In the case mentioned above, there was also consideration of to whom the duty of care is owed. The court concluded that a social worker, like a doctor, owed a certain duty of care to the person in his care, but in the advice given to the employing statutory authority by the social worker (in relation to recommendations to the court about child welfare), the general professional duty was to the employer, rather than to the client. In that particular case, the judiciary decided by a majority that the social workers (for whom the authority were liable) owed no legal duty of care to those children who had been on their caseload (*M (Minor) v Newham London Borough Council; X v Bedfordshire County Council* [1994] WLR 554; see also in [1995] 2 AC 633 and [1995] 3 WLR 152 and [1995] 3 All ER 353). Generally, the courts are reluctant to impose a duty of care on public servants. The House of Lords has imposed a duty of care on professionals in relation to a child who had been in statutory care from a few months old about matters arising while in care (*Barrett v Enfield London Borough Council* [2001] 2 AC 550, [1999] 3 All ER 193). However, it is generally considered unlikely that courts would impose a duty of care in relation to child protection and other areas of field social work (Carson and Bain, 2008), as it might render various social work tasks and roles impossible.

The basic message is that the scope of a duty *to* care depends on your personal beliefs and professional values, whereas a legal duty *of* care is a more precise concept defining who might be sued when a plaintiff alleges negligence.

Standards of care

The next question is whether the standard of care is acceptable. It is a defence that the professional acted in a way that would be considered reasonable by a responsible body of professional opinion. A medical doctor is *not guilty of negligence if he has acted in accordance with a practice accepted as proper by a responsible body of medical men skilled in that particular art* (Mr Justice McNair in *Bolam v Friern Hospital Management Committee* [1957] 1 WLR 582, [1957] 2 All ER 118). This judgement in relation to standards of care is now widely known as the *Bolam test*. The standard of care required is not the best possible practice, nor what the majority recommend nor what most practitioners do. The question is whether a responsible body of co-professional opinion would have supported the decision, at the date of the event and in the circumstances of the case. In other words, pioneering treatments and changes in care services and practices are not prevented, but there must be a level of professional support for the approach taken. Looked at the other way, *a doctor is not negligent, if he is acting in accordance with such a practice, merely because there is a body of opinion that takes a contrary view* (Mr Justice McNair in *Bolam v Friern Hospital Management Committee* [1957] 2 All ER 118, [1957] 1 WLR 582). In Scotland, the equivalent test is that a practitioner *has been proved to be guilty of such failure as no practitioner of ordinary skill would be guilty of if acting with ordinary care* (*Hunter v Hanley* [1955], s. 200).

The courts will seek to ascertain, as a matter of fact, professional standards of practice at the time of the event. It is normally a decision of the appropriate professional body to set standards of care for practice. However, the courts retain the right to be the final arbiter of a professional standard. Examples of a court overruling a professional standard as being too low are extremely rare. There is a crucial role for professional bodies in stating explicitly standards of practice.

The Bolam test must now be viewed in the light of the judgement in *Bolitho v City & Hackney Health Authority* [1998] House of Lords AC232. This case, involving a paediatrician in a hospital, concluded that professionals must be able to give a rationale such as research evidence or a theoretical basis for their views that an approach was justifiable in the circumstances (Foster, 1998). This judgement emphasises the essential place of *evidence-based practice* – using the best available evidence to inform decisions. We discuss this further in Chapter 5.

CASE STUDY **3.2**

Standards of care and reasonable risk-taking

Aquila is 58 years old with learning disability. She has epilepsy, is deaf, and has no speech. She was discharged four years ago to a small (24 bed) residential unit from a long-stay hospital. Staff were keen that she developed self-care skills and an agreed care plan was developed. They knew that she enjoyed baths. Over time she developed skills to take baths on her own, eventually locking others out. For three years, there was no problem. Then one day staff had to break open the bathroom door. She had experienced an epileptic fit, slipped down in the bath and drowned. The case was referred to the coroner.

(Continued)

(Continued)

- *What do you need to know to judge whether this was a sound care plan?*

- *What standards of care might apply in this situation?*

- *What might be done to ensure that the care plan was perceived as sound even if a tragedy or harm ensued?*

- *Who took what risks?*

- *Did the staff have legal power to stop Aquila bathing on her own?*

- *Is it relevant that the organisation had adopted a 'normalisation' policy?*

(See also R v HM Coroner for Reading ex parte West Berkshire Housing Consortium Ltd *[1995] CO/2994/94)*

Causation

If it is shown that a professional with a duty of care has breached his or her duty of care, then the plaintiff must show that the breach has caused injury. The injury might be deterioration in their condition, an adverse outcome, or treatment that they would not have undergone had the duty of care not been breached. The client has to prove that, but for the negligence, he or she would have been in a better position. The aim of compensation for negligence is to put the victim back into that position. Clearly, victims cannot turn back the clock. Financial compensation is based on the level of losses incurred in the past (whether physical or emotional) and those that may arise in the future as a consequence. The question at this point becomes: *would the harms or losses have been experienced even if the standard of care had not been breached?*

Recognised losses

The nature of the loss must be recognised by the courts for compensation purposes. This is one reason for the development of psychiatric diagnoses such as post-traumatic stress disorder (PTSD). This makes them identifiable and recognisable conditions for compensation purposes as well as for developing approaches to helping.

ACTIVITY **3.1**

Traumatic stress as a recognised loss

You were watching the FA Cup semi-final between Liverpool and Nottingham Forest at Hillsborough Stadium in Sheffield on television on 15 April 1989, when you saw the

human crush that led to the match being called off after six minutes. You needed treatment and time off work because you saw your loved ones among the 96 football fans
who perished in the tragedy.

- Could you sue to seek recompense for your lost earnings or medical, mental health or
  social care?

(http://en.wikipedia.org/wiki/Hillsborough_Disaster)

There are three main areas of loss that might be considered for the purpose of establishing a negligence claim: physical injury or loss of functional ability; financial loss;
and emotional loss or shock. This latter category has been recognised increasingly in
recent years, including in relation to the abuse of children. A basic criterion is that the
shock must have been experienced or observed directly.

Foreseeability of losses

The issue of foreseeability of harm can raise major issues in relation to supporting
clients to take reasonable risks in accordance with government policy and sound
professional values and standards. There needs to be clarity about who is taking the
risk. Is the client, informed and with capacity and freedom to choose, deciding to
take the risk? If risks are taken (as they must be in life, by everyone) then sometimes,
unfortunately, harm ensues. If professionals know that harm is possible they need to
discuss it with clients so that they can make an informed decision. The key question
is whether serious negative consequences should have been foreseen and were not.
The sort of *risk-taking* inherent in any independence programme (for example, learning road traffic skills or to use public transport for a person with a learning disability)
requires a *reasonable and reasoned approach* to the level of harm that may ensue
and its likelihood. *Donoghue v Stevenson* [1932] AC 562 550 was a defining judgement which established who owes a duty of care to whom by developing the legal
concept of 'neighbour'. Losses can only be recovered if they are foreseeable; that is,
they are not too remote.

ACTIVITY 3.2

Claudia's walk

*Claudia was a 17-year-old autistic child living in a residential unit who was taken for a
walk by a care worker. Claudia became agitated when she saw Mrs Partington walking
towards her and lashed out at her before the care worker could stop her. Mrs Partington
sued for damages on the grounds of negligence on the part of the local authority that ran
the residential unit regarding their lack of care and control of Claudia.*

(Continued)

59

(Continued)

- *Do you think that the authority or the worker is liable for damages?*

- *What do you want to know about the incident in reaching a judgement?*

- *What do you want to know about standards of practice at the time?*

- *What law or mandatory regulations are relevant if this situation arose now?*

- *How would you decide whether the policies and procedures in the unit were reasonable at the time?*

- *Is it relevant that Mrs Partington has a red and white stick to indicate her visual and hearing impairment and taps this on the pavement as she walks?*

- *In what circumstances would the care worker or the organisation have a right to prevent Claudia from taking a walk? (For a consideration of trespass to the person, see Dimond, 1997.)*

In this case the court held that the local authority was not liable, as Mrs Partington had not shown that Claudia was improperly supervised.

What the duty [of care] involved varied from person to person and, perhaps, from day to day, depending on the handicapped person's mood ... The problem was to balance what was best for the handicapped person with the interests of the rest of the world.

(Partington v London Borough of Wandsworth *[1990] Fam Law 468*)

Liability for risk-taking decisions

A key issue is the consent of the individual with capacity to take risks.

An individual who has the mental capacity to make a decision, and chooses voluntarily to live with a level of risk, is entitled to do so. The law will treat that person as having consented to the risk and so there will be no breach of the duty of care by professionals or public authorities.

(DH, 2007, p22, para. 2.26)

A competent adult who acknowledges and accepts a foreseeable risk would not be successful in suing for negligence. Client consent is a full defence to a claim in negligence, hence the importance of ensuring that this is evidenced in records in any risk-taking situation. However, statutory authorities remain accountable for the use of their funds, which must not be used for inappropriate purposes.

Ultimately the ... authority has a statutory duty of care and a responsibility not to agree to support a care plan if there are serious concerns that it will not meet an individual's needs or if it places an individual in a dangerous situation.

(DH, 2007, Executive Summary, para. 7)

It is not common for a court judgement to clarify the model of decision making used. An exception was the case of *Re JC; D v JC* [2012] MHLO 35 (COP), in which the court identified that in a case of deciding on a statutory will where an adult lacked testamentary capacity, there may be a factor of 'magnetic importance' which may resolve difficulties in identifying benefits and disbenefits.

ACTIVITY **3.3**

Consent to take risks

- *Identify a recent case where you felt uneasy about possible conflict.*

- *What is the most likely threat to your judgement?*

- *At what level of concern did you discuss your judgement with your professional supervisor or line manager?*

- *What recording did you make of the decision process?*

Consenting to take risks

It is generally regarded as your responsibility to ensure that your client is capable of giving consent to whatever care or treatment you are proposing. In multi-professional teams, it is common to look to specific professions to undertake particular tasks so as to create more co-operative working. However, this is not an excuse for a professional abdicating their responsibility for their own care planning with the client and family. In many jurisdictions (including England and Wales) there are mandatory procedures for ascertaining capacity to make decisions through mental capacity legislation. The same principles of good practice apply generally where there is not a specified process.

- *A person must be assumed to have capacity unless it is established that he lacks capacity.*

- *A person is not to be treated as unable to make a decision unless all practicable steps to help him to do so have been taken without success.*

- *A person is not to be treated as unable to make a decision merely because he makes an unwise decision.*

(Brown and Barber, 2008, p5 quoting from the Mental Capacity Act 2005 [England and Wales] Part 1, Section 1, The Principles)

If we disregard for the moment safeguarding decisions and illegal activities by clients, once we have satisfied ourselves that an adult client has capacity to make this care decision we have no right to stop them. If we have concerns about the proposed activity, we must then make a separate decision as to whether we in our profession or organisation are willing to support the care plan. There is an important distinction between people being harmed because of our activities and supporting a person with capacity in a decision-making process where they make an informed decision to take reasonable risks, as a result of which, inevitably, harm will sometimes ensue for some clients, as for any person.

> *An individual who has the mental capacity to make a decision, and chooses volun-tarily to live with a level of risk, is entitled to do so. The law will treat that person as having consented to the risk and so there will be no breach of the duty of care by professional or public authorities. However the local authority remains accountable for the proper use of its public funds, and whilst the individual is entitled to live with a degree of risk, the local authority is not obliged to fund it. In very difficult cases, there will need to be a robust process whereby conflict about the acceptabil-ity of risk or otherwise can be properly debated and resolved.*

(DH, 2007, p22, para. 2.26)

Decisional capacity

Professional judgements about consent and capacity to consent can be challenging in practice, and sometimes small acts present more challenge. In what circumstances has a care worker the right to take mouldering food out of a fridge? What happens if an ambulance is called and the person then shouts: *I don't want to go to hospital!*? When does weight loss become neglect or self-neglect? In terms of the law, compe-tence to consent is a question of fact in each case. There is a general presumption of competence, that is, it is generally presumed that an adult is competent unless it is shown otherwise. The duty is to the competent patient or client. The practice is to include family and relatives (as they are the most likely to complain after the event), but they rarely, if ever, have rights – especially when the patient or client objects. Except as provided under safeguarding provisions in mental health legislation *there is no power at the moment in law for one person to give consent on behalf of another adult* (Dimond, 1997, p36), except that Section 11(7) of the Mental Capacity Act 2005 (applying in England and Wales only) allows for limited power of consent by an individual with a lasting power of attorney regarding continuing treatment but not life-sustaining treatment (Pattison, 2006, p160). The basic principle remains that the pro-fessional must act in the best interests of the client. There is not scope within this book to explore this further. The interested reader is referred to the DH (2007) publi-cation on supporting choice and risk, and to Carson and Bain (2008).

CASE STUDY **3.3**

Enabling a client to understand the risks

Mr Eaton is a man of 88 years who is a widower living in sheltered accommodation. He has health problems and a history of falls, which increases his dependency on his daugh-ter for some daily living tasks. Mr Eaton has been subject to financial and psychological abuse from his daughter, who has threatened to withdraw her support. The theft of the money was not pursued by the police due to lack of evidence and the reluctance of

> *Mr Eaton to pursue the matter. Mr Eaton is registered as a vulnerable adult and my role is to engage the relevant professionals to assess the risks and create a protection plan. In discussion with Mr Eaton it became apparent how highly he valued his relationship with his daughter despite the abuse, and living in supported housing rather than a residential home. I focused my energies on ensuring that Mr Eaton understood the risks and was able to weigh up the consequences of his choice.*
>
> - *At what point does a client's expressed choice become so risky that you decide that an assessment of their capacity to make that decision is required?*
>
> - *What process do you use to ascertain their capacity to make that decision?*

Essentially, the question is whether the individual is unable to make their own decision in relation to the matter because of an impairment of, or a disturbance in the functioning of, the mind or brain. Key issues are:

- a general understanding of the decision to be made and why;

- an understanding of likely consequences of making or not making this decision;

- an ability to understand, retain, use and weigh up relevant information as part of the decision process; and

- ability to communicate this decision (by any means).

(see Mental Capacity Act 2005 [England and Wales]
and Code of Practice)

An informative case regarding capacity to consent was that of *Re: C (adult: refusal of medical treatment)* [1994] 1 All ER 819, where a man suffering from paranoid schizophrenia in a secure hospital refused to have his leg amputated even though the result was expected to be premature death. The court held that he was entitled to make that decision as he was competent, using criteria along the general lines outlined above. If a person lacks the mental capacity to make a decision about a course of action, any decision or action must be made on the basis of what is in the person's best interests. For further consideration of this aspect see Brown and Barber (2008).

Capacity of children to make decisions

In relation to children, the courts have taken the approach that children who have competence should be able to consent to treatment (*Gillick v West Norfolk and Wisbech Area Health Authority* [1985] 3 All ER 402 (HL); *R (on the application of Axon) v Secretary of State for Health (Family Planning Association intervening)* [2006] EWHC 37 (Admin)). This is now generally known as *Gillick competence*, after the former judgement above or as the *Fraser Guidelines*, after Lord Fraser who spoke on the issue in the House of Lords. The Gillick case arose in relation to whether there was a duty on a doctor to tell the parents if they were providing contraceptives to a child under the age of consent (16 years), contraception being regarded as a medical treatment. The judgement might be viewed as protecting doctors against prosecution for knowingly supporting sexual activity by a child below the age of consent, rather than intending to provide the child with complete autonomy or to eliminate a parent's rights when a child grows in competence. However, this approach has been applied by professionals dealing with children and young people in other areas where consent is necessary, although the court judgements above refer specifically to matters related to sexual and reproductive health. When it comes to refusing treatment, the courts do not seem to have applied this rule; instead they tend to allow parents to override consent. Nonetheless, there are examples where Gillick competence seems to be used as a practice principle also in terms of refusing consent such as in the case of Hannah, a terminally ill 13-year-old who was interviewed by a child protection social worker as part of a process whereby she persuaded a hospital to withdraw a High Court action that would have forced her to have a risky heart transplant against her will (Grice, 2008). The interested reader is referred to Walters (2008) and Maguire (2009), which give further references.

Duty to communicate risk – and confidentiality

Giving information and advice to clients is part of a social worker's task. In *Coles v Reading and District Hospital Management Committee and Another* [1963] 107 S.J. 115, the House of Lords confirmed that a doctor (and in similar circumstances, therefore, any other professional) was under a duty to disclose any substantial risk involving grave adverse consequences of following or not following the advice given. The duty to communicate about risks was extended in *Sidaway v Governors of Bethlem Royal Hospital and the Maudsley Hospital* [1985] 1 All ER 643, where the test as to what was required was stated as being the same as in any other case of alleged professional negligence, i.e. the Bolam test in terms of what an appropriate body of co-professionals would regard as reasonable risk communication (viewed in the light of the Bolitho judgement about professionals having reasonable evidence for their opinions, as discussed above).

These precepts were clarified – and possibly expanded – by *Montgomery (Appellant) v Lanarkshire Health Board (Respondent) (Scotland)* [2015] UKSC 11 On appeal from: [2013] CSIH 3; [2010] CSIH 104. The duty to communicate about risks should now be regarded as whether a reasonable person in the position of this client would think that the risk of the proposed intervention was significant in terms of consequences or likelihoods. This judgement seems to set a higher threshold for ensuring that risk communications are personalised to the individual client or family, rather than simply being a matter of getting a document signed (such as for a home care arrangement). Although negative side-effects of the service offered are much less common in social care than in health interventions, the principle is clear: efficient and effective communication is vital, particularly in relation to risks inherent in the intervention. In contentious or high-risk cases, consider agreeing what is adequate written advice with your line manager or professional supervisor, and consider what should be evidenced in contemporaneous records in case of any subsequent challenge.

CASE STUDY 3.4

Mr Coles had a crushed finger and went to a cottage hospital where he received first aid. No anti-tetanus injection was given; he was told to go immediately to another hospital for further examination and treatment. Mr Coles went home and was seen later by his GP. He subsequently died of tetanus. The court held that the hospital was negligent in failing to explain why he needed to go to the other hospital and to have the anti-tetanus injection. Proper communication was that which was reasonably necessary for safeguarding a patient's interests and sufficient to enable the client to be safe if followed.

(Coles v Reading and District Hospital Management Committee and Another [1963] 107 S.J. 115)

- *What information do you provide to clients where possible harm might ensue if the care plan is not followed?*

- *What do you do to ensure that the information is understood?*

It is important that concern for confidentiality does not blind us to the need to share information that might reasonably be expected to help to prevent harm. For example, *W and Others v Essex County Council and Another* [2000] 2 All ER 237 reports how a local authority social services department placed a child who was known to have sexually abused other children with a foster family. The social workers responsible for placing the child withheld this information from the foster carers. The foster child went on to sexually abuse the children of the foster parents. The court found the local authority negligent for failing to disclose full information about the foster child, as it was foreseeable that he or she might abuse (or try to abuse) members of the foster family.

ACTIVITY 3.4

Duty to communicate with carers

As part of an adult placement service, a statutory authority placed a 19-year-old with a history of abusing young children with a host family who had young children without informing them of his past. He then seriously abused their two children (Vale of Glamorgan Council, 2009).

- *What is the responsibility of the authority towards the host family?*

- *What is the responsibility of the authority towards the young man?*

- *What is a reasonable professional decision in such a situation?*

- *What communication would be good professional practice with the parties?*

Despite our general professional value of respecting confidentiality, there are situations where we face a dilemma when we know information *confidentially* which might protect someone from harm. You should be aware that you may have a duty of care to override confidentiality to inform identifiable third parties if there is a specific risk of violence to an identifiable individual (*Tarasoff v Regents of the University of California* [1976] 551 P 2d 334 [USA]). Even if a professional is employed privately by a client or a solicitor on the client's behalf, he or she may still have a legal duty to protect the public from identifiable violence which may override the duty of confidentiality to the client (*W v Edgell* [1990] All ER 835). In particular, child and adult safeguarding systems may require the passing of information without consent where this is justifiable, for example in terms of urgent action to protect someone from serious immediate harm. *This is a complex area and legal advice should be sought urgently if you are facing this type of situation.* The general points that we derive from case law precedents are that professionals should be educated on risk factors (see Chapter 6); should carry out competent assessment (see Chapter 4); and should communicate effectively with other professionals (see Chapter 8). For general education, the interested reader is referred to Monahan (1993) and Kopels and Kagle (1993).

Liability for decisions in teams and groups

Engaging the appropriate range of professionals in making a decision may be viewed (in addition to any other possible benefits or responsibilities) as good risk management. If something goes wrong the blame may be shared by the group. Also one would hope that the group would be less likely to make a poor decision about the care of the client than any professional or profession acting alone.

It should be noted that case law suggests that courts do not recognise the legal liability of a team, unless it is constituted as a *legal person* in its own right (*Wilsher v Essex Area Health Authority* [1986] 3 all ER 801 (CA)). A useful working principle might be to regard each profession as accountable for the decisions that fall within its domain of competence. Similarly, each organisation is responsible for decisions that lie within its purpose, powers and duties. You and your supervisor are responsible for your actions, not other professions or organisations. You must take into account the facts available and the opinions of others in forming your own judgement, and must inform others of the decisions of your profession or organisation. And you must not, of course, sabotage the decisions of others to the deliberate detriment of the client. Each profession must make those decisions that are within its own competence and each organisation those decisions that are within its mandate or statutory function. The group may have some formally defined powers of its own, for example, in relation to child protection, deciding that a child requires a formal safeguarding plan or ceasing one, but such group decisions are generally very limited for the above reason. However, this is not to dampen enthusiasm for multi-professional collaboration, which remains one of the best risk management defences against the culture of blame in which we work!

Legal aspects of decisions under time pressure

Many social work decisions are made with less information than desired, potentially false information and rather less than *full* information. This is a fact of life; what is important is that you have a rationale for your information gathering, your prioritising and your judgements.

If you are operating under tight time pressure and with limited information this might be considered as an emergency. Clearly one cannot expect the same rigour of decision making, or such assurance of positive outcomes, if decisions are made in an emergency. A dilemma is a decision where there is a lack of harm-free options. Many social work decisions might be framed this way. The law acknowledges emergencies where a lower standard of decision making might be acceptable because of pressures such as time and lack of harm-free options (dilemmas) (Carson, 1988; Rogers, 2006; Carson and Bain, 2008, p320). Dilemmas are not easy emotionally (Lipsky, 1980), but it is important to agonise over some dilemmas and to retain a *healthy scepticism* (Laming, 2003). If a tragedy ensues, what is important is that you record at the time the context of the decision making so that time and resource pressures and the lack of options are clear. In an emergency situation a lower standard of care may be acceptable but you need to think how you would answer the question: *why was this emergency not foreseen*? In recording and report-writing, explain the options that are available and the anticipated dangers of each option, bearing in mind how it might look with hindsight.

ACTIVITY **3.5**

Recording judgements under time pressure

- *Consider a recent case where you had to make a judgement or recommendation under time pressure, with less than the full information that you would have liked and where the option you would have preferred was not available.*

- *How did you record the context of these pressures so that it might be recognised subsequently as an emergency situation or dilemma?*

Conflict, confidence and being sued

This chapter has aimed to provide some clarity in lay language on legal aspects of decision making. Uncertainty about rights and responsibilities in relation to the law can inhibit sound approaches to supporting choice and managing risks (DH, 2007, Executive Summary, para. 11). There is, of course, nothing to stop someone commencing an action for negligence against any individual, including a professional. The claim itself may be without merit, but answering such a claim can be stressful. Thankfully, it is rare that a social worker is sued and extremely rare that a social worker is sued successfully! However, you might have to fight a case, which can create much anxiety. A particular aspect that may cause stress is that the loser of the action may have to pay the legal costs of both parties as well as damages. Even though a case against a social worker may be successfully defended, despite 'winning' you may be responsible for some or all of your own costs. Therefore it is essential that you have professional indemnity insurance, such as is available through a professional body like the British Association of Social Workers.

Chapter summary

- As social workers, we are accountable to society, through the law, in the judgements and decisions we make. The law supports reasoned, reasonable risk-taking decision making as something inherent in the professional task.

- You must ensure that a client has the capacity to consent to whatever care or treatment you are proposing, including risk-taking steps towards rehabilitation, independence or better quality of life.

- The law of tort provides underpinning principles that help you to articulate reasoned, reasonable decision making in the face of challenges such as from inquiries, complaints or politicians.

- Seek timely legal advice, through the arrangements in your employing organisation, when you are facing high-risk or very contentious decisions.

- If a court is judging reasonableness, a key point is whether your practice is likely to be judged reasonable by other social workers respected in that field.

- Ensure good communication about risks and decisions, and record evidence of assessment and decision-making processes in sufficient detail in case of challenge. The expectations for communicating about risk are comparable to the standards expected for practice judgements.

- Although multi-professional working is good in principle, you cannot abdicate responsibility to another profession for the decisions that are within the deemed competence of your profession.

- A lower standard of practice might be acceptable in an emergency or where it is clear that no options are 'harm free'; ensure that records demonstrate the relevant context.

- As well as case law, the Human Rights Act and statutes relating to mental capacity are key frameworks for considering the legal framework for risks and decisions.

- Ensure that you have professional indemnity insurance through your professional organisation.

FURTHER READING

Carson, D. and Bain, A. (2008) *Professional Risk and Working with People: Decision-Making in Health, Social Care and Criminal Justice.* London: Jessica Kingsley.

This is an excellent book on legal aspects of risk and decision making, particularly the tort of negligence and 'duty of care', and drawing out the way the law supports as well as challenges decision making by professionals.

Dimond, B. (1997) *Legal Aspects of Care in the Community.* London: Macmillan.

This readable textbook is well structured, clearly written and very accessible to the social worker wanting a detailed grounding in general legal aspects of practice in Great Britain and Northern Ireland, including negligence, trespass to the person and entering locked premises.

Preston-Shoot, M. (2014) *Making Good Decisions.* Basingstoke: Palgrave Macmillan.

This concise and readable book considers decision making from the perspective of a series of books focusing on aspects of law for social workers, and is richly illustrated with case law examples.

White, C. (2008) *Northern Ireland Social Work Law.* West Sussex and Dublin: Tottel.

This is an excellent textbook for social workers on relevant aspects of the law in Northern Ireland.

White, R., Broadbent, G. and Brown, K. (2009) *Law and the Social Work Practitioner*, 2nd edition. Exeter: Learning Matters.

This text gives an overview of legal aspects of practice in the main areas of social welfare statutes (child care, mental health, etc.) and contains useful chapters on the English legal framework for decision making and the Human Rights Act.

The British and Irish Legal Information Institute website (**www.bailii.org**) provides access to freely available British and Irish legal information.

Chapter 4
Assessment, risk assessment and decision support systems

'It is not possible' Cai was saying as we entered, 'and even if it were, the risk is terrible.' Arthur smiled and reached across the board to ruffle Cai's red curls. 'Trust Cai to count the risk.' 'God's honour! That is the truth. I do heed the risk ...' Cai.

(Lawhead, 1989, p120)

Introduction

This chapter focuses on assessment within judgement and decision making, relating assessment to issues of risk, and building on the earlier chapters on client engagement and legal aspects. The main components of assessment are considered as gathering, ordering and analysis of information. Principles of staged and unified ('single') assessment processes are considered as a response to the need for proportionate assessment and effective inter-professional decision making. We have highlighted the need for social workers to have knowledge and skills in using appropriate specialist assessment tools as well as the ability to co-ordinate a range of specialist assessments from different professionals. Theories that underpin health and social care assessment are discussed. We consider the potential for decision aids (including assessment tools) to assist in supporting decision making. The need to develop further methods of analysing assessment data is highlighted, with illustrations of recent developments. The potential of the emerging realm of *decision support systems* is highlighted. It is beyond the scope of this book to discuss the communication skills required to carry out effective assessment, and these foundational social work skills are assumed. This chapter leads on directly to Chapter 5 on issues relating to the professional judgement which has to be made as a result of the assessment process. Aspects specific to risk assessment (predicting harm), safeguarding and service eligibility judgements are discussed further in Chapter 6. Care planning choices involving taking risk following assessment are discussed further in Chapter 7. Using assessment to inform professional engagement in decision processes is discussed in Chapter 8. It is beyond the scope of this book to examine in detail the issues and processes for ascertaining capacity to consent, and the interested reader is referred to Brown *et al*. (2015).

Assessment processes and gathering information

Assessment is the basis for good judgement and decision making (Simmonds, 1998, p177). In the context of this book the aim of assessment is to gather and order information for analysis, so as to inform professional judgement and decision processes about care in the context of risk. *Assessment is a tool to aid in the planning of future work, the beginning of helping another person to identify areas for growth and change* (Taylor and Devine, 1993, p7). The terms 'care' and 'work' are used here to mean the range of possible social work interventions such as *care planning* (including safeguarding, deciding on allocation of services and supporting clients in taking reasonable, reasoned risk-taking decisions), and the wide variety of psycho-social interventions undertaken by social workers with individuals and families (Roberts and Greene, 2002). To give a context to assessing what action needs to be taken, some examples of interventions undertaken by social workers are given below (there is a longer list of interventions for which systematic reviews of effectiveness have been carried out in Chapter 5):

- safeguarding;
- social care planning including decisions regarding resources such as home care workers, family support workers, family centre services, respite and placement schemes, fostering, adoption, day care and support, supported housing and long-term care;
- crisis intervention;
- task-centred casework; problem-solving and solution-focused counselling;
- behaviour modification interventions;
- non-directive and mediating model counselling;
- varieties of cognitive behavioural therapy;
- varieties of family work and family therapy;
- youth justice and family group conferencing;
- narrative life review, including life story work and reminiscence therapy;
- motivational interviewing;
- reality (cognitive) orientation.

The model of assessment and care planning outlined here might be considered as building on an interactionist model of social work (Shulman, 2011), but encompassing also the use of assessment tools as appropriate. Sometimes assessment tools are linked to particular interventions. We discuss this further below in relation to specialist assessment. There is a danger in using assessment tools that those who use them become de-skilled, particularly if they use the tool without understanding its purpose and design (see the study by Gillingham and Humphreys, 2010, of a mix of qualified and unqualified workers). We need to use assessment tools to assist and support the professional judgement and decision process – with an understanding of their design, strengths and limitations – and that is the focus of this chapter. Assessment tools are useful only when used by those with an understanding of the decision options for which it is being used. Otherwise it becomes 'form filling' rather than assisting in an immediate clinical (professional social work) purpose.

Assessment: engaging the client, family and other professionals

Assessment is the process of systematically gathering and analysing information about the client, family and context (Taylor and Devine, 1993):

- beginning to engage a person or family in a helping process;

- to assist in planning how to work together with the client (and family);

- to start to make sense of the issues for all parties;

- to create an understanding of the dynamics of the situation, making use of a professional knowledge base;

- to relate the decision context, risks and issues to law, policy, procedures and standards of practice;

- to identify strengths, and resources that might support a change process;

- to take account of any effect of religion, race and culture on understandings, needs and possible provision of services or intervention;

- to identify concerns for client learning, growth and change relevant to the social work role;

- to ascertain the response to previous interventions and the effectiveness of these;

- to facilitate information sharing between professionals and between organisations;

- to inform decisions about safeguarding and allocation of social care services;

- to establish a baseline against which to measure client progress; and

- to provide anonymised, aggregate information for managing and developing services.

Our focus here is on assessment in terms of gathering, ordering and analysing information to inform a judgement and decision process. The assessment process through which the client and family engage with a social worker and begin to form a trusting working relationship is essential. Tuning-in, scene setting, clarifying your role and reaching below the immediate presenting problem to identify the underlying problems and strengths are essential basic social work practice skills (Shulman, 2011) and these must be applied to the issues addressed here. There are many challenges to professional assessment presented by clients and families with complex needs, including issues relating to uncertainty, emotion, conflict and managing risk (Hood, 2014), and the professional task requires thorough learning of relevant knowledge and skills. A challenge for social work is to engage fully with the client, family and environment, and to use a variety of methods of gathering information because (1) what is relevant may not be readily apparent; (2) clients may not be honest; and (3) diverse perspectives give a more reliable, holistic picture of the situation (e.g. Ferguson, 2010). For general communication skills, the reader is referred to Koprowska (2010) and for the particular challenges of engaging with resistant and aggressive clients, Taylor (2011) is recommended.

The role of the social worker may often include having a leading role in planning the assessment process across professions, as well as contributing appropriately, according to our own sphere of deemed professional competence. This co-ordinating task requires knowledge of the respective contributions of different professions and organisations, and sensitivity to different ways of working. Undertaking such co-ordination is an honour and a tribute to the holistic approach for which social work is renowned internationally. Our challenge is to combine appropriately a holistic overview co-ordinating different professional contributions as appropriate and yet also making our own specialist contribution.

Below are some practice pointers on assessment for decisions:

- gathering an appropriately wide breadth of information for the decision;
- 'thinking the unthinkable' in terms of detecting lies and exploring possible abuse;
- avoiding irrelevant, impertinent and non-cost-effective information gathering;
- appraising the credibility of sources of information;
- considering the influence of the data gathering process on the accuracy of data gathered;
- using direct observation when appropriate;
- recognising how your potential biases may influence your information gathering and analysis;
- recognising how leading questions may influence answers given;
- recognising the effects of memory on memory;
- assessing facts and meaning, i.e. the impact of situations as well as relevant contextual facts;
- recording the source and type of information, e.g. fact, hearsay or opinion;
- recording significant evidence underpinning the decision process;
- recording the understandings about confidentiality and access to information.

Assessment: risk and strengths as well as needs and context

In the early 1990s adult social care greatly expanded in the United Kingdom, with a clearer focus on assessing needs and the design and provision of services to meet those needs. At about the same time, children's services went through a re-orientation towards meeting the needs of families to balance the emphasis on protecting children. The seminal work on assessment and care planning in social work (Taylor and Devine, 1993) was written in this context, delineating key elements which are expanded here into the domain of risk (see Figure 4.1).

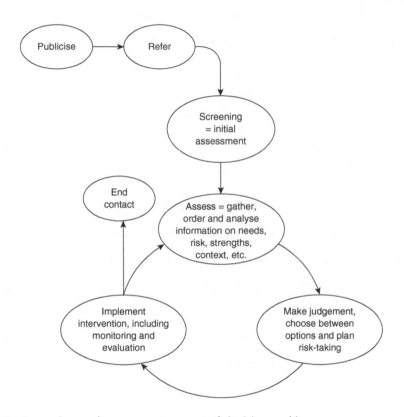

Figure 4.1   Screening and assessment as part of decision making

However, this was in the same year that the Merrett Report (DH, 1993) was published on managing risk in health services. This drew on parallel developments in business and industry requiring directors and senior managers to be aware of the range of risks within their organisation and to record their actions to address the high priority risks. The principles of that report apply equally to social care services, although some additional points would need to be added such as responsibility for functions (powers and duties) vested in the organisation by statute, and protecting clients from harm in their own homes not just as visitors to business premises or within large institutions such as hospitals. A generic conceptualisation of *risk* has developed since that time in social care services (sometimes conceptualised within 'social care governance'; see Taylor and Campbell, 2011). From that time onwards the concept of assessment in social work has broadened increasingly beyond assessing needs and strengths in their context to include a dimension of seeking to anticipate harm that may occur in the future ('risk').

The main focus in this book in terms of *risk assessment* is not so much the type of situation where this seems to be a stand-alone activity such as in preparing for an outing from a children's home, although it has some relevance there. Our main focus is on risk – the assessment of risk in the context of assessing overall needs, strengths and risks, and planning care for an individual – which almost always has inherent risks. In that sense *risk assessment* is an intrinsic part of *assessment* of the individual or family, and the tasks involved in supporting appropriate client risk-taking and planning for risk are intrinsic parts of care planning.

The task of social work assessment now clearly involves a range of elements which span the assessment of needs, risks and strengths. One practical example of incorporating a strengths perspective within assessment is the *Signs of Safety* approach in child protection (Saleebey, 2001; Turnell and Edwards, 1999; Turney *et al.*, 2011; Weld, 2008). This approach includes within the assessment a consideration of:

- **the house of worries** – the client's (child's) perspective on troubling matters;

- **the house of dreams** – the client's (child's) vision of how things should be; and

- **the house of good things** – the client (child's) appraisal of current strengths.

This type of creative approach to embodying strengths as well as needs is potentially adaptable to assessment with adults with various types of needs, and is an area for future development. An important question to ask about any assessment tool is the extent to which it appropriately guides assessment of: needs, context, strengths and risks, and supports the professional in relating these to the professional duties, powers and services available.

Assessment tools: gathering and ordering information

Assessment tools assist in gathering, ordering and analysing information to make a decision. It is important that assessment tools are viewed by professionals as exactly that: 'tools' for a job, or rather for a number of jobs as outlined elsewhere in this chapter as purposes of assessment. Assessment tools are there to assist the professional to do the task required in terms of assisting in the process of gathering relevant information; ordering information in a way that is useful to those engaged in this assessment process; and supporting analysis of the client, family and contextual data gathered in terms of professional knowledge and responsibilities to provide services or protect.

In terms of gathering information, many assessment tools function as checklists, in effect saying to the practitioner *don't forget to gather information on ... and consider this aspect*. Examples include tools used for assessing children in need (DH, 2002), mental health (Morgan, 2000) and older people (McCormack *et al.*, 2008a). Some tools contain prompts for interviews, for example in relation to harm to others and harm to self (Alberg *et al.*, 1996, pp44 and 54). Some tools allow wide discretion for collecting unstructured social history, others have many 'compulsory' questions that must be completed. Some take a middle road, providing a measure of structure such as prompts within an otherwise relatively unstructured template (Taylor, 2012b). Assessment tools should not be allowed to blinker the professional into thinking that assessment is a one-off event that will not be revised (Sidebotham *et al.*, 2016), although on the other hand never-ending 'assessment' must not be used as an excuse for avoiding making a judgement call. And a word of caution to the wise: read the guidance as well as the tool itself so that you understand the principles on which it is based. Looking only at the tool itself may convey a misleading impression as to its potential!

Tested assessment tools are a valuable support for professionals in making rational judgements and decisions. Use of appropriate assessment tools can help to inform and educate newer practitioners and develop practice at a standard based on professional consensus and current best knowledge. Decision processes are becoming increasingly complex and open to challenge (for example, allowing the media into family courts); hence increasingly sophisticated assessment tools are required to support professional judgements.

The use of assessment tools, including risk assessment tools, has a number of advantages, including:

- the clarity and straightness (bluntness!) may challenge the client and facilitate more open discussion with the social worker;

- the questions may help to structure, order and pace disclosure provided the social worker uses the tool appropriately;

- the holistic insights help the social worker to get a more balanced picture of the client, family and context within which to situate the particular referral problem; and

- an assessment tool can give permission to discuss a topic that might have been felt to be taboo.

There are also potential disadvantages to using assessment tools if not used appropriately:

- the coverage of domains or their depth may be inappropriate for this client and service;

- the client may feel under pressure to disclose too much, too soon;

- the tool may become such a routine part of practice that it is used mechanically;

- the assessment tool may set the agenda for the work in an unhelpful way; and

- the presentation of domains for assessment may seem to give them equal weighting in terms of risks that are being appraised (see Chapter 6 on risk factors and predicting harm).

These disadvantages can be addressed through skilled use of appropriate tools, and highlight the false economy of expecting workers with insufficient knowledge and skills to carry out professional social care tasks. A key point for the present book is that the apparent 'equal weighting' of the risk factors on which information is required by assessment tools may distract from developing the expertise required to identify which are the important factors and how they act or interact to affect the situation. We revisit this issue in Chapter 6 in terms of quantifying risk factors indicating the likelihood of some particular undesirable (harmful) outcome that we are trying to avoid. Appropriate knowledge and interpersonal skills are required to undertake assessment effectively; it is not simply a matter of completing forms. Assessment and care planning is a professional responsibility. Appropriate parts of the assessment and care planning tasks might be delegated to staff such as a foster parent or a day care worker, but accountability for supervising the overall assessment and care planning remains with the appropriate professional. Assessment tools must be *used* by the professional, not the professional used (or abused) by the tool! Assessment tools and other decision aids are a support to professional judgement and cannot replace it. No assessment tool can make a decision; it can only inform.

Purposes and theories of assessment

Assessment tools are an important way to apply research and theoretical knowledge to practice in a systematic way (Darragh and Taylor, 2009; see Table 4.1). Findings from rigorous research develop into theories, concepts and pointers for good practice that can be embodied into the design of assessment tools.

In the enthusiasm to develop unified assessment systems that support co-ordinated assessment and care planning, it is important that we do not get carried away into thinking that one assessment tool can necessarily support all the purposes of assessment. Some purposes of assessment tools might be to support the social worker in:

- assessing the risk (likelihood) of harm to or by this person;

- assessing the need for help that lies within the mandate of the organisation (and which may address less-apparent issues underlying the presenting problem and risks);

- determining eligibility for publicly or charitably funded services;

- assessing the likely response of the client to an intervention being considered; and

- determining realistic goals for the care (or safeguarding) plan.

Specialist assessment tools might be designed to address one of these aspects of assessment, as a contribution to the overall assessment. The unifying tool, of course, needs to be designed to be able to incorporate diverse contributions to assessment. An interesting exercise is to look at the assessment tools that are mandated or available in your working environment and to analyse them, according to their primary and secondary purposes, using the concepts in this chapter.

A variety of theories can underpin assessment depending on the purpose of the tool. For example, if you are assessing against eligibility criteria for a service then the assessment tool will need to support you in gathering, ordering and analysing information about current functioning and the need for those services. If you are anticipating the possibility of a behaviour modification intervention you will want the assessment to include consideration of antecedents, behaviours and consequences. If you are anticipating the possibility of a family intervention you will want the assessment (diagnostic) stage to include appropriate dimensions of family functioning. We can consider the theoretical underpinnings of assessment on a continuum (see Figure 4.2). The point is not that a particular tool is good or bad in terms of these dimensions; what is required is a tool fit for its intended purpose.

Table 4.1   Principles of assessment tools to support decision making

Client perspective

- information is gathered once and is appropriate to needs and services;
- proportionate assessment;
- respects the individual;
- client is involved in decision making regarding levels of care and risks;
- client's views and wishes are kept to the fore;
- paints a holistic picture of needs, abilities, strengths, goals and motivation;
- considers effects on quality of life;
- embodies consent to assessment and information sharing;
- if client lacks capacity, facilitates participation and safeguarding of interests.

Family and carer perspective

- captures the role and support of family and carers;
- captures family views and perceptions of the older person's needs;
- acknowledges their right to assessment;
- enriches information gathered.

Professional perspective

- well structured and easily understood;
- realistic and appropriate assessment time;
- facilitates appropriate identification of need;
- standardises principles of best practice;
- reflects a strong evidence base;
- in accord with professional values;
- supports professional judgement;
- simplifies access to information;
- is transferable across services and care processes;
- promotes integrated working and facilitates information sharing;
- guides the collation and analysis of relevant information.

Organisational perspective

- supports the mission, principles and standards;
- in accord with (or adapts) current policies;
- in accord with (or adapts) current service development strategies;
- reduces inappropriate referrals;
- supports effective use of resources;
- promotes integrated ways of working; and
- provides information for managing and developing services.

(Adapted from McCormack *et al.*, 2008a and 2008b and from Taylor, 2012b)

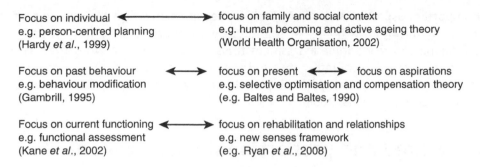

Figure 4.2   Types of theories underpinning approaches to assessment

Assessment tools need to be implemented by people knowledgeable and trained in the skills required not only to use the tool but to appreciate sufficiently the range of interventions and care service options that may follow from the decision, based on the completion of the assessment using the tool. It is not appropriate to consider or teach about assessment tools in isolation, nor even just in the context of 'assessment' skills. Assessment must be considered in the context of the judgements and decisions for which it is being carried out, and with an understanding of risk if the assessment includes an element of considering future harm and courses of action.

Co-ordinating and communicating about care

A key requirement for integrated health and social care provision across professions, organisations and service areas is communication about the assessment stage of decision making. English and Pecora (1994) found that one of the main strengths of assessment processes was to document decisions and to make information more readily available and thus improve communication (Morrison and Henniker, 2006). The development and use of standard unified (or *integrated* or *single*) assessment systems are central to supporting effective communication between professionals.

CASE STUDY *4.1*

Using an assessment tool

My social work career has been entirely in child care work. I have worked in various teams, and with various assessment arrangements. As has been highlighted through some inquiries into children killed by family members, professionals can focus their attention on one aspect of a family situation and neglect other important aspects. I have found that the Common Assessment Framework ensures a rounded, holistic picture of the child, family and circumstances, although you can still give extra attention to aspects that are particularly important.

- *What assessment tool do you use (or contribute to) that provides a holistic picture of the social care needs of the individual (and family or carer as appropriate)?*

- *What are the strengths of this tool, and what are its weaknesses?*

An important aspect of assessment tools is the extent to which they support effective communication with clients. Traditionally, assessment tools were written for professionals to read. Some assessment tools are beginning to word their assessment directly to the client rather than to the professional, even if it is recognised that the assessment will normally be completed jointly with an appropriate professional (McCormack *et al.,* 2008a, 2008b).

Integrated and proportionate assessment

Staged assessment processes have been developed in order to avoid the situation where clients are subjected to unnecessarily complex assessment, and also to ensure that assessment is sufficiently complex where necessary. This desire for proportionate assessment and also to support co-ordination of care has led to *integrated* (or unified or single) *assessment systems* that incorporate more than one stage in the assessment process. Some clients will use the full complexity of the system, whereas others will be assessed using only some parts of the system. The aim of an integrated assessment system is to be suitably comprehensive at each stage as well as to aid communication between professionals and co-ordination of care (Taylor, 2012b).

Specialist assessment tools

Although a particular strength of social work is to bring together specialist assessments into a holistic, person-centred whole for a co-ordinated decision process, there is also a role for social workers in undertaking specialist assessments within their sphere of competence. This is an aspect of social work that is generally underdeveloped at present. Some specialist assessment tools are linked to particular methods of intervention; for example, systemic family therapy or a behaviour modification intervention. Others might relate to particular problem areas facing a client or family such as attachment, carer support, anxiety, depression, stress, anger management or trauma. Professionals proposing to use a particular specialist tool are often required

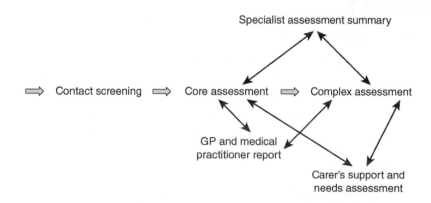

Figure 4.3   Integrated assessment systems: the Northern Ireland Single Assessment Tool for the Health and Social Care of Older People (McCormack et al., 2008b; see also Taylor 2012b)

to undertake a short training course in the use of that particular tool. This should be seen as standard practice in social work, as in other professions.

Usefulness of a specialist assessment tool

I am a senior social worker (team leader) in a family and child care team. Judging the quality of care received by a child is an essential component of any assessment in a child welfare or child abuse context. The Graded Care Profile (GCP) (Srivastava et al., 2003) is a validated tool which offers a standardised framework which allows the component parts of quality of care to be separately assessed against predetermined criteria. The aim of this audit project, undertaken as part of a post-qualifying programme, was to evaluate how well this tool works in assessing child neglect in a busy team. Data were collected from files (to create a profile of recent neglect cases) and from questionnaires completed by social workers in relation to each family where they used the GCP over a three-month period (to gather data on their perceptions of the usefulness of the tool).

Comments on the GCP were particularly positive in terms of its practical usefulness, providing an objective measure of parenting, and as a mechanism to facilitate discussion of practicalities with parents where neglect was a concern. The summary of the GCP is readily transferrable to the standard UNOCINI common assessment framework to enable co-ordination with other professionals and other parts of the process.

(McKillop, 2007)

Using a specialist assessment tool in learning disability

My role is as a social worker within a large hospital for people with learning disabilities. Tariq, a man of 31 years with a minor criminal record, is being considered for discharge. As part of the assessment of Tariq, I completed an Anger Scale and Provocation Inventory (Novaco, 1994) with him. This provided valuable insight into the situations that Tariq found challenging, and added my professional contribution to the overall assessment that shaped his care plan.

- *What specialist tools do you use to contribute to the holistic assessment of health and social care needs?*

- *In what aspects of your practice might specialist tools be useful?*

Analysis in assessment

Sound decision making and management of risk depend on what is done with the information once it is gathered and collated. If a particular type of intervention is being considered, such as family therapy or a behavioural therapy, then the theoretical framework of the intervention will shape the analysis during assessment. Similarly if specialist assessment tools are being used, these will generally have a structure to lead to a reasonably clearly conceptualised conclusion or score.

For analysis in generic social work assessment broader questions might be asked such as in relation to the quality of the sources of evidence.

- How reliable is this information?
  - Is it directly observed by a reliable witness?
  - What is, or might be, the motivation, bias or blinker of the witness?
- Is information corroborated by other sources?
- How does client self-report information fit with information from other sources?
  - What experience is the information coming from?
  - What is, or might be, the motivation of the client in providing this information?
- How does client and family information fit with theoretical understandings such as: human growth, development, ageing, loss and change; family and social functioning and dynamics; social processes of mental ill health, etc.?
- Do I feel uncomfortable when considering this information? Why?
- How might differing or contradictory views be tested or corroborated?
- How does the situation appear if I consciously try to think of the evidence for the opposing conclusion to the one that I am forming?
- How does the situation seem if I try to consider the perspective of hindsight in terms of reasonable, reasoned judgement?
- How would or does my supervisor understand the main issues and dynamics?

Professionals and organisations are increasingly required to provide a rationale for their decisions. The analysis of data gathered as part of assessment needs to become more explicit in informing the decision process. Analysis within assessment often measures such dimensions as functioning level within particular domains, level of complexity, compounding factors, mitigating factors and effects on quality of life. Analysis of patterns of harm and pathways to harm are required using theory to support reasoned judgement and decisions. This helps to develop a working hypothesis as to what causes or perpetuates the problem and how it plays out in the life of the client, family and significant others so that a judgement can be made about an intervention to be offered to the client or family. One of the main weaknesses of assessment tools in current use is the limited support they give for the analysis required to make a judgement, although this situation is beginning to be addressed (Barlow *et al.*, 2012). Some assessment tools explicitly incorporate established risk factors to give the best estimate of the probability of some harm (such as homicide

Support for analysis in child protection assessment tools

Child protection assessment tools were reviewed in terms of the models of analysing significant harm that they embodied. A search of ten databases and two web search engines retrieved over 22,000 potentially relevant references. Three systems of tools were identified:

1. *Comprehensive Assessment Tool (CAT);*

2. *Children's Research Centre-Structured Decision Making (CRC-SDM) = Ontario Risk Assessment Model (ORAM);*

3. *Victorian Risk Framework (VRF).*

Eleven individual tools were identified, of which:

A. *seven were risk-safety checklists:*

   1. *Child Abuse Risk Evaluation-Netherlands (CARE-NL);*

   2. *Child at Risk Field (CARF);*

   3. *Child Endangerment Risk Assessment Protocol (CERAP);*

   4. *Manitoba Risk Estimation System (MRES);*

   5. *Signs of Safety (SoS);*

   6. *Resilience Matrix (RM);*

   7. *Washington Risk Assessment Matrix (WRAM)*

B. *four were family assessments:*

   1. *California Family Assessment and Factor Analysis (CFAFA);*

   2. *Graded Care Profile (GCP);*

   3. *North Carolina Assessment Scale (NCFAS) including Strengths and Stressors Tracking Device (SSTD);*

   4. *Safeguarding Assessment and Analysis Framework (SAAF)*

C. *and two were audit tools:*

   1. *Corby (2003);*

   2. *Ward et al. (2012) (cited in Barlow et al. (2012)).*

or suicide or some particular form of abuse) (Doueck and English, 1993). However, even assessment tools that include reference to prediction in their title or purpose sometimes do not include a methodology for estimating the likelihood of a particular outcome. Assessment tools that are more closely tied to a particular intervention or theory provide more support for analysis and designing the care or intervention, but leave less room for professional discretion. In England and Wales there is now strong encouragement for social workers to develop the knowledge and skills required to be recognised as expert witnesses in court. *Social workers may not be experts for the purposes of FPR Part 25, but that does not mean that they are not experts in every other sense of the word. They are, and we must recognise them and treat them as such* (Munby, 2013, p3). This requires, in particular, greater skills in analysis within assessment, a topic explored in greater depth in Chapters 6 and 7.

RESEARCH SUMMARY 4.2

Decision-making tools such as assessment forms are used increasingly, particularly in determining eligibility for services. This paper is based on a qualitative study of three decision-making tools used in the Danish public welfare services in three domains: (1) employment; (2) child protection; and (3) home care services for older people. Ten interviews with groups of relevant professionals were conducted in relation to each tool, all those in relation to the first two tools being social workers. The common language of such decision tools may shape the client interview, and may demand increased attention to citing the sources of information. If the tool includes normative data, such as on child development, for comparison then it can have a stronger influence on the decision. Categorisation of client needs and of service types may make problems manageable in terms of organisational systems, and can also highlight lack of coherence between needs and services offered. The strength of the linkage to standard categories of services influences the perceived influence, or intrusiveness, of the assessment tool.

(Høybye-Mortensen, 2015)

Perhaps a reason for lack of support for analysis in assessment tools is the complexity of social work decision making. Multiple factors have to be taken into account in social work judgements. Statistical approaches to analysis commonly use some variant of *linear regression* to analyse the impact of particular factors. In effect, this approach starts from the premise that any factor is equally relevant for any person within the population under consideration. So, taking examples from the risk factors for child abuse, the parent's impulse control and the child's disability, and the environmental isolation would be treated as having equal effect on the likelihood of abuse.

An alternative to linear regression is to use a *classification tree,* which has been used in predicting violence by people with a mental disorder (Monahan *et al.*, 2001). In a classification tree model, factors are viewed like branches on a tree so that their influence on the event depends on some factors but not others. For example, the likelihood of a person discharged from prison re-offending might be shown to depend on getting a job and having a family network. In an assessment tool constructed using a linear regression model these two factors would be regarded as contributing independently to the likelihood of re-offending. If the tool were constructed using a classification tree analysis, then it could recognise that the impact of one of these factors might be less if the other is present. The study of such complex decisions is known as *multi-attribute decision modelling* and there are useful examples of this such as the *analytic hierarchy process* although the application to social work is not yet well developed.

Another development to assist in analysis in decisions is to create scales that are perpendicular rather than linear. For example, there might be a concern continuum and a strength continuum, which are regarded as being at right angles rather than opposites of each other. Thus, if situations are scored as *high* or *low* on each scale there are four options: *high concern and high strength*; *high concern and low strength*; *low concern and high strength*; and *low concern and low strength*. Each quadrant might suggest different types of intervention. The scales, of course, could be made more precise by having more than just two points on each, for example a three-point scale of *high, medium* and *low*.

PRACTICE EXAMPLE *4.2*

Assessment tool supporting analysis

An assessment tool has been developed for young people who sexually abuse others with four domains (Offence, Developmental, Family or Carers, Environment), each with a number of question areas based on research and theory. For example, the Developmental domain includes resilience factors, health issues, experience of abuse or neglect, witnessing domestic violence, quality of early life experiences, history of behaviour problems, sexual development and interests. Two continua are used to analyse the information: a concern continuum and a strength continuum, each with high, medium and low markers. A two by two table is then used for each combination of high and low strengths and high and low concerns with indicators of likely key issues and possible service responses for that quadrant. This facilitates communication and a shared understanding of the case across professions and agencies. The third stage of the analysis is to identify the five most important strengths, the five most important concerns and the five most important unknowns.

(Morrison and Henniker, 2006)

Another relevant development is in the field of heuristic models of judgement. Although the idea of weighing up all relevant factors may be appealing at first glance, it seems unlikely that the human brain can compute weightings of large numbers of risk factors in order to conclude with an overall risk level. It seems more likely that *homo sapiens* has developed the ability to select the most relevant information using cues from the environment (Taylor, in press). In undertaking assessment, we are always dealing with an incomplete jigsaw puzzle; the issue perhaps is whether we have enough pieces in place to understand the picture even if it is not perfect. Heuristic models of professional judgement are discussed further in Chapter 5. A broad social work assessment analysis might be linked to conceptualisations of risk such as *vulnerability* and *trigger* factors, as discussed in Chapter 6 or *balancing benefits and harms* as in Chapter 7.

Safeguarding assessments and thresholds

In a safeguarding situation, early stages of assessment are likely to involve making a *holding judgement* regarding safety and stability for the child while developing a common understanding with the client and family as to why the assessment is being undertaken and who is likely to be involved in decision making (Hollows, 2003). Decisions will then need to be made about managing the process of assessment and decision making to engage appropriate people at the appropriate stage.

There are various developments in *risk assessment tools* in areas such as child protection and mental health. In the USA, the focus tends to be on assessment tools that are designed to predict possible harm by being based on the best-researched risk factors. These have the benefit of improving consistency of decision making by providing as clear a benchmark as is available on the likelihood of harm. In the UK, the approach is more often to develop assessment tools that will guide the professional in the task of collating and ordering the data. This has the benefit of not giving a false sense of confidence or misuse of risk factors, but a weakness in not guiding the use of knowledge to inform analysis. Such assessment tools are based on a professional consensus, incorporating a qualitative professional knowledge base informed by research rather than having a clear relationship to the best measures of likelihood of harm derived from research. For some examples of UK tools for assessing child neglect, see Howarth (2007).

Assessment incorporating professional knowledge (primarily based on research) adds rigour to decision making. If the purpose of assessment is to predict the likelihood of harm, then a reliable assessment tool would incorporate actuarial risk factors in its design. It is important to remind ourselves of the limitations in trying to predict harm or any other rare event in relation to a particular individual. Mathematical risk factors can tell us the likelihood of the undesired event more accurately than unaided human judgement, even for those with experience. Thus we may know that an individual has, say, a 20 per cent chance of being abused or of being reconvicted of an offence. However, even the calculated risk factors cannot tell us whether this particular individual is one of the two out of ten who will be abused or reconvicted, or whether they are one of the eight out of ten who will not. Some assessment tools explicitly combine actuarial and clinical factors, and incorporate care planning and management within their format (e.g. RAMAS for mental health; DH, 1998). However, we need to recognise that clinical factors have even more limited predictive value than tested actuarial factors, and as a profession we need to seek further research to test and measure such factors for their validity in prediction.

Another aspect of assessment is the effect of the use of language on the users, both clients and professionals. A narrow approach to assessing risk defined in terms of harmful outcomes and matching against eligibility for resources may limit the vision of participants in assessment by comparison with an approach aiming to build on strengths as well as identifying difficulties. These aspects need to be considered in relation to the expectations regarding safeguarding judgements. Social workers sometimes seem to be expected to act as if accurate prediction were possible, for example to ensure that:

the child is provided with immediate protection in situations where their life is at risk or there is a likelihood of sustaining a serious injury if this action is not taken ....
In situations where there are child protection concerns but the child is not in a life threatening situation or at risk of serious injury or harm, careful consideration is given to the degree of risk, how best to protect the child.

(Social Services Inspectorate, 1993, paras 14–15)

Assessment tools can assist the practitioner in collating and ordering appropriate data, in facilitating communication with clients, families and other professionals, and in supporting analysis through embodying research and theory evidence in the tool design.

Quality of assessment tools

Assessment tools increase the consistency and reliability of assessment (Kemshall, 2008) and hence improve the quality of decisions. We can consider the quality of assessment tools in terms of:

- **validity** – does the tool assess what it purports to assess?

- **reliability** – would two professionals using the same assessment tool with the same client complete the assessment form the same way and reach the same decision?

- **usability** – how easy do users (usually professionals) find the tool to use?

- **open (qualitative) versus closed (quantitative) questions and scales** – to what extent does the tool embody closed questions (supporting ease of judging need and ensuring equity of service provision with other clients) and open questions (supporting gathering the client's perspective on the issues and context)?

- **appropriateness** – is the tool appropriate and tested for use with this culture or type of clients?

Validity is difficult to demonstrate, because to do this properly one needs to know the outcomes of the assessment. For example, if the tool predicts that a particular child will be abused, is the child in fact abused? Alternative methods include using professional consensus methods (McCormack *et al.*, 2007a). Reliability may be tested by arranging for two professionals to each use the same assessment tool with the same client within a reasonably short space of time to see how similarly they complete the tool. Alternative methods include asking professionals to use a tool against a vignette (McCormack *et al.*, 2007b) or with actors trained to role play patients and clients (McCormack *et al.*, 2008d). Usability may be assessed by asking a range of professionals or clients to report on how they find the tool when they use it (McCormack *et al.*, 2008c).

Decision support systems

Decision support systems aim to provide the best, relevant, up-to-date knowledge for decision makers to use in making the decision and at the same time to standardise best practice and reduce variation due to errors of judgement insofar as our knowledge enables us to address these. We could regard various aspects of our professional world as non-computerised decision supports, such as regulations, policies and procedures, and professional guidelines such as those issued by SCIE. A major development in the past 20 years has been the various types of computerised systems now in use to support practice (Lewis, 2010). This growth opens up many new possibilities for supporting professional decision making.

The most far-reaching development has been information management systems that store and provide an ordered structure for data on individual clients. This aids decision making in terms of:

- improving accuracy of data on which a decision is based;

- having the essential information readily available and retrievable;

- knowing who key stakeholders are and how to contact them;

- facilitating sharing of up-to-date client information;

- providing anonymised data for managing the service and its development; and

- providing anonymised data for research, studying population needs and service evaluation.

Slightly more sophisticated systems – sometimes called *passive decision support* – provide a flagging system to focus attention on important aspects of a person's care. Systems can flag up such things as the imminent anniversary of a client's bereavement and the dates of care reviews that are due a specified time in advance. Some systems will flag up if a client has been violent or threatening in the past or if there is other crucial information that someone should know before visiting for the first time. This is particularly useful in situations where a locum worker is covering an urgent referral and has to make a decision while the regular social worker is on annual leave or sick leave.

More in their infancy are what are generally called *expert systems* that provide *active decision support*. These systems provide support based on professional knowledge for assessment and decisions in relation to a particular client situation. Such systems can prompt consideration of relevant legislation, policy, research and professional guidelines relevant to the client assessment. The system may provide access to the relevant documents held on computer or the world wide web or may extract data from a number of sources to provide a unique analysis.

Expert systems aim to provide information that might aid the making of a particular decision by bringing together a range of relevant professional knowledge and applying it to the recorded information that we have about the client, family and circumstances. There is relatively limited use of *active decision support* in social work but this is likely to become more common as our knowledge base and technical resources increase. An increasing number of *care pathways* are being developed, charting the expected rehabilitation and treatment journey of a client with a long-term condition such as stroke, based on professional consensus utilising current best evidence. At present, these are mostly in hospital and rehabilitation settings, but are being developed into community services and for an increasing number of chronic conditions. In due time, we can expect that these will be computerised and used to inform professional judgement about the care of an individual.

RESEARCH SUMMARY *4.3*

Information requirements for decision making

Increasingly, jurisdictions are adopting universal assessment procedures and information technology to aid in healthcare data collection and care planning. Before their potential can be realised, a better understanding is needed of how these systems can best be used to support clinical practice. We investigated the decision-making process and information needs of home care case managers in Ontario, Canada, prior to the widespread use of universal assessment, with a view of determining how universal assessment and information technology could best support this work. Three focus groups and two individual interviews were conducted; questioning focused on decision making in the post-acute care of individuals recovering from a hip fracture. We found that case managers' decisional process was one of a clinician–broker, combining clinical expertise and information about local services to support patient goals within the context of limited resources. This process represented expert decision making, and the case managers valued their ability to carry out non-standardised interviews and override system directives when they noted that data may be misleading. Clear information needs were found in four areas: services available outside of their regions, patient medical information, patient pre-morbid functional status and spouse health and functional status.

(Egan et al., 2009)

Assessment tools could be seen as static, paper versions of expert systems to support decision making. One advantage of a computerised system is that a much wider range of knowledge can be incorporated. A traditional assessment tool has to be based on the most generally applicable knowledge base for the range of clients and families for which it is intended to be used. With a computerised system, only the knowledge relevant to this particular decision need be presented to the professional to inform his or her recommendations. This information can be selected from a large bank of stored data that would be too large for an individual to memorise in detail. Hence the quantity of knowledge that can be incorporated into the system without swamping the human decision maker can be much greater. Such *expert systems* need to be primed with the general knowledge base relevant to the range of decisions being undertaken, and fed with data relating to this particular client, family and context. Expert systems can be built to use the data from client information management systems, but a major challenge is specifying the information to be used to inform the decision. The quality of data going into the decision system is crucial to its effectiveness.

Expert systems could be used to structure an ideal decision process in order to standardise what is currently agreed (through some professional consensus process) to be best practice in that type of decision. Such expert systems can be designed to use various methods to analyse and synthesise the data, whether linear regression or classification trees or some form of 'fuzzy logic' such as neural networks (Garson, 1998) that can give approximate solutions where there are many variables to consider in a decision. There are many issues to be addressed about the complexity and variation of decision situations and the limitations of systems to model these.

Chapter summary

- Assessment is a central activity in judgement and decision making. We consider the main processes to be gathering, ordering and analysing information, and the main domains to be needs, strengths, risks and context. A wide range of purposes of assessment are outlined.

- In order to be person-centred, assessment processes have been developed that are integrated (unified) to co-ordinate contributions across professions, and staged so that assessment is in some measure proportionate to level of need.

- Social workers are particularly suited by training and role to co-ordinate multi-professional assessment in complex cases. Social workers also have a role in using appropriate specialist assessment tools.

- Much attention is often focused on the gathering and ordering of data, to the neglect of how it will be analysed to inform a decision. We consider various approaches to analysis in assessment including statistical, narrative and *psycho-social rationality* approaches.

- Assessment tools are a valuable resource, but must be actively used by suitably knowledgeable and skilled professionals; they are tools for a clinical (professional) purpose, not a form being completed primarily for a management purpose.

- There is an untapped potential for computerised decision aids to support decision making in social work.

FURTHER READING

In recent years it is increasingly possible to access assessment tools online. The interested reader is referred to sources such as:

DASH checklist for domestic abuse: **www.safelives.org.uk/node/516** and at **www.dashriskchecklist.co.uk**

Department of Health and Personal Social Services (2010) *Promoting Quality Care and Guidance on the Assessment and Management of Risk in Mental Health.* Belfast: Department of Health. **http://webarchive.proni.gov.uk/20100917121022/ http://www.dhsspsni.gov.uk/mhld-good-practice-guidance-2010.pdf**

Department of Health, Social Services and Public Safety (2011) *The Northern Ireland Single Assessment Tool: Procedural Guidance.* Belfast: Department of Health. **www.health-ni.gov.uk/sites/default/files/publications/dhssps/guidance-ver-3-jan-2011.pdf**

Department of Health, Social Services and Public Safety (2015) *Adult Safeguarding: Prevention and Protection in Partnership.* Belfast: Department of Health. **www.health-ni.gov.uk/sites/default/files/publications/dhssps/adult-safeguarding-policy.pdf**

Family Outcomes Star Model: **www.outcomestar.org.uk**

Signs of Safety: **www.signsofsafety.net**

Calder, M.C. (ed.) (2008) *Contemporary Risk Assessment in Safeguarding Children.* Lyme Regis: Russell House.

This is a detailed book for the child protection specialist interested in the cutting-edge development of models, theory and research in safeguarding children, the principles of which may be generalised to other client groups.

Milner, J., Myers, S. and O'Byrne, P. (2015) *Assessment in Social Work,* 4th edition. London: Palgrave.

This book contains clear and accessible guidance on assessment linked to intervention approaches and service contexts.

Taylor, B.J. and Devine, T. (1993) *Assessing Needs and Planning Care in Social Work.* Hampshire: Ashgate.

This textbook outlines a sound framework for assessment and care planning that has stood the test of time and illustrates skills based on a practical conceptual model.

Chapter 5

Professional judgement, bias and using knowledge in assessment and decisions

Good judgement comes from experience, and experience – well, that comes from poor judgement.

(Anonymous, quoted in Robertson, 1996, p10)

Introduction

Having set the scene in the earlier chapters in terms of client focus, legal aspects and assessment processes, this chapter focuses on the challenge for the individual professional in making a judgement recommending a particular course of action particularly in a context of uncertainty ('risk'). We consider the framing of decisions and the role of heuristics (short-cuts) and types of bias in professional judgement. The use of professional knowledge in making judgements about individual situations is discussed. Reflective practice and use of professional supervision are illustrated as essential ways to minimise the effect of individual bias and ensure high standards of decision making in uncertainty. Two particular types of professional judgement are considered further in Chapter 6 (relating to judgements against a threshold, such as for safeguarding, service eligibility or inspecting services) and Chapter 7 (relating to balancing benefits against harms, such as in choosing care options). Individual professional judgements often inform supervisory or collaborative decision-making processes, which are the focus of Chapter 8. This chapter considers the use of knowledge within professional judgement about risks and the effectiveness of interventions. For a fuller discussion of shaping an answerable question; identifying relevant research; and appraising and synthesising research to address a practice issue, the reader is referred to Taylor *et al.* (2015).

Reflective practice and learning from experience

How do you 'decide'? Do you simply reiterate the views of your client or the family? Do you just 'go along with' the views of other professionals? If you form your own judgement, how do you explain or justify your opinion? How do you use knowledge – as well as information about the client and context – to inform your recommendation about a plan for care or safeguarding or hospital discharge or re-ablement or recovery in the community? To what extent are your judgements based on an awareness (more or less conscious) of *what might happen if …*? These are some of the issues discussed in this chapter, which focuses on your individual cognitive processes in forming a judgement prior to, or during, engaging in decision processes with your client and organisation. How do we form an opinion about a situation? What basis of knowledge and principles comes into play in our thinking processes? Are we more likely to 'take risks' than people in other professions? As social workers we are decidedly not infallible or all-knowing; we learn by using professional knowledge, concepts, theories and models to aid us in reflecting on our practice. As knowledge and skills become increasingly internalised with experience, decisions may become less conscious and might be described as more 'intuitive', at least in the sense that we may be less aware of the cognitive (analytic) process of reaching the judgement (Benner, 1984). We need to understand the processes of forming a judgement so that we can most effectively learn from experience, build on the best practice of ourselves and others, and teach those newer to the profession. We need to be able to become conscious of the application of our knowledge base – including law, psychology, sociology, human growth and development, mental health, illness, disability, criminology and social policy – so that we can minimise bias in the way that we apply it to the unique features of a particular decision and explain our judgement process to those to whom we are accountable and those who might be learning from us. No professional can 'know everything'; the more important requirement is to recognise that you need to know, and know how to find out what you need to know. This is a key component of reflective practice in relation to using knowledge to inform professional judgement.

An important part of professional skill is to recognise patterns and meanings in the complex information we receive about clients, families and their context. We have to consider these in relation to the professional roles that we carry, including responsibilities for safeguarding, gate-keeping scarce public or charitable resources, and co-ordinating the contributions of diverse professions and organisations into an integrated care process. We might use a model known as *recognition primed decision making* (Klein, 2000) in this facet of our decision making. Because of pressures such as time, rapidly changing circumstances and the need to get a quick overview to identify priority issues, a decision maker may *intuitively* look for similarities with problems tackled previously, which might be more efficient for this purpose than a detailed analytic approach, which time may not permit. By contrast, a more analytic approach would be used if the decision is more unusual or more contested and therefore requires a clearer rationale and justification. Recognising a place for intuitive judgements is not an excuse to avoid the hard work of analysis that may be required to reach a sound, justifiable conclusion in complex cases. Judgements using knowledge and skills at the intuitive end of the spectrum are appropriate in certain contexts and may be the fruit of learning from sound training and years of reflective experience where theory and personal practice have been integrated to generate internalised wisdom.

One way of understanding the multiple factors that have to be taken into account in a professional judgement is through Egon Brunswick's *lens model* (Cooksey, 1996), which illustrates the decision maker using multiple cues for a decision as a parallel to the human eye taking in rays of light from various parts of the scene in view to form an internal image. The decision maker creates an internal representation of the relevant factors as a step in the tasks of seeing patterns and making sense of the data as part of *decision analysis*. It is interesting that research suggests that experts do not use more cues than novices, but rather that they are better at identifying factors that are most relevant to the decision (Gilovich *et al.*, 2002).

Discretion, assessment and professional judgement

All professions have scope for discretion, and that is an essential part of their training and responsibility. No set of procedures could possibly ever cope with the variety of situations that are encountered and which must be addressed in the complex work undertaken by social workers. Almost by definition that is what a professional does: deal with complex situations which are so varied that precisely prescribed procedures are not possible. At the same time, professional judgements are increasingly being challenged in Westernised societies. It is becoming increasingly important that professionals can articulate some basis for their judgements. As discussed in the chapter on legal issues (Chapter 3), one simple way of conceptualising this is to seek reasoned, reasonable judgements. It is not realistic to expect all professionals to make judgements in an identical way. What is important is that professionals can articulate their rationale so that it can be discussed in an appropriate forum such as supervision or a multi-professional meeting. As discussed in the chapter on assessment processes (Chapter 4), one virtue of assessment tools is that they provide in themselves a rationale for what is reasonable in terms of gathering and organising information. The challenge is, then, the analysis of this information (on the client, family and context) using an appropriate knowledge base so as to form a judgement within the discretion appropriate to your role. Discretion is not something fixed in relation to your job title; it can also vary during the work. For example, once you are told certain information – for example about potential abuse or a crime – you may lose some discretion and be obliged (through professional values, organisational policies or in law) to do something in response. One of the key tasks in social work is always to clarify role (Shulman, 2011). This role clarification is in relation to both the client's issue and also in relation to the scope of discretion allowed by your employer (Wallander and Molander, 2014). You need to be clear what discretion you have in terms of shaping decision processes, such as the extent to which you might delay a decision to good effect (see Chapter 9).

RESEARCH SUMMARY 5.1

Professional judgement and reflective learning

Context

Guidance in the UK requires the co-ordination and standardisation of services to protect adults from abuse. However, there remains considerable ambiguity about the basic concepts of abuse and vulnerability. This paper reports an empirical study of factors in professional decision making in relation to identifying and reporting abuse of older people.

Method

A systematic review and a panel of expert practitioners were used to identify factors that might influence professional recognition and reporting of elder abuse. These factors were incorporated into a questionnaire that included randomised factorial survey vignettes and additional questions on decision making. Sets of unique vignettes were completed by 190 social workers, nurses and other professional care managers across Northern Ireland in 2008, giving n = 2261 randomised vignettes used as the units of analysis.

Results

Recognition and reporting were influenced by case factors specific to the abuse event (type and frequency of abuse) while contextual factors (age, gender, condition) did not significantly influence recognition or referring of abuse. Most often respondents provided identical ratings on abuse and recognition scales indicating that they perceived the level of abuse and the need to report as identical, in accord with stated policy. However some practitioners were prepared to under-report (17.4 per cent, n = 393) or over-report (10.7 per cent, n = 241). The variation correlated with wishes of the client, level of training and employment location.

Conclusion

The presence of under- and over-reporting suggests that some practitioners are exercising judgement regarding the most appropriate response to identified abuse. This was most commonly not reporting a single incident of an action that might be categorised as abusive under the procedures.

(Killick and Taylor, 2012)

Context, role and framing judgements

A primary concept in professional practice is to clarify our role in relation to each situation. In relation to decision making, a consideration of role alerts us to seeing ourselves as one player within what is often a complex situation, but nonetheless a useful contributor with a particular range of knowledge and skills. Among professions, social workers tend to have a holistic perspective on situations. The factors that we take into account in order to make sense of a complex, changing mosaic of information may be described as *framing the decision* and *framing the risks.* The narrative by which we construct meaning out of our observations and other client information is an essential component of the 'context' of the judgement. The factors that we need to consider include:

- the problem and who is facing what decision;

- your role and the aim of the social work intervention;

- needs, issues and strengths;

- past events, present situation, prospects;

- family, friends, neighbours, community and supportive groups;

- law, regulations, policies, procedures;

- function of your organisation and services available;

- relevant functions and services of other organisations;

- response to and effectiveness of previous services used;

- values, standards, principles;

- knowledge, research, theory and skills;

- potential bias from using this frame of reference.

Eileen Munro (1996, 1999) has studied how errors of reasoning can influence child protection judgements. One of her key conclusions is that a common problem concerns professionals who are reluctant to change their minds in the light of new information.

> In practice this means that social workers get a 'frame' on a case too quickly, and seek out information that will confirm that view .... A clear awareness of the inherent weaknesses in both practice and the systems of the organisations in which social workers operate could go a long way to reducing the problems.

(Hollows, 2008, p53)

ACTIVITY 5.1

Framing a decision

Recall a recent reasonably (but not exceptionally) complex case.

- *What frame of reference are you using for this decision?*

- *What effect might this have on the decision process and outcome?*

- *Reflect on the mental process that you went through in reaching a judgement.*

(Continued)

(Continued)

- *What were the most important factors considered and why?*
- *How did you process or bring together different aspects of the issue?*

Using knowledge of risk in professional judgement

There is an extensive literature illustrating the diverse perceptions of risk within society. Such varying views of risk will influence the judgements of clients and other professionals as well as ourselves as social workers. In the UK there is a particular challenge in that some of the media and politicians seem at times quite irrational in their determination to blame someone – usually social workers – when there is a tragedy or other adverse event, and no other more important news item on which to focus. A major task for the profession is to contribute towards strengthening the training and public voice of social workers to support us in making judgements that are not clouded by misguided and misguiding media coverage.

Research illustrates the inconsistencies in professional judgements in many areas of professional decision making (Beach and Connolly, 1997; Gilovich *et al.*, 2002), including various aspects of health and social care such as medical diagnoses of physical and mental illnesses (Eddy, 1996, Chapter 29), eligibility and safeguarding decisions in child protection (Spratt, 2001) and decisions about the long-term care of older people (Austin and Seidl, 1981).

> *Between the macro level of governmental risk management initiatives and the micro level of professional communication with an individual service user, there is a less explored domain of how health and social services professionals make sense of such complex issues in reaching a judgement about appropriate care.*

(Taylor, 2006b, p1413)

Because of the multiple conceptualisations of 'risk', it is important to seek clarity of thinking process, as well as avoidance of bias informing a judgement about a situation. In seeking to clarify the facts of the situation the following four prompts may be useful.

1. What patterns of behaviour are apparent from the information at hand?

2. What are the aspects (behaviours) of concern?

3. Is there a changing pattern of behaviours of concern?

4. What strengths are there in the situation?

One particular aspect of risk that is essential to professional judgement is the dimension of predicting harm and making a judgement against some threshold for compulsory intervention or priority access to services. This important topic is the focus of Chapter 6, which from a theoretical perspective includes material on signal (risk) detection and threshold judgements. Another key aspect of risk in relation to professional judgement is weighing up options where a choice is to be made between options for care or treatment. In practice this is normally described as contributing to a care plan or safeguarding plan, or risk plan or discharge plan, or some similar term. This important topic is the focus of Chapter 7, which from a theoretical perspective includes material on subjective expected utility models of judgement and the use of decision trees. This chapter will focus on more general aspects of bias and heuristics (short-cuts) as aspects of professional judgement before going on to consider the use of knowledge within professional judgement.

RESEARCH SUMMARY 5.2

Paradigms for conceptualising risk

Risk management systems are developing rapidly within health and social care services, sometimes within a framework for clinical and social care governance. However, the risk management strategies of organisations need to take into account the conceptual frameworks used by professionals. This grounded theory study used data from 19 focus groups and 9 semi-structured interviews (99 staff in total) to explore perspectives on risk and decision making regarding the long-term care of older people. Focus group participants and interviewees comprised social workers, care managers, consultant geriatricians, general medical practitioners, community nurses, occupational therapists, home care managers and hospital discharge support staff. Social work and healthcare professionals conceptualised risk and its management according to six paradigms: (1) Identifying and Meeting Needs, (2) Minimising Situational Hazards, (3) Protecting this Individual and Others, (4) Balancing Benefits and Harms, (5) Accounting for Resources and Priorities, and (6) Wariness of Lurking Conflict. Professionals seemed to use one paradigm instinctively when asked about 'risk', but switched to other paradigms when faced with alternative issues. The effective translation into practice of risk management strategies needs to address the complex and often contradictory issues facing health and social services professionals (Taylor, 2006b).

Bias in professional judgement

As individuals we may like to have a persona that portrays a perception of all our personal decisions as being supremely rational. However, it may be that the reality of our judgement processes is not quite so robustly logical as we like to portray. Selwyn Hughes (2005, p33) suggests that: *We arrive at some of the greatest decisions of our lives based not so much on reason or logic but what is going on deep within us – in our hearts – and then we look for logical reasons to support our feelings.* Some bias (or error) in any human decision might be attributable to tiredness or emotional exhaustion (McFadden *et al.*, 2015). Some aspects of emotion in decision making have been discussed in Chapter 2. Our focus here is primarily on types of cognitive bias (see Table 5.1).

Does it make a difference to your recommendation if you are the one who will go back to the client to tell him or her about the decision or if you have greater responsibility for the decision (cf. Schwartz *et al.*, 2004)? How does resource availability fit into the decision-making process? How do the needs of other patients and clients affect your judgement (for example, problems of delayed discharge from hospital and the tendency to ignore the unseen clients on the waiting list)? Does it make a difference knowing that this client is related to a local politician, or has threatened to go to the press if he or she does not get what is demanded? Are such influences on the decision outcome (a) legally permissible and (b) ethically right?

Table 5.1   Heuristics and biases

• **Adjustment bias**	Judgements may be influenced by initial information that shapes our gathering and perspective on subsequent information. New information may be selectively processed to support judgements already made.
• **Anchoring bias**	Judging new situations in relation to known 'related' point (for example, regarding normal child development or ageing) but this may be biased by an inappropriate judgement of what is normal.
• **Availability heuristic**	The ease with which a problem or situation may be conceptualised or imagined may influence the judgement made. See also 'recall bias'.
• **Base rate neglect**	Neglecting to pay attention to the underlying (prior) probability of an event occurring perhaps through paying more attention to factors that have less influence on the likelihood.
• **Compression bias**	A tendency to overestimate the likelihood of rare but serious undesirable events (risks) and underestimate the frequency of common undesirable events.
• **Confirmation bias**	A tendency to search for and interpret information consistent with one's prior beliefs, knowledge and experience.
• **Credibility bias**	We may be more inclined to accept a statement by someone we like.
• **Framing effect**	The wording used to describe a situation may influence the way in which a decision is perceived, and this may influence the judgement made. Common framing effects may relate to highlighting aspects of the purpose or consequences of the choice, and whether positive or negative goals or risks are emphasised.
• **Fundamental attribution error**	A tendency to emphasise internal characteristics in understanding other people's behaviour, but more often recognising situational factors as justifying our own.
• **Hindsight bias**	A tendency to view past events as being more predictable than they seemed to people at the time.
• **Illusion of control**	Humans tend to underestimate future uncertainty because we tend to believe we have more control over events than we really do.
• **Illusory correlation**	Although learning the cues that signal danger, social approval or other consequences is an essential human skill, information received may be inappropriately weighted.
• **Loss aversion**	A tendency to want to avoid the possibility of loss and pain more than seeking the possibilities in benefit and gain.
• **Omission bias**	The preference for harm caused by omissions over equal or lesser harm caused by acts.
• **Optimism bias**	An incorrect expectation of positive outcomes in care planning.
• **Over-confidence**	We have a tendency to be over-confident about the extent and accuracy of our personal knowledge.
• **Prejudice**	Bias from conscious or unconscious stereotyping.

- **Recall (or representativeness) bias** Recent and dramatic cases or incidents in the team or the media can have an undue effect. People have a tendency to overestimate the likelihood of types of events that are familiar from their experience or where an event of this type becomes well known through conversation or the media. See also 'availability heuristic'.

- **Repetition bias** A willingness to believe what we have been told most often and by the greatest number of different sources.

- **Wariness of lurking conflict** Staff may be anxious in case they are assaulted, subject to complaints, sued, censured, criticised by inquiries, the media or politicians, etc.

(Compiled from various sources including Baron (2008); Baron and Ritov (2004); Breckon (2016); Chapman and Elstein (2000); Fiedler (2017); Hardman (2009); Jones and Harris (1967); Kahneman and Tversky (2000); Kühlberger (2017); Luft (1969); Macdonald and Sheldon (1998); Munro (1996); Pennycook and Thompson (2017); Taylor (2006b); and Thompson (2002)).

CASE STUDY 5 . 1

Avoiding potential bias

Terence, aged 15, is on probation for stealing a car. My role is to advise, assist and befriend him with a view to reducing the likelihood of him re-offending and also to assess the risk that he presents to others so as to protect society. In seeking to help Terence I am aware that I need to understand his world. My own upbringing was very different from his: he had no father or father-figure; he is living on a housing estate with a high crime rate; and he is under pressure to conform and has received threats from peers and adult criminals. At each point where I am seeking to help him to take positive steps forward, I have to consciously avoid the bias of my own upbringing.

- *What expectations do you have from your own upbringing and life in terms of such aspects as how to bring up children, how to respond to social pressures or threats or bullying, how to manage money, etc.?*

- *How can you tune-in most effectively to the circumstances of your client?*

- *How do you hold out for them hope for growth and challenge for change?*

On the other hand, errors may occur because of a lack of anchoring a judgement. For example, risk factors indicating a higher probability of abuse may be insufficiently understood or used, theories may be used that are untested, and theory and research may be used unsystematically (Munro, 1996). As humans we need categories and labels (which we relate to known *anchors* of knowledge) to make sense of the world; as professionals we need them to determine need and eligibility for services. The very mechanisms that enable us to learn and take complex decisions are the same mechanisms by which we may be open to bias.

Heuristics in professional judgement

The cognitive processes that might lead to bias may also be essential shortcuts or *heuristics* that aid us as human beings in making complex decisions in everyday life. Such heuristics are invaluable in simplifying decisions. It is neither possible nor efficient to go through life undertaking a detailed analysis for every decision. Such a journey would take us towards *analysis paralysis* or mental illness! The development of such heuristics can also be seen as part of the learning process by which we generalise from previous knowledge of similar decisions (Reynolds, 1942) and in response to the challenges to the human brain in processing large amounts of information (Miller, 1956; Dodds *et al.*, 2012). We build on our decisions by creating internalised rules to help us to achieve the same result more efficiently in similar situations. The subsequent judgement is more efficient and possibly effective because of our previous experience, but also it may be biased by previous experience. A variety of ingenious experiments have been conducted in this field (Kahnemann *et al.*, 1982; Kahnemann and Tversky, 2000). Most of this research tends to focus on innate human heuristic decision making as biases in terms of the way that they might distort our decision making.

Gary Klein (2000) has studied how people in work situations make decisions under time pressure. He focused particularly on fire-fighters and military contexts, but the findings are relevant to the time pressures and high-risk situations in social work. Klein's *recognition primed decision model* is novel in how the decision maker evaluates possible courses of action by visualising them. In this way, the similarities to previous experience of decisions may become apparent. This then informs the individual in terms of appraising urgency, deciding what further information is required and judging the likelihood of success of the proposed plan.

In certain situations, decisions may be worse because of information overload rather than improved by additional information. Malcolm Gladwell (2006) conducted a selective overview of research across diverse fields of human endeavour to illustrate how sometimes the use of limited information may lead to sound judgements. These arguments are not to suggest that initial rapid judgements are always correct, nor that more intuitive judgements cannot be trained and educated. For example, many studies have been conducted on bias and approaches to combating prejudice (e.g. Dasgupta and Greenwald, 2001; Enosh and Bayer-Topilsky, 2015). Awareness of bias can prompt us to create mechanisms and processes that will minimise the possibility of bias and enable us to gather rapid information that is less biased.

These ideas have a resonance with the *bounded rationality* approach to decision making studied by Herbert Simon (1957) and by Gerd Gigerenzer and colleagues (1999). Their argument is that it is not efficient to attempt to make all decisions based on amassing comprehensive information that is weighted (and given probabilities if uncertain) and then computed to give a decision. The bounded rationality school of thought suggests that whilst some (perhaps more serious) decisions might be made in this way, it is not the normal or natural approach in everyday life (Taylor, 2012c). As man has evolved, decisions about survival have to be made based on limited information, and conscious of the 'cost' of seeking further information.

A conclusion from these various perspectives on bias in professional judgement is that the structuring of the decision and the risks is crucial. It has been suggested that experts give problem definition more attention than novices, and structure problems at a more abstract level (Gambrill, 2008). Conclusions from research about the need to be aware of the decision context lends support to the traditional social work focus on holistic assessment and case history.

ACTIVITY 5.2

Avoiding bias

- *What benchmarks (anchors) am I using in judging client behaviour?*

- *Is my practice influenced by previous experiences: (a) growing up; (b) at work; (c) adult life outside work?*

- *What strengths and dangers are there for professional decisions in anchoring decisions in your own previous experience?*

- *Am I unduly influenced by recent or dramatic events?*

- *What ways are there to moderate against inappropriate bias?*

- *How do you learn from life and work experience yet avoid bias?*

- *On what am I basing my estimate of the probability of harm (or success)?*

- *Am I giving due weight to the various sources of information?*

- *Am I ensuring that I do not discriminate on such grounds as sex, ethnic origin or political persuasion?*

- *Am I unduly confident or over-optimistic?*

- *What would it take to change my mind since the last assessment point?*

Using professional knowledge to inform judgements

Although experience is a valuable source of knowledge (Campbell *et al.*, 2016), social workers who rely solely on personal experiences to inform their practice run the risk of bias (Darragh and Taylor, 2009, p149). We need to use sound professional knowledge in our judgement to be transparent and fair in our decision processes, and to achieve the best outcomes for clients. This has come to be known in recent decades as evidence-based practice, although the essential principles are not new. The origins of social work in Western democracies might be viewed as rooted in efforts to apply the question 'what works?' to the endeavours of Christian and socialist charitable activities in the nineteenth century. The essence of evidence-based practice is not that professional expertise will be rejected in favour of some mechanistic method. Rather, evidence-based practice is about consciously identifying, understanding and using the best available relevant knowledge to inform practice decisions. It involves having skills such as being able to appraise the quality of research rather than treating something as completely authoritative when it lacks rigour; being able to consciously apply research and theory to practice; and for social workers in appropriate roles to contribute to the development of the profession's knowledge base through well-designed research on priority topics. Professional knowledge is important in decision making for the following reasons.

- *Well-informed decisions by social workers are vital to the immediate life opportunities and outcomes for clients and their families.*

- *Well-informed decisions may be regarded as a right for clients whose long-term wellbeing depends in part on social care decisions which can have a substantial impact over time.*

- *Where there are high risks and compulsory powers are exercised, requiring best evidence provides safeguards in the decision-making process.*

(Marsh *et al.*, 2005, pp3–4)

A growing number of organisations seek to distil and disseminate *best evidence* into a digestible format for busy practitioners and policy makers, utilising a variety of approaches (Walter *et al.*, 2004). In the United Kingdom, the Social Care Institute for Excellence (SCIE) promotes *better knowledge for better practice* in social care. There is encouragement for the development of knowledge and skills in identifying relevant research and in synthesising robust studies to inform practice, including both assessment and interventions (Taylor *et al.*, 2015). When considering the usefulness of knowledge to inform our practice, there are two key questions:

- How robust or rigorous is the knowledge in its own right?

- How relevant is the knowledge to this client situation?

For the social worker who is a researcher, the challenge may be to design and carry out studies that will have the greatest credibility in informing practice within available resources. For the social work practitioner, we often have to rely on *good enough* studies and accept that ideal studies are not available and perhaps not achievable within legal, ethical and resource constraints. A key issue is to understand the limitations of the knowledge that informs our decisions (Taylor *et al.*, 2015).

RESEARCH SUMMARY **5.3**

Information search

Introduction

The aim of this study by Rami Benbenishty and colleagues was to identify the ways in which decision makers search for information and use it to reach their risk assessments and their recommendations of whether to remove children from home. The decision-making processes of social work professionals, social work trainees and non-professionals were compared in terms of how they are influenced by information on physical abuse to a child, and what additional information beyond the initial referral they regarded as a priority.

Method

Three convenience samples of 100 subjects each were used: certified social workers, social work trainees and students in the BA programme in the School of Business Administration. Minimal referral information was provided on a case of alleged child abuse and respondents were asked to make initial judgements and recommendations on the case. A list of available additional information cues about the case was then provided, and respondents were invited to identify what further information they wanted from this list. The information provided to each group of respondents was manipulated so that half received a version describing clear signs of physical abuse and the other half of each group received a version that did not include clear signs. The study combined the two traditions in decision research of 'policy capturing' and 'process tracing'.

Results

Information on signs of physical abuse had significant impact on risk judgements, removal recommendations and information search patterns. There were significant differences between the three groups in their assessment of risk and recommendations for removal. Non-professionals tended to assess higher risk, recommend removal more often, and were influenced by information on physical abuse more than the other two groups. Professionals and trainees looked for more information than the non-professionals, particularly when there were no clear signs of physical abuse. In general the three groups selected information in a similar sequence: (1) signs of physical abuse; (2) quality of mother's and father's relationship with the child; (3) child's relationship with his parents; (4) child's development; (5) parent's personality and functioning; (6) parent's childhood history; and (7) family's relationship with its social environment. However, there were some differences in the sequence in which sub-categories of additional information were selected within this general result.

(Benbenishty et al., 2002)

CASE STUDY 5.2

Using knowledge to inform a judgement

Benjamin is 12 years old and recently moved from primary to secondary school. His parents separated just prior to his change of school and his grandfather, to whom he was close, died shortly afterwards. His school attendance presented no problems at primary school, but his attendance at secondary school has been unsatisfactory and he has been referred by the school to the Education Welfare Service. Studies show that limited school attendance is a factor in mental health problems and social isolation, and also increased involvement in crime. Lengthy absence from school makes reintegration progressively harder. One conclusion of the assessment was that Benjamin's development had been arrested by the shock of his parents' separation and his grandfather's death. Benjamin's need to behave like a much younger child playing with cuddly toys was understood in terms of Bowlby's theory of attachment. Applying this knowledge base, I proposed a care plan to build self-esteem and confidence through a series of small successes using a task-centred approach.

- *What other knowledge might have been used to inform work in this case?*

- *For a recent case of your own, what knowledge base could usefully inform your judgement?*

- *How can you access the knowledge that you require?*

103

RESEARCH SUMMARY 5.4

Initial judgements: heuristic or bias?

Context

This study by Sybil Carrère and John Gottman tested the hypothesis that how a discussion of a marital conflict begins – in its first few minutes – is a predictor of divorce.

Method

The marital conflict discussion of 124 newly wed couples was coded using the Specific Affect Coding System. Positive emotions were classified as: joy (+4), humour (+4), affection (+4), validation (+4) and interest (+2); negative emotions were classified as contempt (−4), disgust (−3), defensiveness (−2), belligerence (−2), stonewalling (−2), domineering (−1), anger (−1), whining (−1) and sadness (−1); weighted as indicated. The data were divided into positive, negative, and positive-minus-negative affect totals for five three-minute intervals.

Results

Couples were followed up for a six-year period and 17 divorces occurred during that time. The first three minutes of data for both husbands and wives was predictive of marital outcome over the six-year period. For husbands this prediction improved as data on the two groups of husbands (in couples staying together compared with those divorcing) diverged in the remaining 12 minutes; for wives the prediction remained equally strong for the remaining 12 minutes as it had been in the first three minutes (Carrère and Gottman, 1999).

Follow-up studies

In a subsequent publication, John Gottman presents data from a range of studies on this topic. On the basis of detailed analysis of one hour of couple discussion, methods of analysing relatively brief interactive data can predict with 95 per cent accuracy which couples will have divorced within 15 years (Gottman, 2000).

Using knowledge of the effectiveness of interventions

A crucial area where research could provide less biased knowledge than individual experience is on the effectiveness of interventions (Taylor, 2012a). We want to know whether clients in similar situations achieve better outcomes with one intervention rather than another. Sadly, many management systems are designed to gather data on performance outputs rather than on outcomes for clients and families which could be used to inform professionals.

> *To rule out other factors that might influence the outcome (such as family factors, age, and changes in society more generally), the best approach is to assign participants randomly to two groups, one (the 'experimental' group) that receives the intervention being studied and one (the 'control' group) that does not. This basic design is known as a randomised controlled study.*
>
> (Darragh and Taylor, 2009, pp149–50)

There are ethical as well as practical challenges in undertaking experimental studies in social work, and much research to be done if we are to make the substantial progress that is necessary to inform practice most effectively.

Decisions about types of interventions should be based on robust knowledge of *what works*. We might well question the value of a single research study, particularly as evidence in highly contested decisions such as in court. There is steadily increasing recognition that a *systematic review* of research (Coren and Fisher, 2006; Taylor *et al.*, 2015) is of more value than any one individual study. A *systematic review* embraces:

- an explicit process of searching databases to retrieve all relevant research on the topic (Taylor, 2003; Taylor *et al.*, 2003; Taylor, Wylie *et al.*, 2007; McFadden *et al.*, 2012; Stevenson *et al.*, in press);

- an explicit process of deciding which studies to include in terms of content and quality (Taylor, Dempster *et al.*, 2007); and

- an explicit process for combining (synthesising) the studies to produce a unified message to inform practice (Fisher *et al.*, 2006; Taylor *et al.*, 2015).

Creating a systematic review that synthesises all relevant, high quality research on a particular topic is a time-consuming and skilled job requiring collaboration between professionals and information scientists. There are a number of initiatives in publishing systematic reviews which are of interest and value to social workers; some examples are in the Further Reading section at the end of this chapter.

Most systematic reviews at the present time are on the effectiveness of interventions, although a few exist on other topics such as client perceptions of services (e.g. Fisher *et al.*, 2006) and professional judgements (e.g. Killick and Taylor, 2012).

The *Cochrane Collaboration* library contains something approaching a hundred systematic reviews of the effectiveness of interventions that might be carried out by social workers (some requiring post-qualifying training), including the following:

- family and parenting interventions in children and adolescents aged 10–17 with conduct disorder and delinquency;

- advocacy interventions to reduce or eliminate violence and promote the physical and psycho-social well-being of women who experience intimate partner abuse;

- family therapy for attention-deficit disorder or attention-deficit/hyperactivity disorder in children and adolescents;

- cognitive behavioural interventions for children who have been sexually abused;

- individual- and group-based parenting programmes for the treatment of physical child abuse and neglect;

- parent training support for intellectually disabled parents;

- multi-systemic therapy for social, emotional and behavioural problems in youths;

- kinship care for the safety, permanency and well-being of children removed from the home for maltreatment;

- behavioural and cognitive behavioural training interventions for assisting foster carers in the management of difficult behaviour;

- independent living programmes for improving outcomes for young people leaving the care system;

- parent-mediated early intervention for young children with autism spectrum disorder;

- psycho-social and pharmacological treatments for deliberate self-harm;

- family therapy for anorexia nervosa;

- psychological treatments for bulimia nervosa and binging;

- self-help and guided self-help for eating disorders;

- marital therapy for depression;

- psycho-social interventions for cocaine and psycho-stimulant amphetamine related disorder;

- psychological treatment of post-traumatic stress disorder (PTSD);

- interventions for learning-disabled sex offenders;

- reminiscence therapy for dementia;

- validation therapy for dementia (=Reality Orientation);

- non-pharmacological interventions for wandering of people with dementia at home;

- massage and touch for dementia;

- interventions for preventing falls in elderly people;

- discharge planning from hospital to home;

- smart home technologies for health and social care support.

It is all too easy to assume that there is evidence of the effectiveness of interventions just because there is local enthusiasm for their implementation (see, e.g., McGinn *et al.*, in press). The Cochrane and Campbell Collaboration libraries are a robust source of evidence of effectiveness, and a good starting point for planning interventions. It is beyond the scope of this book to discuss evidence of effectiveness of interventions in detail. The interested reader is referred to Taylor (2012a).

CASE STUDY **5.3**

Using research on effectiveness of interventions

As a Guardian-ad-Litem I am responsible for a case where Paul (aged 8 years) has been cared for by his mother who has an addiction problem. Paul was recently admitted to care on a voluntary basis as his mother knew that she was not coping well with him, but Mrs Roberts has now requested that Paul be returned home. However, the child care social work department responsible for safeguarding children is concerned that she is not yet fit to resume custody of Paul. The legal advisor for Mrs Roberts is arguing that she no longer has an addiction problem, having been to a well-known treatment programme.

- *What do you need to know about theories and research on addiction?*
- *What studies are there of the effectiveness of treatments for addiction?*
- *What do they tell us about recovery times and patterns?*

Using knowledge of the application of interventions

While it is important to know what types of interventions are most effective in particular sorts of situations, it is also important to understand helping processes in making a judgement on what intervention is appropriate. The views of clients can help to sensitise us to crucial issues. Some of the knowledge that is useful but less tangible and less amenable to generalisable research might include:

- perceptions of key stakeholders about *this problem* and possible ways forward;
- knowledge of resources to implement the proposed care plan or helping process;
- knowing what is needed to help the client to engage with the helping process (transport? child care? emotional challenges?).

We need to know what works and we need to know what is required to make it work in this particular situation. You need to know what works well for you as well as challenging yourself to extend your repertoire of skills. Personal experience is perhaps better in helping to adjust a method to the immediate situation than judging what works generally. There is research that suggests that a sound approach is to undertake thorough preparation but allow for flexibility in the pressures of the live decision situation (Gladwell, 2006).

There is a challenge for professionals in using and in demonstrating the use of knowledge to inform practice decisions. For social work in particular, we have challenges in our weak and diverse knowledge base as well as the increasingly intense societal demands on our judgements. The profession needs to develop its knowledge base through improving the quality and quantity of research and theory to support policy, management and practice. The interested reader is referred to Taylor *et al.* (2015) on the identification and use of research to inform practice, and to Campbell *et al.*

(2016) on undertaking social work research to create useful knowledge. The former includes detail on various approaches to synthesising knowledge to inform practice.

Professional knowledge and reflective practice

A primary mechanism for professional development is reflecting on your practice in relation to professional knowledge and on your knowledge base in relation to practice experiences. Having the self-awareness to relate judgements to law, regulations, policies and procedures, and professional knowledge is a safeguard against bias. Such professional knowledge may be drawn from theory and research on such issues as risk factors, causes of problems, and the effectiveness and processes of interventions. Donald Schön (1983) describes *reflection-in-action* as thinking on one's feet, involving looking to personal experiences, connecting with personal feelings, and attending to theories in use; while *reflection-on-action* entails building new understandings that inform individual actions in the situations that unfold, with the new understandings emerging after the encounter.

ACTIVITY **5.3**

Prompts to aid reflection on your professional judgements

- *What was my role?*
- *What was the goal of the decision and intervention?*
- *What was the issue (risk) on which I had to form a judgement?*
- *What information about the client, family and situation was most significant in shaping my judgement?*
- *How did the decision appear from the perspective of client problem solving?*
- *What assumptions influenced my judgement?*
- *What alternative options were considered?*
- *What alternative causal explanations were considered?*
- *What justified the decision?*
- *What professional knowledge informed my judgement?*
- *What research or theory underpinned this knowledge?*
- *What additional information or knowledge would I have liked to have had?*
- *What emotions and challenges were there in this decision situation?*
- *What skills did I use?*
- *How could my judgement have been improved?*
- *What learning from this might inform my judgements in future?*

Increasing experience generally reduces the conscious element of decision making. Professionals internalise judgement processes (and become more 'intuitive' in common language) as their experience and professional knowledge increases. Emotion can influence any human judgement, perhaps varying with changing life circumstances. Judgements must be continually checked back against the framework of legislation, policy, procedures and standards which underpin the service. For all these reasons, it is important to step back regularly to reflect on the basis for our judgements, and to continue to extend our knowledge base to inform practice.

Chapter summary

*   In making judgements about situations you may be influenced by your own childhood and by recent or dramatic life and professional experiences. We need to recognise such influences in order to avoid bias in our judgements.

*   The frame of reference that you use for a decision and when conceptualising a risk should be an explicit sound structure for a decision process and avoid inappropriate influences.

*   A greater awareness of the heuristics, or short-cuts, that we use in everyday judgements – such as rapidly identifying the most important information and recognising how a situation has parallels with previous experience – assists us in improving practice through reflective learning.

*   There is a challenge for the profession in creating, accessing, appraising, synthesising and using the best available evidence to inform practice. It is important that you have a rationale for important judgements that you make.

*   Reflective practice, professional supervision and robust, supportive systems in organisations supporting evidence-based practice are emphasised as tools to minimise the effect of individual bias and ensure the highest standards of decision making.

FURTHER READING

Benner, P. (1984) *From Novice to Expert: Excellence and Power in Clinical Nursing Practice.* Menlo Park, CA: Addison-Wesley.

This book captures something of the professional journey to having a more internalised knowledge base and greater ability to identify and respond to subtle cues that might be missed by those less experienced.

Gambrill, E. (2005) *Critical Thinking in Clinical Practice: Improving the Quality of Judgments and Decisions*, 2nd edition. Hoboken, NJ: Wiley.

This thorough book by an esteemed social work academic addresses many aspects of applying knowledge to practice judgements. Note that the word 'clinical' as applied to social work is used here, as commonly in North America and Australasia, to indicate therapeutic or helping practice with individuals and families (as opposed, for example, to safeguarding, case management or community development activities).

Gibbs, L. (2003) *Evidence Based Practice for the Helping Professions: A Practical Guide with Electronic Aids.* Pacific Grove, CA: Brooks/Cole.

This attractive book and accompanying web-based learning materials take as their mission: *Placing the client's benefits first, evidence-based practitioners adopt a process of lifelong learning that involves continually posing specific questions of direct practical importance to clients, searching objectively and efficiently for the current best evidence related to each question, and taking appropriate action guided by evidence.*

Gigerenzer, G., Todd, P. and the ABC Research Group (1999) *Simple Heuristics That Make Us Smart.* New York: Oxford University Press.

This is one of the most accessible of the publications emerging from the bounded rationality school of research on decision making, which takes as its premise that the failure to use comprehensive balancing of values and probabilities of each option is not a sign of irrationality, but is a human response to managing vast amounts of information most effectively. Seen in this light, what might be viewed as biases may be seen more easily as rational heuristics to simplify complex decisions.

Taylor, B.J., Killick, C. and McGlade, A. (2015) *Understanding and Using Research in Social Work.* London: Sage.

This readable textbook focuses on practical skills in shaping an answerable practice question; identifying relevant research; appraising its quality; and synthesising research findings to inform practice. It is the ideal complement for the material in this chapter in terms of applying knowledge to practice.

North–South Child Protection Hub (NSCPH) (**http://members.nscph.com**)

The aim of the NSCPH is to enhance and share child protection knowledge by providing access to:

- local, national and international research in the field of child protection;

- RoI, NI and UK national policy documents and guidance;

- reports of child protection inspections and inquiries;

- executive summaries of serious case reviews;

- coverage of child protection news and events.

Safeguarding Adults at Risk Information Hub (SAaRIH) (**www.saarih.com**)

The SAaRIH project is an online central information resource for practitioners, managers, researchers, educators and policy makers (across all relevant disciplines and agencies and sectors) with an interest in adult safeguarding and protection. The aim is to provide a single point of focus for individuals to access relevant and current information to assist them with understanding, practice and decision making in relation to vulnerable adults.

Cochrane Collaboration (**www.cochrane.org**): undertakes systematic reviews of the effectiveness of health and social care interventions;

Campbell Collaboration (**www.campbellcollaboration.org**): undertakes systematic reviews of the effectiveness of interventions in justice, education, social welfare and international development; and

Social Care Institute for Excellence (**www.scie.org.uk**): commissions and provides summaries of systematic reviews to guide good practice in social work in the UK.

Chapter 6

Judgements about safeguarding and service eligibility, and predicting harm

Amphitryon to Sosias: 'But tell me, by your conscience now: is there a shade of probability in anything you tell to me as truth?'

(Heinrich von Kleist [1777–1811], 1962 edition, p26)

Introduction

This chapter extends the initial consideration of professional judgement in Chapter 5 with a focus on what may be the most difficult judgement calls in social work: judgements involving considering whether a situation crosses a *threshold* or 'line'. In social work, these judgements may be about compulsory intervention on behalf of society (such as to protect children or adults with a particular vulnerability), eligibility for provision of services or an appraisal of the quality of social care services as 'good enough' if you are in a regulatory role. These types of judgements often involve the crucial issue of attempting to predict harm as an aspect of professional decision making, even when the focus is on eligibility for services rather than safeguarding. This has become a key dimension of assessment and professional judgement as discussed in previous chapters, spurred by feelings of blame in our 'risk society'. These types of judgements relate to diverse practice issues from protecting children to supporting independence steps by people with a disability, as well as attempts to predict and thereby prevent such undesirable outcomes as abuse, homicide, suicide, hospital admissions, accidents and re-offending. We consider in particular the extent to which professionals can predict harm. The purpose of this chapter is to develop an understanding of general principles of predicting harm. It is beyond the scope of this book to provide data on specific risks, although we give some indication of where we would like to see the profession develop in this regard. This chapter highlights the issues involved in any assessment process where we are attempting to make a *yes–no* decision, as there will always be some people incorrectly identified as *at risk* and some incorrectly identified as *not at risk*. This chapter extends the chapter on professional judgement in general to consider a specific aspect of professional judgement that links also to assessment and decision processes. Actuarial and clinical prediction methods are explained and discussed in terms of their application in social work. We consider the social work role in relation to clarifying the mandate for intervening compulsorily in family life, and making a *criterion-based judgement* in relation to threshold criteria for statutory measures to protect an individual. These precise statistical methods are followed by a consideration of *risk cluster* and *heuristic* approaches to professional judgement. This chapter thus focuses on a key aspect of individual professional judgement intrinsic to assessment (see Chapter 4), and which will then often inform collaborative decision making as discussed in Chapter 8. For more on assault and aggression 'risks' the interested reader is referred to Taylor (2011).

Risk, blame and predicting harm

After some human tragedy occurs, it has become commonplace in the UK media to hear a message along the lines that 'they' (often referring to social workers, but occasionally to other professionals also) should have been able to predict and prevent the harmful outcome. A major challenge in social work practice is the apparent expectation of some media and politicians that social workers and other professionals should be able to precisely predict harm that may be caused to a human being, normally by another (violence, abuse) or by themselves (self-harm, self-neglect, avoidable accidents) and be able to prevent that harm occurring. In the words of Eileen Munro:

> *Ideally [professionals] should protect all children who are at risk of abuse while not disrupting any family providing adequate care. Abused children should return only to families who have changed and no longer pose a threat to their offspring. These ideals however are impossible to achieve.*

(Munro, 1996, p793)

There are also dangers in the profession focusing so much on the rare and (by definition hard to predict) most undesirable outcomes (such as in response to media and political pressures) that the good that social work can do is neglected, the profession comes under unreasonable criticism, and hence we provide less for the vulnerable in general (McDonald and McDonald, 2010; see also Barlow and Calam, 2011). This chapter explores how risk factors may be used to inform professional judgements and decisions and the limitations to human ability to predict harm (or anything else). Where the purpose of assessment is to help us to better understand harm which might or might not occur in the future, the points discussed in this chapter will be relevant to effective assessment processes and the design and use of assessment tools. Assessing the likelihood of harm is a particular focus in safeguarding decisions, where society provides statutory mandates for safeguarding measures to *protect this individual and others* (Taylor, 2006b; Tooth, 2009) from serious harm. We consider organisational responsibilities in relation to the *blame culture* in Chapter 10.

The classic text by Brearley (1982) might be viewed as opening up the concept of *risk* in social work. Although social work has many ideas relevant to risk and its assessment and management, it was not until the 1980s and 1990s that it was conceptualised as such (DH, 1993). Since then, there has been an increasing focus on *risk* in social work as a way of thinking about our work. Increasing areas of social work are now being conceptualised in terms of assessing and managing *risk* of future harm rather than exclusively on meeting appropriate presenting needs.

'They should have detected that he was a real danger to himself and others,' said Mrs Linda Abram regarding her son Michael Abram, later diagnosed as paranoid schizophrenic, who broke into George Harrison's home on 30 December 1999 and stabbed him several times (quoted by Bunyan (2001) 'Doctors "let off hook" in report over ex-Beatle's attacker', Daily Telegraph, *24 October). Oxford Crown Court jury in 2000 accepted that he was insane at the time and ordered indefinite detention.*

- *Who are 'they'?*

- *What is their responsibility?*

- *Could they have detected that he was a real danger?*

- *To what extent can such assaults be anticipated*

The focus on the likelihood of possible harm is most prominent in the areas of child protection (abuse), mental health (in relation to both homicide and suicide) and criminal justice (preventing re-offending), although protection of vulnerable adults from abuse and intra-familial ('domestic') violence are receiving increasing attention. The justification for providing services is increasingly conceptualised in terms of *risk* rather than *need*. However, what must be clearly understood is that there will always be a degree of error in any prediction about the future well-being of a client or family.

> *Since risk assessment is, by definition, making judgements under conditions of uncertainty, there is an unavoidable chance of error. It is impossible to identify infallibly those children [or other clients] who are in serious danger of abuse [or other harm]. Professionals can only make fallible judgements of the probability of [the undesirable event occurring].*

> (Munro, 2008, p40)

Risk factors and predicting from experience

How will we as professionals predict harm? The starting point might be to look first to form a judgement based on intuition. Inevitably, this will be based on life experiences (both as a child and as an adult) that are often subconscious. With professional training we might more consciously draw on a knowledge base that includes such areas as human growth and development, psychology and sociology, as discussed above. With practice experience we can draw increasingly on our experience of similar cases, transferring knowledge to new situations by analogy. We may also draw on colleagues, utilising whatever knowledge and experience they have and can articulate with us. This type of process of forming an opinion based on a wide-ranging, useful but ill-defined body of practice knowledge and experience is known in the literature as a *clinical* approach to prediction.

There are several challenges in attempting to predict some undesirable event (for example, violence or abuse) using such a *clinical* approach:

- Judgements are often over-reliant on self-report of the person being assessed.

- Professionals may be exposed to a non-representative range of clients.

- Professional perceptions may be subject to bias such as more recent or more dramatic events having undue impact.

- Professionals may be subject to bias from economic considerations, political pressure and personal and societal prejudice.

- Professionals often get limited feedback on the outcomes of their interventions.

    Psychiatrists and psychologists are accurate in no more than one out of three pre-dictions of violent behaviour over a several-year period among institutionalised populations that have both committed violence in the past (and thus had high base rates for it) and who were diagnosed as mentally ill.

(Monahan, 1981, p48)

We discuss below the significance of the frequency with which an event occurs (*base rate*) for the accuracy of prediction. I would not suggest that social workers are any more, or less, accurate than other professions at attempting to predict harm!

Can we improve on such intuitive approaches by developing more thorough methods? A key avenue for exploration is obviously to look at how often in the past a similar event has occurred. If we could understand past events better, perhaps we could improve our predictive ability. We might ask what factors correlate with harm occurring. If we knew that, we might look out for such factors in future situations. This is called an *actuarial* approach. We aim to calculate the probability of harm to or by this individual on the basis of the frequency with which this event has occurred in the past.

The factors that are found to correlate with a specific undesirable outcome are generally known as *risk factors*. A risk factor is a feature that is found more often in the risk situation than in equivalent non-risk situations. For example, a parent having a mental health problem is only predictive of child abuse if a significantly greater proportion of parents who abuse their children have mental health problems than among parents in general. The strength of a risk factor depends on how common the factor is amongst the undesirable situations (abuse, crime, neglect, suicide, etc.) compared to how common it is amongst the population in general (known as the *base rate*). It is possible in principle that a risk factor might be found only in the undesirable situations, but this is not the case in practice. Sometimes a risk factor may be very rare in the general population but much more common in the undesirable situations, giving a risk factor that is strongly predictive of the undesirable harm occurring. Sometimes the difference in the incidence between the undesirable situations and the general population may be rather smaller, giving a weakly predictive risk factor.

It is common to talk about *static risk factors*, being the ones that are not amenable to change, and *dynamic risk factors*, which are. For example, the extent of previous convictions is the best predictor of future criminal activity. As this cannot be changed by an intervention, it is a static risk factor. By contrast having employment is a dynamic factor; this may change. In work with offenders we need to know about the strongest risk factors – whether static or dynamic – in order to assess the risk (likelihood) of re-offending. But in order to engage with offenders in constructive interventions to reduce re-offending, we need to focus on dynamic factors that are amenable to intervention. Dynamic factors are more recently being considered as sub-divided into those that are *acute dynamic factors* (which includes most of those commonly considered such as family support, employment, accommodation, physical and mental health, and cognitive and emotional aspects such as affect and stress) and those that are *stable dynamic response mechanisms* (such as substance abuse, supervision compliance, coping efficacy, criminal attitudes and criminal associates) (Jones *et al.*, 2010).

In order to use *risk factors* that correlate with some particular harm (such as abuse or neglect) occurring, we can learn from approaches in the insurance industry. Actuaries calculate the likelihood of a ship being lost to storms or pirates and the value of a ship and its cargo to calculate the insurance premium accordingly. For example, if one ship in a thousand were lost then the insurance premium would need to be one thousandth of the average value of a ship and its cargo in order for the insurance company to break even (not counting operating costs).

Clinical and actuarial approaches to predicting harm

Similarly, there are *actuarial* approaches in health and social care that seek to identify factors that correlate with particular (usually undesirable) outcomes (Munro, 1999; Kemshall, 2008). The same statistical approaches can in principle be applied to identifying the factors that correlate with any *social ill-health* or *social dis-ease*. The best developed actuarial approaches in social welfare work are in the prediction of re-offending (e.g. Hood and Shute, 2000; Maung and Hammond, 2000; Raynor *et al.*, 2000), homicide and violence by people with mental illness (e.g. Monahan *et al.*, 2001), suicide (e.g. Gunnell, 1994) and, to a more limited extent, child abuse (e.g. Macdonald, 2001). This knowledge can be used to inform professional practice, for example through the design of assessment tools (McCormack *et al.*, 2008a and see Chapter 4). From such research, we can identify factors that increase or reduce the probability of the outcome we are trying to avoid.

Some risk factors for child abuse compiled from various sources are given in Table 6.1. Some risk factors for violence by people with mental health problems are in Monahan *et al.* (2001), Fazel *et al.* (2009) and Volavka and Swanson (2010), although there are many other studies. The following fairly reputable-looking websites give risk factors, although the research sources are not clearly documented:

- intimate partner violence: **www.emedicinehealth.com/domestic_violence/page3_em.htm** (see also Straus, 2009);

- elder abuse: **www.helpguide.org/mental/elder_abuse_physical_emotional_sexual_neglect.htm#risk.**

RESEARCH SUMMARY 6.1

There are many studies of the risk factors for admission of older people to institutional care, using a wide variety of research methods. The main findings can be grouped as:

- *client needs:*
  - *cognitive functioning;*
  - *physical functioning;*
  - *medical condition;*
  - *presentation of needs;*
- *demographic factors;*
- *services currently received;*
- *client choices;*
- *family support;*
- *capacity of family to cope.*

(Taylor and Donnelly, 2006b)

In our field of work, we can start with a wide population base and narrow down to more precise estimates of the likelihood of harm occurring. For example, if there are approximately 80 child homicides a year in England and Wales (Creighton, 2004a, 2004b) in a population of approximately 12 million children, then a first estimate of the probability of any particular child in England and Wales being deliberately killed by another person this coming year is 80 in 12 million or 1 in 150,000. If we have more precise data about sub-groups of children we can make more accurate estimates. For example, if we knew that urban children were three times as likely to be killed as children living in rural areas (I know of no evidence for this, it is purely an example) and there were equal numbers of children living in rural and urban areas, then the likelihood of homicide for a child living in a rural area would be 20 in 6 million (1 in 300,000) and for a child living in an urban area it would be 60 in 6 million (1 in 100,000). If we were to calculate the effect of identified risk factors such as those in Table 6.1, we could make a more precise estimate.

Table 6.1   Risk factors for child abuse

Risk Factors (1) Parents and parent-figures
- *Previous convictions for violence*
- *Parents' mental health*
- *Parental conflict and intimate partner violence*

- *Parents' experience of being abused or observing abuse*
- *Locus of control (impulse control)*
- *Parenting skills and expectations of the child*
- *Conflict resolution skills*
- *Parents' self-esteem*
- *Substance or alcohol misuse*
- *Employment*

Risk Factors (2) Child

- *Premature birth*
- *Developmental history*
- *Learning disability*
- *Physical disability*
- *Temperament and behaviour*

Risk Factors (3) Family

- *Attachment*
- *Family dysfunction and stress*
- *Poverty and housing*

Risk Factors (4) Environment

- *Social isolation and lack of support*
- *Social and educational resources*
- *Cultural and social values*

(Compiled from Bridge Child Care Consultancy, 1995; Dalgleish and Drew, 1989; Hagell, 1998; Hindley *et al.*, 2006; Johnson *et al.*, 2015; Macdonald, 2001; Milner, 1995; Pritchard *et al.*, 2013)

RESEARCH SUMMARY 6.2

Pritchard et al. (2013) undertook two rigorous studies of factors correlating with child homicide. First, using World Health Organisation data, the correlation between child homicide (children under 14 years) and relative poverty (using four validated scales) was studied. There was no correlation between child homicide and relative poverty, although there was a significant correlation between overall child mortality and relative poverty. Second, data on 4 per cent of the UK population were compared to identify the risk factors that correlated with the 22 homicides that occurred in that region over a ten-year period. The largest number of child homicides (8) correlated with mothers having mental health problems, and the next largest numbers correlated with fathers having mental health problems (4) and situations where there was a step-father in the family network with previous convictions for violence (4). The data were then compared with the prevalence of these situations in the whole population studied. By comparison with the prevalence of the 'problem' in the general population, a step-father in the family network with previous convictions for violence was by far the largest risk factor, approximately five times larger than mothers with mental health problems.

(Continued)

(Continued)

Questions: If, by current standards, this is viewed as a robust study for its purpose:

- *What does it add to the study that overall child mortality rates were also studied, and that this data did show a statistically significant correlation?*

- *Do you think that poverty might be a risk factor for other domains of child abuse or neglect even if not for child homicide, and if so why?*

- *Should we identify mechanisms (e.g. alleviating poverty) by which we can engage with families and motivate their engagement with services even if these are not in themselves risk factors (problem areas)?*

- *What challenges might there be in extending the study method to include a wider range of countries?*

(Pritchard et al., 2013)

It is possible to express the probability in terms of the increased likelihood of harm to, or by, this individual. Table 6.2 illustrates *risk factors* for suicide, which have been calculated in terms of how much more likely it is that an individual will commit suicide if they are described by that factor. For example, a person who is unemployed, a farmer or a doctor in England and Wales is twice as likely to commit suicide in any particular year as the average person in the whole population (Gunnell, 1994 (see Table 6.2); see also lists of unquantified factors in American Psychiatric Association, 2003, and Bryan and Rudd, 2006).

Table 6.2   Suicide risk factors (England and Wales) (Gunnell, 1994)

- *First 4 weeks after discharge from psychiatric hospital – male *200*
- *First 4 weeks after discharge from psychiatric hospital – female *100*
- *History of parasuicide *10–*30*
- *Alcohol abuse *20*
- *Drug misuse *20*
- *Samaritan client *20*
- *Current or ex-psychiatric patient *10*
- *Prisoner *5*
- *Doctor *2*
- *Farmer *2*
- *Unemployed *2*

Note:* For a person with the characteristic, multiply the average suicide rate for the population by the factor given.

Risk factors: static, dynamic, clusters and strengths

Researchers often focus on particular clusters of risk factors, because the issues have to be made manageable conceptually and in order to complete studies with limited resources. *Risk factors* may be considered in categories such as:

- *historical or developmental factors;*
- *dispositional or personal factors;*
- *symptom (presenting issue) factors; and*
- *contextual or situational factors* (see Righthand *et al.*, 2003, p35).

What is important for practice is to identify the risk factors that present the greatest threat (Jones, 1998) and that are amenable to influence, and to indicate how these will be addressed in the care (or safeguarding or risk) plan. Although the relative importance of risk factors has been explored for predicting certain types of re-offending and for homicide and suicide by people with mental health problems, the work on risk factors in child abuse and many other areas of social work is less well researched (Taylor and Zeller, 2007). Studies often identify *static* risk factors such as age, gender and past events which are not amenable to intervention. What is of more interest to us is *dynamic* risk factors such as anger, impulsivity and thought patterns which might be a target for helping a client to change and hence reduce the likelihood of harm.

Another form of analysis with less precise risk factors involves the creation of categories. For example, Agathanos-Georgopolou and Browne (1997) create three categories – high, medium and low probability of the undesirable event – in relation to predicting physical abuse of children (see Table 6.3). Risk factors may be incorporated into professional assessment tools, which we discuss further in Chapter 8. An under-researched area is the converse of 'risk factors' – factors that reduce rather than increase the likelihood of the unwanted harm. This has been studied most prominently in the justice sector as 'desistance' – factors that reduce the likelihood of re-offending. Another example is the work by Reeves *et al.* (2015, p44) on factors that mitigate the risk of suicide:

- willingness to talk about issues, thoughts, feelings;
- capacity for expressing emotion;
- having a key person in whom to confide;
- other important attachments;
- having regular contact with a counsellor or social worker;
- support of family, friends, community;
- involvement in activities, hobbies, etc.;
- sports or other physical activity;
- successful strategies for coping;
- an agreed crisis plan.

Table 6.3   Risk factors for violence (Monahan et al., 2005; Juby and Farrington, 2001; Leventhal and Brooks-Gunn, 2000)

1. Demographic

   a. Male
   b. Young age
   c. Socially disadvantaged neighbourhood
   d. Lack of social support
   e. Employment problems
   f. Criminal peer group

2. Background history

   a. Childhood maltreatment
   b. History of violence or sexual assault
   c. First violent at a young age
   d. History of childhood conduct disorder
   e. History of non-violent criminality

3. Clinical history

   a. Psychopathy
   b. Substance abuse
   c. Personality disorder
   d. Schizophrenia
   e. Executive dysfunction
   f. Non-compliance with treatment

4. Psychological and psycho-social factors

   a. Anger
   b. Impulsivity
   c. Suspiciousness
   d. Morbid jealousy
   e. Criminal or violent attitudes
   f. Command hallucinations
   g. Lack of insight

5. Current context

   a. Threats of violence
   b. Family or other interpersonal discord or instability
   c. Availability of weapons
   d. Availability and use of support services

Exploring mitigating factors (strengths) and the interplay between risk factors and strengths is an area for future research in social work.

Statistical prediction in practice

The majority of studies show that *actuarial prediction* is more accurate than *clinical prediction* (Meehl, 1954; Dawes *et al.*, 1989; Johnson *et al.*, 2015), despite measures by professionals to avoid bias. It is rare to find a study showing *clinical prediction* to be more accurate than *actuarial*. There are a number of reasons why this is common sense. First, factors that are studied and refined for actuarial prediction are those identified by clinicians (i.e. professionals, including social workers) as being the most worthy of study. As further factors are identified by professionals, they are defined more closely and studied so as to determine whether or not a particular factor really does influence the outcome. They thus become *risk factors* amenable to an *actuarial* approach. Second, human beings are sometimes inconsistent with their own *decision rules* due to stress, tiredness or emotion. Some actuarial tools modelled precisely on an individual decision maker's own rules can predict more consistently than the individual on whom it is based. We need to strengthen professional practice with actuarial (statistical prediction) approaches to overcome the inherent bias of each professional relying on their own individual experience only, whilst also recognising the limitations of actuarial tools. It is important not to assume that the level of detail required on domains within assessment tools reflects the weighting of that factor in terms of risk (likelihood) of a particular harmful outcome that is to be avoided.

RESEARCH SUMMARY *6.3*

Grove and Meehl (1996) appraised 136 studies comparing clinical with actuarial prediction in various fields including medicine, psychology and mental health. Of the 136 studies, 64 showed that actuarial prediction was more accurate; 8 showed clinical prediction as more accurate; and in the other 64 studies there was no significant difference between actuarial and clinical prediction.

Having argued that actuarial methods of prediction based on the measured frequency of past events is superior to unaided professional judgement, we now outline the major difficulties facing any attempt to predict future events in relation to a particular individual. We focus on the prediction of possible harm, but the same argument applies to the prediction of the possible benefits of decision outcomes as discussed in Chapter 7.

Generally, major foreseeable harm that may befall individuals is addressed in terms of insurance for people or organisations that are facing the same type of undesirable outcome (car accident, home fire, burglary, travel disruption, etc.). Such situations require us to predict the likelihood (and costs) of undesirable consequences across a range of similar situations. For example, in car insurance the likelihood of harm is now calculated in relation to sub-sets of drivers. Young drivers are sometimes charged higher car insurance premiums because studies have shown that young drivers are more likely to have accidents. In this context it is sufficient to predict that this group of drivers is more likely to have accidents and to charge higher premiums to those that fit the criteria.

Health and social care professionals seem on occasions to be expected by some of the media to predict harm by or to an identified individual, which mathematically is totally different from predicting the general level of harm to a population (Littlechild and Reid, 2007). This apparent expectation is equivalent to expecting an insurance company to predict which *particular* young drivers will have an accident! As another example, on a population level we may be able to do an experiment to show that a certain type of advertising of washing powder produces a measurable increase in sales. That is quite different from trying to predict whether an identified Mrs Smith will alter her purchasing behaviour in response to a particular advertising campaign! Our professional task is intrinsically about predicting individual human behaviour. Human beings have the free will to choose, and the outcomes of their decisions are not always rational or predictable.

RESEARCH SUMMARY 6.4

Barlow et al. (2012) undertook a systematic review of tools to support analysis of significant harm in child protection. Their review involved thorough searches on five bibliographic databases and two web search engines. The review identified: three systems of tools; eleven individual tools; and two audit tools. All tools included (a) methods of assessing a range of aspects of harm at different stages in the assessment process; (b) criteria for operationalising the assessment domains; and (c) guidance about the synthesis and analysis of the data collected. Tools were classified into the following types, and key points for supporting analysis within assessment and professional judgement were drawn out:

1. *Risk assessment tools based on historical and static predictive factors*

   • *both actuarial and consensus types*

2. *Strengths and needs assessment tools*

   • *measure dynamic factors, usually defined as 'needs'*

3. *Response priority decision trees*

   • *to improve consistency and clarity across workers*

4. *Permanency, placement and reunification checklists – same models as (1)*

5. *Audit tools for use retrospectively.*

(Barlow et al., 2012)

False positives and false negatives

Trying to predict rare events such as abuse among a large and diverse population presents particular problems, as can be illustrated. Imagine that we have an assessment tool that we are proposing to use to predict some particular undesirable harm. There are four possible outcomes, in that the assessment tool will:

• correctly predict the harm (called a *true positive* because the tool correctly identified the thing that we want to predict); or

• indicate that harm will not occur, but it does (called a *false negative*); or

• correctly predict that harm will not occur (called a *true negative*); or

• indicate that harm will occur, but it does not (called a *false positive*).

No prediction tool will be 100 per cent accurate. For our purposes we will describe a 90 per cent accurate tool as one that is 90 per cent accurate in predicting harm and 90 per cent accurate in predicting that harm will not occur. When you undertake Activity 6.1 you will have a graphic illustration of the challenge in using an assessment tool to predict harm. Table 6.4 illustrates its application in trying to predict suicide (as an example of an undesirable harmful outcome) using real data.

ACTIVITY **6.1**

Using an assessment tool to predict harm

Assume that you have a test that is 90 per cent accurate at predicting harm and in predicting that harm will not occur. The task is to predict a rare event (such as abuse, violence or suicide) that occurs in 1 in 10,000 people per year in the population served by your team, assumed for this activity to be a population of 100,000 people. In the table below, the first column represents situations where the tool predicts that harm will occur, and the second column that it will not. The upper row is where harm does in reality occur, and the lower row where it does not. The task is to identify issues in using the tool by calculating how many are correctly and incorrectly identified by completing the four angle brackets <1>, <2>, <3> and <4>.

TOOL: REALITY:	Yes harm	No harm
Yes harm	*<1>* *True positive*	*<2>* *False negative*
No harm	*<4>* *False positive*	*<3>* *True negative*

As you can see, the crucial issue is not so much the *false negatives*, the situations that we unfortunately miss because of the limitations of our tool. The real issue is the many non-risky situations that are identified as being *risky* with consequences for rights of individuals and for workloads of professions, teams and organisations. In this case, about 150,000 people would be wrongly identified as being at risk of suicide. Trying to predict rare events such as abuse, violence or suicide in a large population presents particular problems.

> *False negatives are extremely easy to spot with the benefit of hindsight. False positives on the other hand often can't be spotted even after the event because we can never be sure what would have happened .... But the fact is that false positives can also be a disaster for a child. A false positive might mean a family broken up, a child separated from parents in order to avoid a perceived danger, which in fact would never actually have come to pass.*

(Beckett, 2008, p46)

Table 6.4   Using a 90 per cent accurate tool to predict suicide

The suicide rate for Northern Ireland in 2006 was 227 males and 64 females (Northern Ireland Statistics and Research Agency (NISRA), 2007). For our purpose we will treat this as approximately 300 suicides in a population of about 1.5 million, i.e. 2 in 10,000 people in the year. Could we use a screening (assessment) tool incorporating risk factors to identify these people so as to target services?

- Approximately 300 people commit suicide, so approximately 1,499,700 do not.
- With a 90 per cent accurate tool, we will correctly identify 270 (90 per cent) of the 300 suicides that actually occur (true positives) and will fail to identify 30 (10 per cent) of the suicides (false negatives).
- We will correctly identify 1,349,730 (90 per cent of 1,499,700) situations where no suicide occurs (true negatives) and will incorrectly identify 149,970 (10 per cent) individuals as being likely to commit suicide when they do not (false positives).

TOOL: REALITY:	Yes harm	No harm	Total
Yes harm	270	30	300
No harm	149,970	1,349,730	1,499,700
Total	150,240	1,349,760	1,500,000

Signal detection theory focuses on the challenge in identifying *what* information is relevant to the decision amidst the vast amount of irrelevant data (*noise*) present to the decision maker, as applied in diverse fields such as identifying enemy aircraft from radar-screen blips. The pioneering work of Len Dalgleish in social work might be considered within this approach (Dalgleish and Drew, 1989). If the task is to predict the likelihood of abuse, then there are four options. If there is a signal (abuse) then a *yes* response is a hit and a *no* is a miss; if there is no signal (no abuse) then a response of *yes* is a false alarm and a *no* is a correct rejection (of this case leading to abuse). Dalgleish considered the influences on a social worker that might increase the likelihood of *correct yes* and *false alarm* (such as an overriding concern not to miss any instance of abuse), and the influences that might increase the likelihood of *correct no* and *incorrect rejection* (such as an overriding concern not to disrupt families where this is not warranted).

Base rates and other challenges in prediction

A key challenge to the use of prediction data in health and social services assessment is that statistical prediction is less useful in predicting the likelihood of events (such as abuse, violence or self-harm) that occur only rarely (Gigerenzer, 2015; Munro, 2008). This problem leads to many fallacies in reasoning, even in some inquiries into child abuse tragedies (Parton *et al.*, 1997). The sensitivity of the assessment tool in correctly identifying situations where the harm will occur, and the specificity in correctly identifying the situations where harm will not occur, has to be related to the incidence of the harm within a particular population of people during a stated time interval.

One of the key findings in the literature pertaining to human aggression and interpersonal violence is that violence is very difficult to predict ... violence is a rare event, and rare events are inherently difficult to predict because of what is known as the base rate problem. Put simply, if an event occurs one time in one hundred thousand ... it is exceptionally difficult to predict the one time in one hundred thousand that it will occur.

(Righthand *et al.*, 2003, pp33–4)

Of course, to make a calculated prediction from among those referred to a social work team (provided the numbers analysed are sufficiently large) should be more accurate as the incidence of the undesirable harm is likely to be higher in that group of people than in the whole population. Similarly, predicting re-abuse (on which there is very little research) may give scope for greater accuracy than predicting abuse among the general population. In general, whilst we must make as good use as we can of risk factors (and undertake much more robust research on these), we must recognise (and be able to explain to others) that even the best risk factors can only provide some numerical indication of likelihood. A statistical calculation of the likelihood of harm is useful to inform professional judgement, but cannot replace it.

RESEARCH SUMMARY 6.5

Risk factors for child maltreatment were selected from amongst the 20,000 items in the National Survey of Child and Adolescent Wellbeing (NSCAW). A sample of 5,501 children in the Child Protection Services section of the NSCAW who were in the care of their biological parents at the close of the investigation were split randomly into one group on which to create a model using risk factors to predict maltreatment, and a validation group with which to test the model. Bivariate (maltreatment vs no maltreatment) correlations were examined at 12, 24 and 36 months. Following analysis of covariance (to identify factors that essentially measure the same thing), items that were highly associated (>0.7) were combined into a single factor, and the Burgess method used to create a simple risk scale summing significant factors.

• *Look up the references to find the conclusions of these studies on risk factors.*

(Shlonsky, 2007; see also Shlonsky and Wagner, 2005)

Predicting harm: achievements, challenges and prospects

Predicting serious re-offending by known serious offenders is probably the best researched area of prediction studies relevant to social work. The best statistical (actuarial) tools in this area are achieving overall accuracy rates of about 70 per cent over a ten-year period (Thornton, 2007). This is useful to underpin a professional judgement, and such risk factors built into an assessment tool will support staff in focusing their minds on key issues. However, even at this level of accuracy we must be conscious of its limited use in practice in terms of prediction. *Trying to predict serious offending (even amongst known serious offenders) is the researcher's equivalent of hunting a needle in a haystack* (Beaumont, 1999, p84). The tools available for predicting harm in other areas of social work such as abuse, suicide and neglect are more limited.

ACTIVITY **6.2**

Repeat Activity 6.1 above, using a prediction tool with 70 per cent accuracy.

Consider the implications for practice of the false positives.

The problems of false positives as well as false negatives are greater with a less accurate tool. But in case you are tempted to retreat from this statistical endeavour, recall that professional (clinical) judgements alone almost always achieve less accurate predictions when compared! Although these alternatives have been contrasted here, in practice social workers make use of assessment tools that embody both tested (actuarial) factors and those that are less thoroughly researched but based on professional consensus. Professional (clinical) factors (i.e. knowledge of child and family perspectives, professional knowledge of nuances of family and cultural context, etc.) come into their own in the care planning stage of intervention, and we discuss this more fully in Chapter 7.

Criterion-based judgements and decision policies

Every day social workers ask themselves questions along these lines:

- Is this family safe for this child or can it be made safe?

- Does the possibility of harm to this child require removal from the family?

- Is this parent's recovery from addiction, etc. sufficient for this child to return home?

- How safe is this person with a disability living with this level of independence?

- What harm might this person with mental illness do to himself or herself?

- What risk (probability and seriousness) of harm does this person pose to others?

- To what extent does this older person understand the risks they are taking?

We recognise that safeguarding measures by their nature often require client choice to be overridden in the interests of another person or the individual themselves.

There is a delicate balance between empowerment and safeguarding, choice and risk. It is important for practitioners to consider when the need for protection would override the decision to promote choice and empowerment (DH, 2007, p30, para. 2.50).

In these types of decisions the task is to draw a line between dangerous and safe situations; situations requiring safeguarding or not. Such thresholds (criteria) are common in social work – for example, thresholds of significant harm, criteria for approved social workers regarding compulsory admission of patients to psychiatric hospital and eligibility criteria for social care services. The implication of policy guidance is often that there is a threshold. The task is to identify whether the *risk* puts the child or vulnerable (using the term very broadly) adult above or below the threshold so that the vulnerable individual (in this document a child) *is provided with immediate protection in situations where their life is at risk or there is a likelihood of sustaining a serious injury if this action is not taken* (Social Services Inspectorate, 1993, para. 14).

Although major thresholds are outlined in statutes, regulations and organisational policies, we also use decision policies and thresholds created by professional standards. Examples might be where a judgement has to be made about parenting ability, or the safety of a person who is elderly or disabled living alone. Sometimes, such thresholds are incorporated into tested assessment tools, which we discussed in Chapter 4.

> *The basic problem addressed by practice policies is that most health [and social work] decisions are too complicated to be made on a one-by-one, day-to-day basis .... If every practitioner attempted to do this [making the entire decision from scratch] for every decision, the result would be either mental paralysis or chaos. Practice policies have been used for centuries to help solve this problem by enabling practitioners and researchers to analyse decisions before the fact, cast the conclusions as policies, and apply the policies to simplify future decisions. While many decisions can be addressed only on an individual basis, others recur frequently in similar forms. It is these 'generic' decisions that are the targets of practice policies.*

> (Eddy, 1996, p18)

There are many judgements in social work about how a particular situation relates to some criterion such as whether a child is 'in need' or 'at risk', or whether an individual or family meets some criterion for receiving publicly funded or charitable services. The essential judgement and decision task in such situations might be described as a *criterion-based judgement* or as a *threshold judgement* (Taylor and Killick, 2013). In other words, the task is to decide whether this situation is above or below the *line,* using a *decision policy* to give consistency. A *decision policy* is a set of rules for making a decision in a defined range of situations, created and adopted by an individual, group or organisation in order to simplify decision processes or to standardise decision outcomes. Such decision policies may come from legislation, regulations and guidance of government; aims, principles, strategies, policies and procedures of organisations; personal and professional values; theoretical models and research; and understanding and interpretation of patterns from experience of similar situations.

Such decision policies enable organisations and individuals to be more consistent in their decisions, and thereby have greater credibility (Taylor, 1999). Such decision policies may use thresholds to define eligibility for services, as in the example for publicly funded child care services below:

1. *Base Population*

2. *Children with Additional Needs*

3. *Children in Need*

4. *Children with Complex or Acute Need.*

(DCSF, 2009)

We might view *standards* and *regulations* as inflexible decision policies, mandating what must always be done. By contrast, *guidelines* serve as recommendations or reference points that should be followed generally but an argument can be made for adapting them to individual circumstances. Despite efforts to clarify thresholds for decisions, there is still scope for professional discretion to take account of individual circumstances of the client or family in safeguarding or service eligibility decisions. If there is no mandatory decision policy, or you are still undecided after applying all external relevant decision policies, then you might consider using your own professional decision policy. If the application of relevant decision policies still leaves much scope, an individual approach to the decision (or these factors of the decision) may be more appropriate, *balancing benefits and harms* as discussed in Chapter 7.

Practice issues in predicting harm and safeguarding decisions

The capacity of any person to predict a particular harmful event through either experiential (clinical) or statistical (actuarial) methods is limited.

> *Research therefore cautions us that [in mental health] as in other fields such as medicine and child protection there is no such thing as a 'risk free' assessment .... There are **no** criteria which enable us to place individuals into sharply defined, once-and-for-all categories of 'dangerous' or 'not dangerous' [or at risk of a particular harm, etc.]. Rather there is a continuum of statistical risk with uncomfortably limited predictive capacity.*

(Perry and Sheldon, 1995, p18)

Rather than seeking to define an individual as *a risk* or not, it is often more productive to consider *relevant environmental and personal variables, and their inter-relationships both now and historically* (Jones, 1998, p91). Some factors will carry greater weight in seeking to predict harm. Statistical methods of looking at the interaction effects between risk factors will undoubtedly increase the accuracy of our predictions beyond an intuitive approach in time. However, the development of methods for combining risk factors within a practice tool is still in its infancy in social work.

Thresholds and creativity for a safeguarding intervention

I am a social worker in a community mental health team for older people. Mr Gardner is an 81-year-old man with Alzheimer's disease. Mr Gardner has consistently refused to allow care workers or family to light his fire, even in the coldest weather. There is no other heating in the home. The manager of the home care worker has recently informed me of the increased risk due to lack of heating. Mr Gardner's insight into the risks was impaired, and the family advised that he was always very adamant when he had made up his mind. Mr Gardner absolutely refused to consider moving elsewhere; he had lived 40 years in this house and said that he sensed his wife's spirit in the home even though she had died years earlier. In discussions with other professionals it was agreed that there was a substantial risk of serious physical harm to Mr Gardner.

The possibility of needing to initiate a compulsory removal under mental health legislation for his well-being prompted consideration of alternative solutions to manage the risk. On the basis of an assessment of capacity it was clear that Mr Gardner was unable to make a competent decision regarding this issue. The consultant psychiatrist suggested that an electrical safety heater might be placed behind a table at the far end of the living room without Mr Gardner knowing. This could safely raise the temperature of the room to a level that would reduce risk, and thereby avert the need for a distressing removal from his home. This was regarded as being in his best interests.

- *Think of a recent situation where you have faced an ethical conflict because a client is putting themselves in danger through not recognising a serious threat to their health and well-being?*

- *What are the main issues in resolving such dilemmas?*

As a competent professional you should be knowledgeable on risk factors for the safeguarding areas of your practice. No less might be expected by a court or an educated member of the public. However, you also need to be able to explain why such *prediction* is limited in its usefulness in relation to individuals. We are not just assessing the situation now, but are concerned about what harms might occur in the future in the light of changing circumstances and possible professional interventions (Hollows, 2001). We also need to be aware of the emotion that may arise. A false positive in a medical test may elicit an emotional response of 'Phew!' when you discover subsequently that you do not have the illness after all; in social work a false positive may be a child taken into care inappropriately and a family wrongly disrupted.

Risk factors work well for strategic planning of services. You can estimate relatively accurately across a large population how many homicides, suicides and abuse cases are likely to occur each year and use this information in planning services and setting budgets. The much greater challenge – perhaps impossibility – is in predicting harm to a particular individual. Use risk factors whenever available to assist in forming a judgement, but beware of their limitations. *Lists of risk factors, therefore, can do no more at the present time than suggest to practitioners that they might look again at their established or settled perceptions of risk* (Perry and Sheldon, 1995, p19). In practice, we more often use *fuzzy* approaches to considering the relative level of risks and the interplay between them, as discussed more fully in the next chapter.

Use of risk factors may raise ethical issues of stigma and bias. For example, poverty is a risk factor for child abuse (i.e. a child living in poverty is more likely to be abused than one who is not) (Macdonald, 2001). However, it remains a fact that most children living in poverty are not abused. We must be wary of false positives (as above) as well as false negatives. As reports predicting possible harm containing statistics (such as might be derived from prediction-based tools) can have an air of authority about them, it is important that we give a warning about the limitations of such figures, while at the same time demonstrating how they have informed our professional judgements and actions.

One of the dangers is that our attempts to put language to the complex and inter-related concepts involved in judgement and decision making itself steers our thinking in ways that we have not anticipated. In particular, we need to be wary that once we start talking about *risk* we do not become trapped in a situation where neither professionals nor organisations are prepared to describe a situation as *low risk* for fear of consequences if something goes wrong. The use of alternative terms such as *concerns* may help in developing a deeper understanding of behaviour in its context (Morrison and Henniker, 2006).

Mitigating factors: strengths and desistance

The focus on risk factors must not blind us to the importance of recognising mitigating factors that reduce risk. In terms of practice approaches and skills this is often referred to as 'strengths-based practice'. In the criminal justice world the concept of 'desistance' refers to a similar domain, i.e. the factors that support a convicted criminal to avoid criminal behaviour in future. In this case, for example, having a network of peers who are not involved in crime may be an important desistance factor.

CASE STUDY **6.3**

Resilience and protective factors

Jack and Ruby Harris are in their late twenties and have two children aged 3 years and 5 years. Social work involvement began two years ago due to Ruby's mental health problems and alcohol misuse. There are concerns about the children's welfare when in the care of their mother. Resilience and protective factors in this situation are that both Jack and Ruby are engaging with services to get help, the children present as happy in the family home, and Jack is supportive to his wife and can recognise when her mood is deteriorating.

Psycho-social rationality: (1) risk clusters: vulnerability, trigger and mitigating factors

Perhaps because of the caution that is required in using numbers to convey the correct message, qualitative approaches are used more often in practice. If the knowledge about risk factors does not exist in sufficient detail to inform actuarial prediction of harm, we can use *risk cluster* approaches to decision making (Taylor, 2012c). We will consider three main aspects:

- factors that predispose the harm to occur, which we will call here *vulnerabilities*;

- factors that induce the harm to occur, which we will call here *trigger factors*;

- mitigating factors or *strengths* that might reduce the harm or its likelihood.

Vulnerabilities are also known as *predisposing factors* (Brearley, 1982), *background hazards* (Kelly, 1996) or *historical determinants*. *Vulnerabilities* are those factors about the client, family or situation that are identified, on the basis of some imprecise knowledge of risk factors, as making the situation undesirable. *Trigger factors* are also known as *hazards* (Brearley, 1982), *situational hazards* (Kelly, 1996) or *situational determinants*. *Trigger factors* are factors that may trigger or precipitate harm occurring. A *strength* is a factor that mitigates against the undesirable harm occurring. As examples, the age of the child and the parents' inability to manage alcohol may be a *vulnerability*. A social event at a pub or the child crying may be a *trigger factor*. In this scenario the *harm* to be avoided is an alcoholic binge resulting in assault on the child, and a *strength* may be a close neighbour who has looked after the child at her house overnight if the parents are out late. This type of analysis underpins an increasing number of assessment tools and models for considering 'pathways to harm' (Sidebotham *et al.*, 2016). Strengths, or mitigating factors, may be identified through comparative research such as, for example, the study by Reeves *et al.* (2015) on the effect of unemployment and financial indebtedness on male suicide across countries.

CASE STUDY 6.4

Vulnerability, trigger and mitigating factors

Miss Auriol and children, Caitlin (age 9) and Donna (age 7): analysis of risk factors:

Vulnerabilities (factors pre-disposing towards harm):

- *history of Miss Auriol hearing voices telling her to harm her children, which has in the past resulted in admissions to acute psychiatric care;*

- *children unable to see Mr Brown (father of Donna) due to allegation of sexual assault;*

- *Miss Auriol is usually reticent to talk about her mental health issues.*

(Continued)

(Continued)

Triggers (factors that induce harm):

- *possible relapse in Miss Auriol's mental health;*

- *Miss Auriol and Mr Brown's relationship may become volatile again.*

Strengths (mitigating factors that may reduce harm):

- *Miss Auriol and Caitlin and Donna are staying with family members at present;*

- *Miss Auriol's mental health appears stable.*

ACTIVITY *6.3*

Vulnerability and trigger factors

Case One

Samuel was involved in a road traffic accident as a child, which led to mental and physical impairments. He is now 33 years old and has epileptic fits, weakness down his right side and stumbles on uneven surfaces. He presents a danger to others, particularly females, and is assessed as Level 1 on the Multi-Agency Sex Offender Risk Assessment and Management Procedures. The pre-disposing vulnerabilities include his low self-esteem, social isolation and low motivation. The triggers that might precipitate a problem include how a female is dressed, photographs of females especially if only partly clothed and drinking alcohol.

Case Two

Amelia Williams is aged 48 years and has a learning disability and some physical disability. She lives with her mother, Mrs Williams, who has been diagnosed with dementia. Vulnerabilities were identified as being that Amelia requires supervision and assistance with mobility and relies on others to maintain an awareness of danger, and that Mrs Williams is becoming less aware of dangers and it is anticipated that her mental health will deteriorate with time. Trigger factors were identified as being that there are considerable amounts of time when they are alone without support and that Mrs Williams' other daughter (who has been providing support to them) is under stress and her contribution to the care arrangements is in danger of breaking down.

- *Identify the vulnerability (pre-disposing) factors in a recent case.*

- *Identify the trigger (precipitating) factors in a recent case.*

- *How do the vulnerabilities and triggers interplay?*

- *In what ways is it helpful to consider these separately?*

Vulnerabilities may include dynamic risk factors where we might work with clients and families on underlying problems to reduce the likelihood or severity of a harmful outcome. Trigger factors indicate situations to avoid or manage more carefully, so as to reduce harm. If it is not possible to undertake a calculation of the probability of harm it may be helpful in practice to consider these types of factors and the sort of interplay between them that might occur as the client or family situation evolves. Appendix 1 gives some pointers towards designing or completing an assessment using these concepts. Another group of approaches to understanding professional judgements are *heuristic* models (Gigerenzer and Gaissmaier, 2015; Mathew *et al.*, 2016; Taylor, 2012c; Taylor, in press), as introduced in Chapter 5, and these have potential application in this context. A *heuristic* is a simple rule by which a judgement or decision is made. In the face of the impossibility of the human brain to process dozens of risk factors (Miller, 1956), each with its own numerical likelihood, some researchers and theorists propose that humans use simple heuristics which may work even better – and in particular more speedily – than

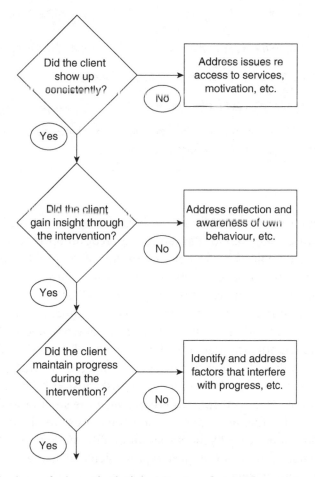

Figure 6.1   Beginnings of a hypothetical decision tree for making a judgement about the progress of a client during an intervention

extensive computation of benefits and harms. Heuristic approaches to front-line child protection decision making are recommended for investigation into their possible usefulness in a UK government report (Kirkman and Melrose, 2014). One particular heuristic that may be useful is a *decision tree*, a series of questions that capture the essence of the judgement process effectively and efficiently (see Figure 6.1). A *decision tree* designed specifically to incorporate the least number of steps possible for an effective decision is known as a *fast and frugal tree*.

ACTIVITY 6.4

Lockett and Naudé (1998) propose a simple conceptualisation (risk cluster, in the terminology of this book) of factors to consider in a judgement such as a social worker might make about a compulsory emergency mental health admission: (1) mental state; (2) risk; (3) family and community support system; (4) family carer's view; (5) medical view; (6) compliance; and (7) history.

Task:

- *How does – or should – a social worker weigh these up against each other?*

- *Which is the most important, or the first, to consider?*

- *Is there any factor that would be irrelevant if a certain other factor were not present?*

- *Could you create a list of three or four key questions that provide a simple conceptualisation of key elements of your judgement process?*

The consideration of heuristic approaches does not mean that professional behaviour is less skilful or demanding. Rather, it is a recognition that a skill learned by experience in any domain is being able, more quickly and with more certainty, to select and use an appropriate simple decision rule. Heuristic approaches might be viewed as building on the *risk clusters* conceptualisation discussed above, but developing that approach into models that could be tested. Heuristic models are at a very early stage of consideration in relation to social work, and it should be noted that *heuristic* models are proposed as viable within small-scale domains, rather than having wide generalisability across contexts. Figure 6.2 illustrates the domain of psycho-social rationality models as building on risk clusters to provide some structure to professional judgement somewhere between the strict probability models of expected utility and actuarial prediction, and the almost totally unstructured narrative explanation approach. Psycho-social rationality models seek to embrace the science of prediction with the art of making professional judgement, using knowledge but not de-skilling professionals.

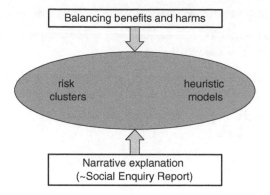

Figure 6.2   Psycho-social rationality models: the art and the science of professional judgement

Chapter summary

*   The focus of social work has moved over the past few decades from improving people's welfare when they present asking for help to trying to manage the possibility of harm in the future. Some media and politicians seem to expect social workers to be able to predict all future harm.

*   *Risk factors* give an estimate of how much more likely this individual is to come to harm, or cause harm, than an average member of the population. There are limitations in the extent to which risk factors can predict harm to or by a particular individual. *Risk factors* can, however, provide a useful basis for assessment and for focused discussion with the client, family and colleagues.

*   *Risk factors* that have been tested through thorough research are the best tools we have to inform decisions about the likelihood of harm. Where available, risk factors can inform judgements in relation to diverse practice issues from child protection to independence steps by people with a disability, as well as attempting to predict homicide, suicide and re-offending.

*   In any assessment process where we are attempting to make a yes–no prediction about individual behaviour there will always be some incorrectly identified as at risk of harm and some incorrectly identified as not at risk, as well as those correctly identified.

*   Where the social work role involves compulsory intervention in family life it is important to clarify the mandate for action. A *criterion-based judgement* is often required in relation to threshold criteria for statutory measures to protect an individual.

*   Practical concepts and tools to support this aspect of professional decision making fall within a broader concept of *psycho-social rationality* or *structured decision making*, and include considering *risk clusters* such as vulnerabilities, triggers and mitigating factors, and refinements of simple *heuristics* by which humans make everyday decisions.

FURTHER READING

Gigerenzer, G. (2014) *Risk Savvy: How to Make Good Decisions*. New York: Penguin.

This is a popular book highlighting the dilemmas and common misunderstandings about probability, for example regarding the likelihood of success or undesirable side effects.

Monahan, J., Steadman, H.J., Silver, E., Appelbaum, P.S., Robbins, P.C., Mulvey, E.P., Roth, L.H., Grisso, T. and Banks, S. (2001) *Rethinking Risk Assessment: The MacArthur Study of Mental Disorder and Violence*. Oxford: Oxford University Press.

This is a detailed book outlining improved approaches to predicting harmful events, in this case in relation to violence by people with a mental disorder.

Chapter 7

Risk-taking care choices: values, gains and hazards

Sarayu laughed. 'I am here Mack. There are times when it is safe to touch, and times when precautions must be taken. That is the wonder and adventure of exploration, a piece of what you call science – to discern and discover what we have hidden for you to find.'

'So why did you hide it?' Mack inquired.

Why do children love to hide and seek? Ask any person who has a passion to explore and discover and create. The choice to hide so many wonders from you is an act of love that is a gift inside the process of life.

(Young, 2008, p132)

Introduction

This chapter focuses on making judgements and decisions where choices about care and intervention are to be made that involve risk-taking as part of the assessment and care planning process. This complements Chapter 6, which focused on decisions relating to threshold (such as safeguarding and service eligibility) judgements, and both these chapters augment the initial consideration of professional judgement in Chapter 5. We begin this chapter by considering the way we value health and social well-being, and the motivation to reduce harm and disease in society. We discuss the tensions between the principles of health and safety at work legislation to take *reasonable steps to protect others from harm*, and the professional role and responsibility to take reasonable risks and to support clients in taking reasonable risks to further care plan goals such as greater independence, motivation, quality of life and re-uniting families. We consider briefly the personal safety of staff. This chapter then focuses on the social worker making judgements involving *balancing benefits and harms* and supporting clients in doing the same, drawn from the well-established *expected utility* models of decision making. A key issue in the development of personalised social care services, re-ablement and recovery models is professional accountability in supporting client risk-taking as discussed here. The term *care plan* (and similarly the verb 'care planning') is used in this book as a generic term to include local and contextual variations such as 'case plan', 'protection plan', 'hospital discharge plan', 'prison discharge plan', 'safeguarding plan', 'home care services plan', 'individual risk management plan', etc. This chapter extends our consideration of professional judgement towards aspects particularly relevant to care planning and decision-making processes regarding this.

Risk, health and social well-being

'computer systems now at risk of cyber attack'

'financial transactions at risk of default following banking crisis'

'concern at climate risk and extreme events spreads'

'research finds risk of side effects with new medication'

'help for at-risk children is "unsatisfactory and inconsistent".'

(National Audit Office, 2016)

Risk is essentially about uncertainty, and as such pervades all of life and occupies much of our social discourse and public policy debates. Is it ever appropriate to *take risks* or should we, morally or legally, always seek to *avoid risks*? Will you stop using a computer or a bank or medicines because there are *risks* involved? How can we justify risk-taking in decisions; for example, a business making a *risky* investment decision or a health and social care authority supporting a *risky* patient or client care plan? Risk-taking may be regarded as foolhardy and reckless disregard for safety, cultural norms, and the welfare of oneself and others. Risk-taking may also be viewed as a positive attribute in society, for example courage in battle; bravery in facing challenging natural environments; the witness of martyrs (Hughes, 2008). It has been argued that we live in a *risk society* (Beck, 1992) because risk has a different significance than in previous historical eras (Gigerenzer, 2015). One of the side effects of technological and social advances means that we sometimes need specialised expertise to identify and assess the dangers we face – including the expertise of social workers!

ACTIVITY **7.1**

Risk-taking in everyday life

- *What risks do you consciously take in your everyday life – living at home, going to work and undertaking recreational activities?*

- *What are the dangers and what are the potential gains in these activities?*

- *How do you justify to yourself taking these risks?*

- *What mental process do you use to justify taking risks that provide opportunities for growth, understanding and change?*

- *How does your decision process differ in relation to occasional risks compared to risks that are a regular part of your life?*

Health and safety at work

As societies have evolved they have developed increasingly sophisticated mechanisms to protect the health and well-being of their citizens. From simple beginnings, legislation about health and safety at work has now become a major feature in many countries. Such legislation was a response to the increasing number of deaths and accidents during the Industrial Revolution, perhaps caused by such aspects as the higher concentration of people into larger workplaces and the greater use of machinery.

The current underpinning statute in Great Britain is the Health and Safety at Work Act 1974, and in Northern Ireland the Health and Safety at Work (NI) Order 1978. The Health and Safety Executives established by this statute aim to *prevent death, injury and ill health in workplaces* (HSE, 2009a).

Table 7.1   Health and safety law: what you need to know

What employers must do for you

1 *Decide what could harm you in your job and the precautions to stop it. This is part of risk assessment.*

2 *In a way you can understand, explain how risks will be controlled and tell you who is responsible for this.*

4 *Free of charge, give you the health and safety training you need to do your job.*

5 *Free of charge, provide you with any equipment and protective clothing you need, and ensure that it is properly looked after.*

10 *Work with any other employers or contractors sharing the workplace or providing employees (such as agency workers), so that everyone's health and safety is protected.*

What you must do

1 *Follow the training you have received when using any work items your employer has given you.*

2 *Take reasonable care of your own and other people's health and safety.*

3 *Co-operate with your employer on health and safety.*

4 *Tell someone (your employer, supervisor, or health and safety representative) if you think the work or inadequate precautions are putting anyone's health and safety at serious risk.*

(HSE, 2009b, extract)

The general approach is that employers and those who create risk are responsible for managing it, and that employees have a right to protection but also a duty to care for themselves and others (see Table 7.1). In our context, *others* might include staff in your own or other organisations, and visitors to work premises including users of services. As the focus of the legislation is workplace health and safety, what is less clear is the definition of *a place of work* for those such as a home care worker or foster parent, and the implications of extending legislation designed for factories, mines and offices into people's homes (Taylor and Donnelly, 2006a).

Minimising situational hazards

The Health and Safety Executive defines a *hazard* as something that may cause harm. Relevant examples might be a slippery mat on the floor in the home of an older person or poor hygiene by someone with a learning disability. A *risk* is considered as the chance that somebody could be harmed by a *hazard* and an indication of how serious that harm could be (HSE, 2009d). The following points help to assess the risks in your workplace.

ACTIVITY 7.2

Look at the website of the Health and Safety Executive and identify publications relevant to your work such as those relating to:

Stress: **www.hse.gov.uk/pubns/stresspk.htm**

Slips and trips resulting in falls: **www.hse.gov.uk/pubns/hsis2.pdf**

Violence at work: **www.hse.gov.uk/pubns/indg69.pdf**

Working alone in safety: **www.hse.gov.uk/pubns/indg73.pdf**

1. *Identify the hazards.*

2. *Decide who might be harmed and how.*

3. *Evaluate the risks and decide on precaution.*

4. *Record your findings and implement them.*

5. *Review your assessment and update if necessary.*

(HSE, 2009d)

ACTIVITY 7.3

Risks in your work role

- *What does 'risk' mean in your job?*

- *What types of risks are involved in your work?*

- *What are the harms that you are trying to help clients to avoid?*

- *What are the most serious risks?*

- *Do you ever 'take risks' at work and, if so, what sort of risks?*

- *Do you justify taking these work risks in some way and, if so, how?*

- *Are we 'gambling' with clients' lives? Why not?*

- *What degree of risk is reasonable to take, and why?*

This approach might be referred to as *minimising situational hazards* (Taylor, 2006b). When there are hazards inherent in an activity, whether for a client or a colleague, it makes sense and is required that we consider how possible harm can be avoided. Such activities may be part of a detailed care plan for an individual or a group activity in, for example, a day centre or residential facility.

Personal safety

Personal safety concerns are an aspect of *health and safety at work*, and add to the complexity of decision making in social work. The number of assaults on social workers, care workers and allied professions is appallingly high (HSE, 2009c; Newhill, 1996). Safeguarding roles frequently bring conflict with abusers and alleged abusers who may already have been violent to others. In addition to assault there are less tangible dimensions that must be taken into account in making judgements, such as threats and verbal aggression. It is beyond the scope of this book to do more than outline some key pointers for personal safety, and point to sources for further knowledge and skills development (Taylor, 2011). Some key aspects of personal safety for front-line staff are to:

- understand the context and possible predisposing and trigger factors (see below) for aggression with your client group and setting;

- avoid and manage situations that are likely to be scenes of dangerous conflict, such as when undesirable news must be given;

- manage a safe environment as far as possible, such as being aware of potential weapons, escape routes, available assistance, etc.;

- learn skills in defusing an aggressive situation;

- learn breakaway techniques to escape from being held by an aggressor;

- learn skills and develop team work in control methods if you are in high-risk work (such as a children's home, day centre for people with learning disability or psychiatric ward).

CASE STUDY 7.1

Personal safety of staff

Fred (aged 51 years) is deaf and partially sighted. He is generally unkempt and unshaven, and sleeps in his clothes unless he is prompted. He is neglected or shunned by his family. Fred requires a home care service to provide support for personal hygiene and dressing

(Continued)

(Continued)

as well as day care to improve his socialisation and personal care. He is inclined to be perceived as invading people's body space which might be attributable to his combined sensory impairments. Because of concerns by staff about such mannerisms, initially two home care workers were allocated to care for him at all times, even though this is not required in terms of functional needs.

The plan was to reduce this to one worker (in line with his functional needs) after three months. However, the home care workers are not comfortable with reducing to just one worker because they perceive him as a threat and because they feel isolated as mobile phones don't work in the rural locality of his home. The risk manager advised that if the staff perceive this situation as threatening then their perceptions must be used to guide the decision and as the social worker managing the case, I amended the care plan accordingly.

- *What options are possible in similar situations that you face?*

- *What ethical issues are raised by one person being allocated additional publicly funded resources in such situations when resources are limited?*

Reasonably practicable steps to protect people from harm

Having identified a hazard, *the law in European Union countries requires you to do everything reasonably practicable to protect people from harm* (HSE, 2009e). While health and safety legislation has been of tremendous value in reducing deaths, injuries and illness there are some conflicts inherent in this approach for the social worker. What is a *reasonably practicable step*? Thus it is usually *reasonable* and *practicable* to move electrical cables to a position that will minimise the likelihood of someone tripping and being injured if we take for granted the decision that the computer will be used on this particular desk. When it comes to personal care tasks in somebody's own home, it may not be so obvious what constitutes *reasonably practicable steps*. To what extent do we accept the person's normal lifestyle arrangements as *given* and work around these? To what extent do we insist on change (or withdraw services) if persuasion is not effective (Taylor and Donnelly, 2006a)?

Social work judgements are complex as we often have to operate outside of controlled environments. Sometimes our clients make minor spontaneous decisions which have more serious consequences than expected. Examples might be a young person in residential care being led astray by a friend while on a social activity with peers, or a frail elderly person standing on a chair to change a light bulb rather than asking for help. Risks taken by a client as part of employment, social or recreational activities (for example while a resident in a home, member of a day centre or in receipt of home care or family support services) will often involve an element of possible harm yet would not be considered as unacceptably *risky* by most people in society. The level of the dangers might range from crossing the road to get on a bus to go to work or the cinema, through taking the risk of getting mugged while visiting friends or shopping to undertaking something more adventurous (*risky*) such as playing football or mountain walking. Where do individuals in society draw the line? To what extent should our support for clients' choices reflect our own values, our profession's values, society's values or the values of clients' sub-groups within society? Where clients have impaired capacity, such as those with dementia, the responsibility on others to make decisions about risk – and by implication also *risk-taking* – increases (Manthorpe and Moriarty, 2010). Engaging with the challenges of these types of decisions is also part of the social work role, as well as more considered judgements such as safeguarding and long-term care decisions.

Balancing this tension between rights and risk-taking is a core area of knowledge and skill in social work practice. Government policy in the UK is beginning to recognise this and provide some support for proactive rather than defensive approaches to managing risk through supporting reasoned and reasonable client decision making:

> [T]here will often be some risk, and ... trying to remove it altogether can outweigh the quality of life benefits for the person.

> (DH, 2007, p9)

> The Health and Safety Executive endorses a sensible approach to risk, which seeks to address these concerns. Health and Safety legislation should not block reasonable activity. Through the care planning process risk assessments are undertaken which should also fulfil the requirement under health and safety legislation, providing the risk to both the person using the service and their family carer are considered.

> (DH, 2007, p26, para 2.35)

Balancing client rights with care worker health and safety

> The assessment of A&B, two young disabled people, identified that they liked and responded positively to swimming and to horse riding, but the application of manual handling regulations meant that they were unable to do either. The court decided that the rights of care staff to a safe working environment had to be balanced against the rights of A&B to undertake activities they enjoyed. This meant that the risks to the health and safety of the staff must be kept to a minimum that was consistent with A&B being enabled to exercise their human rights. Article 8 is not an absolute right, but any interference with it must be justified and proportionate. In the first place it was for the local authority to formulate its manual handling policy and to make the appropriate assessments.

> (DH, 2007, p23, extract; see also *A and others v East Sussex County Council and another* [2003] All ER (D) 233 (Feb))

Can we justify taking risks?

Health and safety legislation focuses on taking reasonable steps to avoid possible harm, but everyday life and care decisions inherently involve making choices and taking risks. An everyday example of taking a risk might be deciding whether to cross a road when there is a gap in the traffic, balancing the time saved against that spent waiting, and bearing in mind the possible pain and other consequences of being knocked down. How do we understand or conceptualise such risk-taking decisions?

We take the premise that a rational decision is made to achieve some sort of benefit – interpreted broadly to include such things as good health, financial gain and social independence – or to ensure one's own moral integrity. Taking risk is intrinsic to human decision making, and hence to social work practice in advising and supporting clients to make decisions.

ACTIVITY 7.4

Risk and allocating blame

* *Is playing a sport a foolhardy risk-taking exercise?*

* *Should people who play sports and get injured be regarded as having self-inflicted injuries?*

* *Does your sense of blame depend on the sport?*

* *How does your view relate to your understanding of the rules of the sport, your perspective on the benefits and your knowledge of the dangers?*

* *What might justify taking the risks inherent in the sport?*

[P]erceived risk [i.e. possibility of harm] must be tested and assessed against the likely benefits of taking an active part in the community, learning new skills and gaining confidence. What needs to be considered is the consequence of an action and the likelihood of any harm from it.

(DH, 2007, p4)

Taking a risk cannot be justified on the basis that no harm in fact occurs after the decision is made. At the time that the decision is taken, the outcome is not known. Sometimes a risk-taking decision will result in an undesirable outcome and sometimes it will not, by the very nature of the fact that we are talking about decisions in uncertain situations. The justification for taking the risk must be established at the time the decision is taken and can only be based on what is known at that time.

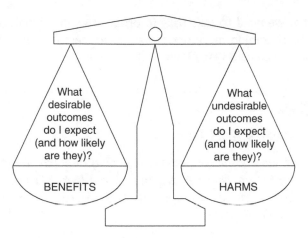

Figure 7.1   Balancing potential benefits and possible harm

Drawing on everyday life, the justification is generally in terms of the potential desirable outcome of the decision. We cannot know the outcome for certain, but we make a judgement as to whether the potential gain is worth the possible loss (see Figure 7.1). This is regarded as a basis for a good, informed decision or sound professional advice (Carson and Bain, 2008).

Child development and risk-taking

Amid increasing concerns about the dangers to children from drugs, abuse and violence on television and computer games (Porter, 1986), the state intervenes increasingly in decisions that were once made entirely by families, for example in areas such as health, well-being, safety and education. A side effect of some of the well-intentioned policies and services to improve the life chances of families (Social Exclusion Task Force, 2008) may be to limit the exposure of children to the challenges and judgement calls essential for growth into responsible adulthood. *During the past decade the list of 'don'ts' applied to children has, according to media reports, proliferated to include a rash of ... activities from snowballs and conkers to football during school breaks and more besides* (Ball, 2007, p58). It is not clear whether this rapidly developing aversion to taking risks is really in the best interests of children, or even whether the number of accidents has decreased. The unintended consequences of such decisions as driving children to school rather than letting them walk or use public transport – such as loss of independence, exercise and opportunities to socialise – are a negative side effect of the laudable desire to ensure that certain foreseeable harms – such as encounters with paedophiles – are avoided. Accidents are increasingly regarded as preventable, with implications for many social work judgements when we must make justifiable recommendations about diverse matters including child-rearing practices.

The paradox is that we need to take risks to progress as individuals and as a society, but we seem to be becoming more risk-averse, or at least fearful of being blamed if an undesirable outcome ensues (see Table 7.2).

CASE STUDY **7.2**

Balancing benefits and harms

Karim is 19 years of age and has a moderate learning disability. He is due to go on a respite holiday where the provider has facilities for outdoor activities, including a rope traverse across a river. Karim has heard about rope traversing from his (non-disabled) brother and is very keen to do this.

- *Will you recommend that Karim be allowed to do this activity?*

- *If so, how would you justify this judgement?*

- *What safeguards against possible harm would you want to see in place?*

- *Does the suitability of the activity for other young people with similar physical ability but no learning disability have any relevance?*

- *What possible benefits are there for Karim in undertaking this activity?*

- *Would you weigh up the possible benefits against the possible harm in some way, and if so, how?*

- *What would you want to do to ensure that the decision was seen as sound if an accident did occur?*

The Health and Safety Executive has become concerned at the possibility of over protection of children and their lack of risk experience. A degree of managed risk is necessary for children's development ... Sensible risk management is NOT about stopping well managed recreation and learning.

(HSE, 2009f)

Potential benefits in risk-taking decisions

To support social workers in these complex risk-taking decisions, the Department of Health acknowledge(s) *that there will often be some risk, and that trying to remove it altogether can outweigh the quality of life benefits for the person* (DH, 2007, p9). The task is not simply judging how much of the likelihood or consequences of possible harm should be removed. Rather, the decision may be essentially about justifying the possibility of harm by evaluating the possible benefits of the course of action. *By*

Table 7.2   Myths about health and safety regulation

Myth:	*Children need to be wrapped in cotton wool to keep them safe, November 2008*
Reality:	*Health and safety law is often used as an excuse to stop children taking part in exciting activities, but well-managed risk is good for them. It engages their imagination, helps them learn and even teaches them to manage risks for themselves in the future. They won't understand about risk if they're wrapped in cotton wool. Risk itself won't damage children, but ill-managed and overprotective actions could. (HSE, 2008)*
Myth:	*Health and safety rules take the adventure out of playgrounds, March 2009*
Reality:	*We're all for playgrounds being exciting and challenging places. Children should have fun in them, get fit, develop social skills and learn how to handle risks. What's important is to strike the right balance – protecting children from harm while allowing them the freedom to develop independence and risk awareness. Exciting and challenging playgrounds do this, poorly maintained or badly designed ones don't. Health and safety laws don't stop children having fun but ill-considered and overprotective actions do. (HSE, 2009g)*

taking account of the benefits in terms of independence, well-being and choice, it should be possible for a person to have a support plan which enables them to manage identified risks (DH, 2007, p10).

This process of *balancing benefits and harms* entails verbalising with clients, and recording potential gains from the decision as well as possible harms that might ensue. A critical issue will be helping the client to clarify the relative value that they place on a particular benefit or harm. This is making explicit what is often considered implicitly in making a judgement about whether or not to *take the risk*. Potential gains for clients in risk-taking decisions include:

- rehabilitation;
- skills development;
- self-esteem;
- self-control;
- independence;
- quality of life;
- motivation;
- co-operation in treatment and care;
- supportive relationships;
- satisfying relationships;
- participation in society.

CASE STUDY 7.3

Discussing benefits and harms with clients and families

Mrs Heaney is a 79-year-old woman living alone. She has had increasing memory problems during the past few years and there have been concerns about her ability to continue living at home. Mrs Heaney visits neighbours in an agitated state and has been found wandering the streets at night unable to find her home. I had a discussion with Mrs Heaney and her son and daughter about the possible benefits and risks in staying at home versus entering residential care.

After discussion the perceived benefits of staying at home were: a fuller family life; Mrs Heaney's right to choice and to live in her own environment; the enjoyment of the companionship of friends and neighbours of long acquaintance; the opportunity to remain active and engage in activities that she enjoys; and Mrs Heaney would remain independent with family and community support. The perceived risks of staying at home were: Mrs Heaney's lack of co-operation with home help support; probability of inadequate nourishment due to missed meals; limited compliance with medication; risks associated with fire lighting; risk of agitation and distress due to loneliness; and risk of wandering out on her own when distressed.

In the family discussion the perceived benefits of Mrs Heaney being admitted to residential care were: Mrs Heaney's needs would be met in a safe environment; she would have adequate warmth, nourishment and medication; her mental state and wandering could be monitored; there would be companionship of other residents; and there would be supervised access to activities and outings of her choice. The perceived risks of admission to residential care were: possibility of greater depression due to confinement; loss of independence and freedom; risk of falls in an unknown environment; risk of infections; and the possibility of increased confusion.

The consideration of each option in terms of potential benefits and possible harm was a helpful way to structure the discussion with the client and family. The key issues were clearly identified and discussed.

CASE STUDY 7.4

Potential benefits in a care plan

Grace is 37 years old and has been a patient in a psychiatric hospital for six months. She has been expressing suicidal thoughts throughout her stay, having been admitted when she intended to commit suicide. The decision is whether to permit a period of home leave. I found it helpful to articulate some of the benefits of a period of home leave or a day pass, to bear in mind alongside the more frequent consideration of the possibility of Grace harming herself:

- *reduce the growing dependency on the hospital staff and environment;*

- *reduce detachment from her home community;*

- *promote Grace's own coping skills and independence;*

- *develop support in the community from her father;*

- *taking a step forward, in discussion with Grace, that begins to move more responsibility back to her when she is ready;*

- *begin the process of Grace using community rather than hospital supports to grieve, with support from her family and a counselling service.*

Values and conceptualising risk-taking decisions in assessment

Our clients come to us as members of the same society as ourselves, with their own needs, tensions, perspectives and values in terms of risk-taking and decision making (Scott-Jones and Raisborough, 2007). Whilst there are situations where social workers are involved in making care plans (such as safeguarding plans) without full agreement of all parties (see Chapter 8) and also in situations where people lack capacity, there has been some exploration of how clients and carers conceptualise *risk* (Stevenson and Taylor, 2016 and in press), including children (Thom *et al.*, 2007), older people (Moriarty *et al.*, 2007), those with dementia (Buri and Dawson, 2000) and people with learning disability (Manthorpe *et al.*, 1997). Clients may also have different perceptions of what actually constitutes *risk* (Ryan *et al.*, 2001). Wynne-Harley (1991) explored the concept of *voluntary risk-taking* from the perspective of the rights of the older person. Boeije *et al.* (2004) studied the risk perception and seriousness of wheelchair dependence in people with multiple sclerosis. A key issue is how your clients and their families value the possible outcomes of a decision in which they are engaged with you.

Sometimes, people's response to taking a risk depends on the degree of voluntariness. Our exposure to possible harm may vary from voluntary situations (for example, choosing to walk on mountains in stormy weather conditions or to visit a nightclub that will involve travelling home at a more dangerous time of day) to involuntary (for example, we have limited control over the spread of epidemic diseases or exposure to the electromagnetic radiation inherent in the use of electrical appliances such as mobile phones and televisions). The *fear factor* may be increased as a result of the danger being unknown, loss of control in the situation, lack of reliable information or a sense of unfairness in who suffers (Calman *et al.*, 1999).

RESEARCH SUMMARY **7.1**

Parents' perceptions of risks to children and their management

Freel identified low-income, urban African-American families with their two- and three-year-old children as a population at high risk for injuries. Parents created safe environments for their children by changing their household environment to make it safer, by having rules banning hazardous objects, spaces and activities, and by monitoring or watching the child. When rules were transgressed, parents used discipline, usually reasoning along with corporal punishment or commands, to both stop the behaviour and to teach future safe behaviour. Parents said that they were influenced by many factors such as their perceptions of the children's knowledge about danger, how much control they had over the possible injuries, to what extent they could prevent injuries to their children and their beliefs about children needing freedom to play, explore and exercise their growing physical skills.

(Freel, 1995)

CASE STUDY **7.5**

Positive and negative indicators

Mrs Rodriguez is 67 years of age and has a problem with alcohol addiction. Her son Alberto lives with her occasionally. One of the areas identified in the assessment was the risk of family breakdown. On the negative side, Alberto is beginning to disengage from caring for his mother because he finds her depressed mood and erratic eating and sleeping increasingly difficult to cope with. On the positive side, family and friends do maintain contact with Mrs Rodriguez at present, and generally have positive feelings towards her.

It is important that a consideration of possible harm or loss is not limited to the particular individual who happens to be your *client* at this moment. Professionals have responsibilities to consider a wide range of risks including possible harm by clients to themselves; harm to other patients and clients, friends, neighbours, co-residents, other tenants; dangers to yourself and colleagues including, for example, foster parents and home care workers; risks to the organisation and to workers in other organisations; and dangers for the general public.

The consideration of risks and the decisions that must be made are a central part of the professional task of assessment and care planning, although consideration of these was not so central in textbooks published in earlier decades. We might consider the following client, agency and worker issues in the stage of the working relationship where choices between risk-taking options must be made.

1. Client issues:

   a. needs and risks;

   b. strengths and limitations (personal, family and community);

   c. motivation and stress;

   d. energy for change or maintenance;

   e. clarity of working agreement with the professional(s);

   f. trust in the worker;

   g. client values.

2. Agency issues:

   a. legislation, regulations, guidance;

   b. policy, procedures, standards for services;

   c. engagement with the client, family and community;

   d. resources; service configuration and availability;

   e. systems for managing decision making and risk;

   f. multi-agency networks;

   g. monitoring and recording systems.

3. Worker issues:

   a. use of theory for practice to understand the client and family situation (e.g. crisis intervention; Maslow's hierarchy of needs; family dynamics);

   b. skills in engaging with the client and family;

   c. skills in identifying meaningful goals and achievable objectives;

   d. skills in engaging the client and family in real 'work' or precision in service allocation;

   e. use of a practice theory for engaging with the client and family (e.g. task-centred case work, etc.);

   f. resource planning;

   g. social work values.

(Adapted from Taylor and Devine, 1993, p43)

Balancing values of benefits and harms

When faced with choosing between two or more alternatives, we might well start by listing (at least mentally) the desirable and undesirable aspects of each option. For an everyday example consider the choice you face regarding going on holiday or buying a car, where the positive and negative points of each option are compared. In relation to care decisions, the same model might be used although the issues are likely to be of greater importance for the individual's future well-being. The outcomes in everyday decisions might be evaluated in terms of the gain or loss of money or pleasure, as well as more basic needs of life such as health and security. In care decisions the priority is more often about benefits to health and social well-being, and possible harm, whether from other people or accidents, so the terms *benefit* and *harm* are used here. This model of *balancing benefits and harms* is adapted from a well-established judgement model known as *expected utility* (Baron, 2008; Hardman, 2009). This approach is based on the premise that the decision maker maximises the expected value of the outcome of the decision. That is to say, you choose the option which seems to offer, on balance, the greatest beneficial outcome when you weigh up the benefits (potential desirable outcomes) against the harms (possible undesirable outcomes). Although there are studies demonstrating a range of minor ways in which people in practice do not follow the rules of *expected utility* (Friedman *et al.*, 2014), it remains the starting point for most discussions of choosing between options as a form of decision making.

The distinction between considering only possible harms when we make a decision and weighing possible harms against possible gains is in certain respects a parallel in modern *risk language* to the traditional ethical debate between *non-maleficence* (i.e. first, do no harm) and *beneficence* (i.e. the duty to do good). Concerns about health and safety legislation and fear of litigation seem to be influencing professionals to focus more on avoiding harm and thus to avoid some more positive approaches to promoting health and social well-being that involve greater inherent danger. This balancing of benefits and harms might be undertaken quite simply by listing factors in two columns.

> *In particular in cases involving, as they so often do, the weighing of risks against benefits, the judge before accepting a body of opinion as being responsible, reasonable or respectable, will need to be satisfied that, in forming their views, the experts have directed their minds to the question of comparative risks and benefits and have reached a defensible conclusion on the matter.*

> (Lord Browne-Wilkinson, in *Bolitho v City & Hackney Health Authority*, 1998, p1159)

Balancing potential benefits and possible harms

The professional role often involves a balancing of possible gains against possible harm, whether as a process of individual *professional judgement* or collaboratively in a decision process with a client or family. This balancing type of decision making may involve relationship factors, judging the appropriate 'demand for work' (Shulman, 2011), and ensuring that client motivation and trust is maintained. Although we discuss these decisions here primarily in a cognitive way, there are normally emotional aspects to consider as well as the need for reflection on the personal propensity for risk-taking or risk-aversion as a potential bias (see Chapter 5).

ACTIVITY **7.5**

Identifying potential benefits and possible harms

Identify potential gains and possible losses in these situations.

- *a toddler walking along a low garden wall when mum is not watching;*

- *a teenager sneaking out of the window to go to a nightclub when Dad has said 'no';*

- *an older person hospitalised after a stroke walking across the ward for the first time;*

- *a person with a disability moving to greater independence in supported housing;*

- *Charles Blondin walking across the Niagara Falls on a tightrope (this 55-year-old French acrobat performed this feat and then repeated the stunt blindfolded pushing a wheelbarrow a few days later. The Chicago Tribune, 4 July 1859, **www.discovergreeneville. com/andrewjohnson/articles.php?r=4**);*

- *a recent situation on your caseload.*

It is important to be clear that balancing benefits and harms is not *gambling*. Decisions about health and social care are important matters to patients and clients. *Gambling* would imply that the decision process itself is undertaken for enjoyment rather than because the outcome is important. We support people to achieve *worthwhile*, normally agreed life goals in accordance with professional values, the purpose of the organisation by which we are employed (i.e. care-related goals in a broad sense) and the legal and policy parameters of our society. This is the answer to any accusation that we are *gambling with clients' lives* by supporting risk-taking.

ACTIVITY **7.6**

Weighing up possible benefits and harms

Consider the situation of a young man with moderate learning difficulties. It is identified as part of his care plan that he would like to learn to use public transport independently and that this would be helpful for his future life and his family.

- *What are the potential benefits of facilitating his request?*

- *What are the potential hazards in facilitating his request?*

(Continued)

(Continued)

- *What might be the vulnerabilities and trigger factors?*

- *What strengths might he have that might improve the success of the plan?*

- *How would you maximise the potential gains in a care plan?*

- *How would you minimise the potential for harm in a care plan?*

Likelihoods of benefits and harms

In reality the potential benefits and the possible harms resulting from our decisions are not certain. For a fuller approach, this *balancing benefits and harms* should consider the likelihood of harm occurring and the likelihood of achieving the desired benefits.

ACTIVITY 7.7

Patterns, severity and probability of risks

Consider the risk in a recent case in terms of:

Risk identified	Pattern of risk	Severity of risk	Probability of risk
Insert here a clear description of the risk identified	*1 Isolated* *2 Occasional occurrence* *3 Repeated occurrence* *4 Established pattern*	*1 Mild* *2 Moderate* *3 Serious* *4 Fatal*	*1 Unlikely* *2 Likely (expected)* *3 Highly probable* *4 Certain*

- *In what ways does this framework help you to discuss risk issues with your supervisor and colleagues in other professions?*

- *What are the main strengths of using a tool like this?*

- *What are the main limitations of using a tool like this?*

The generally accepted formula is that *risk=hazard (severity or value placed on the undesirable outcome) times the likelihood (probability of that outcome)*. In other words, we should multiply the seriousness of the particular outcome by the likelihood of that occurring in our balancing of options. Thus, we would multiply the value that is placed on the beneficial outcome by the probability (likelihood, chance) of achieving that, and would multiply the (negative) value that is placed on an undesirable outcome (consequences) by the likelihood of it occurring. In practice, such formulae cannot be used precisely. A good care plan probably has to address as a priority those areas that are high in severity even if low in likelihood of occurrence, as well as those that rate as high risks overall taking into account both severity and likelihood.

CASE STUDY **7.6**

Weighing likelihood and severity

Mrs Ferguson is aged 79 years and is suffering from dementia. She lives alone but has a son and daughter-in-law living nearby. In assessing Mrs Ferguson, I applied the scoring system in my employer's risk assessment which rates frequency as rarely (1), occasionally (2) or frequently (3), and which rates severity as low (1), medium (2) or high (3). I then multiplied these to give a score for the overall degree of risk.

- *Mrs F loses her purse in the house and blames her daughter-in-law.*
  - *severity 1 * frequency 1=overall risk 1*

- *Neighbours in adjoining flats who are usually very helpful to Mrs F (and help to maintain her at home) are complaining that her visits at strange times are becoming a nuisance.*
  - *severity 2 * frequency 2=overall risk 4*

- *Mrs F leaves the cooker on inadvertently on occasions, presenting a fire risk.*
  - *severity 3 * frequency 1=overall risk 3*

- *Mrs F is not bathing herself properly and is refusing to co-operate with home care staff in this, resulting in the possibility of sores.*
  - *severity 1 * frequency 3=overall risk 3*

The scoring system helped me to communicate more clearly about concerns with other professionals. However, I do not think that the overall scores necessarily reflect the priorities for action. The high severity risk (setting fire to the block of flats) must be a high priority despite not having the highest overall score. Similarly, the two areas that scored 3 overall are not equally deserving of priority attention.

Decision trees

Where we have detailed information on the values of appropriate stakeholders in the decision, and the likelihood of each possible outcome, a *decision tree* may be used to assist in analysing the alternative outcomes. The essence of a static decision tree is to:

- identify the options being considered;

- identify the possible outcomes for each option;

- add the likelihood of each outcome occurring; and

- add the value placed on each of these outcomes.

These latter steps are akin to the model above in judging severity and likelihood of a particular harm. The difference with a decision tree is that it can also show beneficial as well as harmful outcomes (positive values as opposed to negative values ascribed to particular outcomes) and how particular choices depend on other decisions. This is described here as a 'static' decision tree, as it shows (or 'models') the decision as being at a point in time. A 'dynamic' decision tree is one where a sequence of two or more decisions is included. Sometimes, professionals struggle emotionally to give an estimate of the likelihood of a particular outcome, perhaps feeling that this in some way diminishes their whole-hearted endeavours to help the client or family. The realism required to recognise that our best efforts will not always achieve complete success is essential to professional helping. Creating and discussing a decision tree may well assist in clarifying options and the likelihood of success; in no way should it be allowed to diminish the efforts to help the client or family (see Figure 7.2).

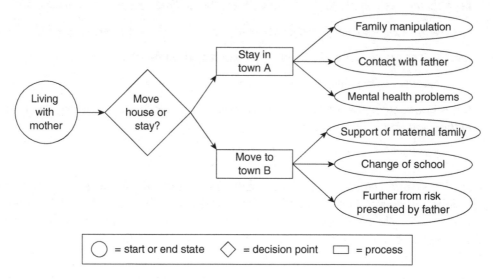

Figure 7.2 Example of a decision tree regarding child placement options (without values or probabilities)

In practice it is uncommon to have sufficiently detailed data to calculate likelihoods with useful accuracy for social work decisions. If you are supporting a client in making a decision, you might consider creating simple categories of value (e.g. very (un)desirable, (un)desirable, don't care) and likelihood (highly likely, may happen, unlikely to happen) to aid the discussion of options. The interested reader is referred to Dowie (1993) or Dowding and Thompson (2002) for further detail.

Chapter summary

- Care planning choices follow on directly from professional assessment, which involves client, worker and agency dimensions.

- The health and safety at work legislation in the European Union has achieved much in reducing harm and disease in our society. As employees, we are required to take reasonably practicable steps to avoid death, injury and illness in social care workplaces.

- There are some tensions between the principles of health and safety legislation and the professional responsibility to support clients in taking reasonable risks to further care plan goals such as greater independence, rehabilitation, motivation and quality of life.

- Reasoned, reasonable risk-taking decision making is an intrinsic function of the professional role in care planning to enable clients and families to achieve worthwhile, care-related life goals.

- We can use a model of *balancing benefits and harms* to conceptualise the social worker making this type of care-planning, risk-taking judgement and supporting a client in taking an informed decision about *risk-taking*.

- A *decision tree* can be a useful model to conceptualise this process of *balancing benefits and harms*, and facilitating communication with the client about the decision.

FURTHER READING

Baron, J. (2008) *Thinking and Deciding.* Cambridge: Cambridge University Press.

This fairly heavy textbook gives a detailed consideration of the strengths and paradoxes of the well-researched models of decision making generally known as *expected utility*.

Brearley, P. (1982) *Risk in Social Work.* London: Routledge & Kegan Paul.

This classic text was one of the forerunners in exploring the concept of risk as applied to social work. Paul Brearley pioneered the concepts (using different terminology) of vulnerability, trigger factors, strengths and mitigating factors in social work decisions.

Health and Safety Executive in England

www.hse.gov.uk/index.htm

Health and Safety Executive in Wales

www.hse.gov.uk/welsh

Health and Safety Executive in Scotland

www.hse.gov.uk/scotland

Health and Safety Executive for Northern Ireland

www.hseni.gov.uk

Health and Safety Executive Bookfinder

www.hsebooks.com/Books/default.asp

The Health and Safety Executives are the enforcing authorities for health and safety in a range of work situations including district councils, government departments, hospitals and nursing homes. The websites provide a wealth of attractive materials, including details of legislation and current policy issues in support of their mission to *prevent death, injury and ill health in the workplace.*

Chapter 8

Collaboration, communication and contest in assessment, risk and decision processes

Give every man thine ear, but few thy voice;
Take each man's censure, but reserve thy judgement ...
... This above all: to thine own self be true,
And it must follow, as the night the day,
Thou canst not then be false to any man.

(Lord Polonius, *Hamlet* Act I, Scene 3, William Shakespeare
(1564–1616), Andrews and Gibson, 2005)

Introduction

This chapter focuses on decision-making processes with others, including how risk is communicated. In Chapter 2, we considered the task of engaging and supporting clients and families in decision and risk processes. In this chapter, we consider the engagement of colleagues from other professions and organisations in assessment processes, and contested decisions. The focus is on contributing your professional judgement within a broader arena where decisions are made. We discuss inter-professional working in relation to decision-making processes and communicating about probabilities ('risks') of harm or success. We consider rights and conflict, where decisions are contested, and making an argument for a professional opinion particu-larly in court. Legal aspects of risk communication and of decision making in groups were considered in Chapter 3.

Collaborative decision making

'All the options are bad, and some look worse to different people; how do we choose the least-worst?!' 'Do we really need to invite Joan to the case conference? It will be a case of "group think" and everyone following her ideas!' The role of the social worker is often to co-ordinate specialist contributions to decision making into a holistic, person-centred picture and to identify key issues to be addressed in a co-ordinated decision process, often involving explicit management of risks. This demands knowledge of the roles of other professions and organisations, and skills in managing the decision process. Social workers may have a specialist assessment role in addition to their co-ordinating role, which was considered in Chapter 4 in relation to assessment. Key tasks in engaging stakeholders in decisions include:

- taking account of relevant values, principles and protocols;

- ensuring that appropriate people are engaged at the appropriate stage in the process;

- managing an effective decision-making process if you have a co-ordinating role;

- clarifying with stakeholders (client, family, professionals and organisations) what is expected of them and what they expect of you, for what purpose and within what timescale;

- giving all parties an opportunity (and sometimes support) to make effective, timely contributions, sharing facts and expressing their opinions appropriately;

- ensuring that you are clear on your role and the powers and duties of your organisation, and that these are communicated clearly to others;

- clarifying how the decision will be implemented;

- informing parties of the decision outcome.

The importance of engaging appropriate professionals on the problem-solving task which lies at the heart of much of our decision making should not be underestimated. The range of perspectives brings a breadth of knowledge and skills to bear and provides checks and balances. A joint decision process will normally increase ownership of the decision. Consensus processes help to anticipate possible consequences ('risks') of the decision and reduce conflicts that might occur later. A more complex collaborative process is likely to be appropriate when the value (positive or negative) placed on the outcome (such as whether a child requires state care) is high, where there is a wider range of options to consider, and where a greater diversity of information (for example about needs) has to be considered. A more complex process takes more time and resources, and that has to be justified.

In all that follows in this chapter, regard must be paid to the comments in Chapter 3 on liability for decisions in teams and groups. Our current understanding of the law is that organisations must not act *ultra vires*, and individual professionals must only make decisions within their competence deemed by virtue of their professional training and registration. Although this chapter focuses on encouraging multi-professional and multi-agency collaboration, it is essential that this does not lead to a situation where 'the group' presumes to tell a particular profession or organisation what it must do. Each profession and organisation should be regarded as being responsible for the decisions within its own competence. Those decisions should be made explicitly in the light of information from other professions and organisations, and taking into account their intentions or decisions. A useful working principle might be to regard each profession as accountable for the decisions that fall within its domain of deemed competence. Similarly, each organisation is responsible for decisions that lie within its purpose, powers and duties. This provides an essential foundation for trust and robust group decision processes.

ACTIVITY **8.1**

Contributors to decisions

- *Recall a recent reasonably complex case.*

- *Who was involved in making the decision?*

- *Who else should have been involved, ideally?*

- *What was your contribution to the decision?*

- *What was the contribution of other key stakeholders?*

- *How might the various contributions have been more effective?*

- *What structure was used for the decision-making process?*

- *How was the decision process managed and by whom?*

- *How did you influence this?*

- *What knowledge underpinned your approach?*

Multi-professional assessment and decision making

Different professions and organisations have distinct roles, statutory or otherwise, in relation to decisions about care (including safeguarding and other interventions). There may be a statutory or policy requirement for partnership in specific areas of practice (Taylor, 1999). There are an increasing number of protocols or procedures being used to shape inter-agency working, particularly in relation to child abuse and intimate partner violence. There is not scope within this book to discuss the various tools used in different countries and regions in detail, and in any case these change over time. Rather our focus is on the essential professional knowledge and skills that are required to engage in these processes effectively regardless of client group or context.

A key practice skill in inter-professional working is to respect the roles and responsibilities of others, and not to demean any.

Inquiry findings

Inquiries show that too narrow a medical view of mental illness offers an inadequate framework for assessing and managing risk, while an over-reliance on social factors without sufficient attention to medical treatment and medication is potentially as unsafe.

(Reith, 1998, p180)

It appears essential that a psychiatric patient with a severe psychiatric illness whose recent history is not known should be assessed by a social worker .... Given the psychosocial nature of the impact of schizophrenia and other severe psychiatric illnesses on the patient, relatives and carers, it is important to ensure that a multidisciplinary and multi-agency approach is always adopted.

(Wood *et al.*, 1966, Recommendation 1)

Open and honest, yet tactful, communication is essential to clarify issues and develop mutual understanding. This involves trust and mutual respect, and takes time to develop. It is important that participants in the decision are confident in the process and feel safe to raise their issues even if some disagreement may ensue. Clear communication also involves using language that others can understand, talking in terms of their own experience where possible. The task of combining client and family information with knowledge to make a judgement (see Chapters 5, 6 and 7) is extended to include ensuring that all participants in the decision contribute appropriately. This requires sufficient access to the information and knowledge, and communication about the reasoning processes of participants. The development of sufficient common language among participants is an essential to effectiveness in this complex task.

The benefits of inter-professional collaboration in decision making must not blind us to the challenges that can occur in reconciling competing objectives. We may need to challenge opinions on occasion as well as seek compromises. *The training of social workers must equip them with the confidence to question the opinion of professionals in other agencies when conducting their own assessment of the needs of the child* (Laming, 2003, Recommendation 37). This questioning of the opinions of others must, of course, be done respectfully. We, as social workers, should also anticipate our opinions being challenged. Rational argument for professional judgements is considered in Chapter 5. There may also be tensions about issues such as a duty to inform other professionals about evidence of possible violence conflicting with a duty of confidentiality towards a client. You can develop multi-professional decision making by:

- being clear about your professional role and confident about your contribution within that role;
- seeking to understand the tasks of other professionals and organisations and respecting their roles;

- seeking to develop trust through timely, open and honest communication, fulfilling promises and acting with integrity;

- clarifying processes of decision making: options, perspectives and context;

- using social work skills appropriately, such as empathy (for example, regarding the uncertainties of making a decision), clarifying (for example, options) and challenging (for example, values and stereotypes of clients and other professionals); and

- focusing on what is in the best interests of the client, family, community or society.

Decision making in groups

Collaborative decisions are often made in group meetings. Our focus here is on multi-professional groups meeting for such purposes as a child protection case conference, a strategy meeting or a panel to allocate publicly funded resources such as home care or admission to institutional care. Good communication skills are required, but these may be insufficient to ensure as effective participation in decision making as you would like (Hitzler and Messmer, 2010).

There may be value in bringing people together for a decision process, such as being able to see a fuller picture as information is shared face-to-face; creating a new synthesis or understanding as problems and issues are discussed; dealing with any conflict of facts or opinions; co-ordinating activities; getting commitment to an agreed, integrated action plan; and laying a foundation for future collaboration where communication may be less direct through telephone or email. Be aware though that convening a group has a cost in terms of time and often travel. Pressures of work mean that professionals will want to be clear about the value of coming to a meeting rather than communicating by form, letter, telephone or e-mail.

CASE STUDY 8.1

Collaborative decision making

Miss Fulton is a 75-year-old woman with schizophrenia who lives alone. She also has chronic obstructive pulmonary disease (COPD), which makes her short of breath and prone to chest infections. She was admitted to hospital after a fall. My role was to support her in planning her future living arrangements. The stakeholders in the decision making included Miss Fulton and her family, various professionals in the community rehabilitation team and the manager of the home care workers. I liaised with each of these and sought consensus for a care plan.

- *In what circumstances is it particularly desirable to convene a meeting of stakeholders regarding care and risk decisions?*

- *In this case, who should be involved in which decisions?*

The decision about who to invite to a meeting may raise the issue of inclusivity versus the need for a small enough group of appropriate people for constructive interaction and the achievement of a decision within the necessary timescale. By definition, participants are there to influence each other but with respect for other participants. This is a particular application of social work listening skills! There are many parallels between social group work as taught on social work training and the skills required to lead a group of professionals. Leading a decision-making group involves the following tasks:

- prepare agenda and ensure that required information is available;

- clarify forms of address;

- clarify the purpose of the meeting, roles and responsibilities;

- promote participation by emphasising mutual gain from collaborating in the decision process;

- skilful chairing, to keep the discussion focused without unduly stifling new ideas;

- legitimise the sharing of facts and opinions, building a culture of mutual respect for participants with their distinct roles, knowledge and skills;

- create a co-operative climate, including addressing obstacles to the group's decision making;

- enable all to participate, including supporting those less able to do so;

- build on the strengths of groups for decision making such as generating a range of ideas and alternatives and gaining ownership of decisions made;

- ensure that the individual meeting fits within the overall decision process (e.g. timing of court hearings, roles of and reporting by sub-committees, reporting to senior managers);

- clarify issues, agreements, disagreements and confidentiality, and manage conflict constructively;

- allow time for appropriate reflection and consultation;

- manage the process and the time;

- ensure that the group makes decisions that it is charged with making;

- ensure that the group does not make decisions beyond its remit;

- ensure clear recording of decisions and disagreements.

Group decision processes

Sometimes it can be difficult to identify exactly when and how a decision in a group was made (Hitzler and Messmer, 2010). It may be that the group needs a stronger reason to change things than to default to the minimal decision to continue with the situation as it is ('if it ain't broke, don't fix it'). The presentation of information by people in groups is never without bias. Indeed, professionals are expected to incorporate their own assessment into their presentation of facts, so as to enable others to understand what sense they make of the client and family information. It is commonplace to present information, or opinions, in the context of its relevance to the decision being made.

A group decision compared to an individual decision has the advantage of the possibility of drawing on wider knowledge, skills, experience, resources and ideas. It may also generate 'ownership' of the decision. Disadvantages of group decision making are the potential for conflicts of interests, perspectives, aims and values which may make consensus difficult to achieve. However, communication in a group about risks and decisions may have the effect of challenging assumptions and requiring participants to clarify their language so as to reach a common understanding. Engaging appropriate stakeholders may be a painful process! But listening to the range of relevant opinions will generally improve the decision, provided that distracting and ill-informed comments can be disregarded as inappropriate!

The quality of group decision making might be thought of as comprising elements such as (Hirokawa *et al.*, 1996):

- information resources available;

- quality of effort of group members;

- quality of thinking of group members; and

- the decision logic of the group, which might be regarded as primarily 'rational' or 'political' (Senge, 1990).

What decision does a group make by comparison with the decisions that the individuals would make by themselves in isolation? Will the group judgement be different if the individuals discuss the decision by comparison with the average judgement if the members consider identical information without discussion? As people interact in a group they may behave differently and may make different judgements. Janis (1982) highlighted various mechanisms that might lead to *groupthink*:

- a view of the group as invulnerable and as holding the moral high ground, which leads to excessive *risk-taking*;

- closed-mindedness that stereotypes some members (perhaps other professions) or discounts their views for some reason (such as not being present);

- pressures to conform to the majority view, whether expressed or only felt by individuals fearing criticism if they voice a counter view.

Janis (1982) also derived some proposals from his research to help to protect against group pressures, some of which are incorporated into the pointers below.

- Group leaders should not state their personal preferences early in the discussion, but should encourage those who might be regarded as least powerful to speak first.

- Group leaders should encourage dissenting views so that the group can consider alternative perspectives and options.

- Groups should periodically take time to reflect together on their group processes, in an environment of openness and honesty.

- Groups should periodically invite external people with expertise to attend and to critique the group process.

Obviously, the application will depend on the type of group (in particular its mandate and longevity) and on the types of decisions being taken.

RESEARCH SUMMARY *8.1*

Variation in professional judgements

A study compared the judgements of case managers (social workers) with a multi-professional panel comprising medicine, social work and nursing. Generally, the case managers estimated the risk of the older person requiring institutional care during the coming months higher than did the panel members. There was low level of agreement amongst panel members, but more than there was between the panel and case managers. Interestingly, the social workers on the panel agreed more with other panel members than with the case managers even though these were social workers. The authors concluded that the low reliability of decisions underscored the complexity of the decision situation. The variation might also be due to factors such as case managers knowing detail about the clients and their families that is not conveyed in the written materials; panel members having an appreciation of wider issues due to their role; organisational pressures being greater on panel members; or case managers having to go back to clients to convey in person the rejection of their request for services.

(Austin and Seidl, 1981)

Early research and theory suggested that the effect of a group may be to make a decision that is more risky than the average of the decisions that would be made by the same individuals acting alone without group discussion. This became known as *risky shift*. It was speculated that this increased risk-taking effect may be because:

- the group members became more familiar with the decision topic and became more comfortable with taking greater risk (familiarisation theory); or

- the sort of charismatic personality willing to take risks is also more likely to be the sort of personality to get others to go along with thier way of thinking in the group (leadership theory); or

- individuals feel less responsibility for the outcome in a group (crowd effect); or

- risk is valued as a positive social norm, so that individuals tend to move in this direction under the influence of the group (risk as value theory) (Stoner, 1968).

More recent research suggests that the effect may be due to the social norm of riskiness attached to a particular option. In other words, some types of decisions may produce a *cautious shift* (the group decision is less risky than the average of the individual judgements) while others produce a *risky shift*. These findings led to the general demise of the first three theories above, while the *risk as value* theory adapted itself to become a *risk or caution as value*. While risk-taking might be given social value in some contexts (e.g. bravery in battle), caution might be valued in others where risk-taking might be viewed as reckless (e.g. doing something for a dare) and hence might lead to a *cautious shift*. The direction of the *choice shift* may be towards the social norm rather than necessarily towards greater risk-taking.

There is little research on group decisions involving social workers. The work by Farmer and Owen (1995, p145) on child protection case conferences illustrated how the process of *assessing risk* in such groups can sometimes lead to *accumulating concerns* and a disproportionate sense of impending harm, and thus to more *risk-averse* group decisions than the judgements of individuals acting alone. This perhaps reflects the views of wider society, which might choose less risky options than professionals. Their research highlighted how pressure can be experienced to conform to the majority view in the meeting. However, there is some evidence that child protection case conferences assume a more extreme position than the average of the members individually, whether more *risk-taking* or more *risk-averse* (Kelly and Milner, 1996), perhaps because of the need to make a clear decision with an explicit justification.

Communicating information for decisions

Professional communication is a central theme of inquiries into homicides and suicides by people with mental illness (Boyd, 1996) and into child homicides (Munro, 2008). Effective communication involves consideration of the language that we use for conveying messages to others.

> *The Department of Health must establish a 'common language' for use across all agencies to help those agencies to identify who they are concerned about, why they are concerned, who is best placed to respond to those concerns, and what outcome is being sought from any planned response.*

> (Laming, 2003, Recommendation 13)

In all fields of social work, we need precise language so as to enable effective decisions. However in the wording of the decision outcome, it may be helpful to consider a range of degrees of precision of language, rather than a dichotomous 'clear' versus 'unclear' language. It is helpful on occasions to use language consciously to encompass a range of acceptable meanings. Effective communication involves consideration of such aspects as:

- who – role clarity;

- when – timeliness;

- what – level of detail to provide;

- why – clarity of issue and expectation of response by recipient, urgency;

- how – in person, telephone, e-mail, letter, fax, group discussion;

- recording – who, when, what, why and how.

PRACTICE EXAMPLE *8.1*

Comments in an assessment report

Does 'Mrs Smith has disturbed sleep', mean:

- *Mrs Smith calls out occasionally in the night, waking her daughter?*

- *Mrs Smith gets up usually once a night to go to the toilet but manages this safely on her own?*

- *Mrs Smith frequently gets up in the night and wanders downstairs and tries to open the outer door?*

Conceptualising and communicating risk for decisions

The research and theoretical literature on risk and on decision making sometimes seem worlds apart from each other! However they are interconnected in ways yet to be studied. One domain where they inter-connect is in relation to risk communication amongst members of a group that is charged with making a decision. There are crucial issues about the way that the group exchanges risk-relevant information, how these are combined and how a decision is reached (Russell and Reimer, 2015). Complex information must be considered, and the 'dynamics' and nature of the individuals in the group will affect how that information is processed by individuals and discussed.

We conceptualise *risk communication* as the exchange of information between individuals receiving services, family members and professionals about possible harm and potential benefits in client situations and care options, so as to inform decision making about care (Stevenson *et al.*, in press). Different stakeholders will understand risk differently. The way in which risk information is communicated may shape the recipient's understanding of the facts of the situation. Although much of the literature considers risk in numeric terms (how likely some harm is to occur), in social work the emphasis tends to be more on the seriousness (value) of the outcomes than their likelihood (Stevenson and Taylor, in press). The term 'risk' is often replaced with terms such as 'concerns' or 'unanticipated events'. Social work by its nature is concerned with daily life, and the conceptualisation of 'risk-taking' in daily life can be even more diverse than the use of the term 'risk' in terms of harms. People tend to focus on what they want to achieve or what they have always done, often without clearly articulating what risks they run in the process. The conceptualisation of 'risk' in social work needs to include at least:

- the types of possible harms ('risks') for your area of work;

- the social constructions of risk used by clients and families as well as the objective measures of the likelihood of identified possible harm that may ensue (this is discussed below);

- approaches to dealing with risk including acceptable risk-taking, risk tolerance and risk-aversion; and

- some understanding of how risk relates to making a judgement and decision making (Stevenson *et al.*, in press).

By 'social construction of risk', we mean the ways in which the seriousness or likelihood of undesirable events is understood by people when it does not correspond in some way with established factual measures of the likelihood of that harmful outcome. An individual's social construction of risk may change with their level of knowledge about those types of situations; through their discussions with family members and professionals; with the experience of crisis which may have brought them to seek services; through efforts to create or understand the 'meaning' of life events and situations; and through the application of their own moral principles and beliefs about the world.

Communicating risk: likelihoods

Risk communication is an essential component of effective multi-professional working, during both assessment and intervention phases of care. Professional judgements are informed by an effective risk discourse, leading to greater transparency of decision making. When care is being delivered, effective monitoring of risk requires clear communication. In seeking to communicate about 'risk', it is important to recognise that the 'lens of risk' (Heyman *et al.*, 2010) may vary from one person to another. It is not easy to communicate accurately about uncertainty and likelihoods, especially about the possibility of harm. If people are asked whether they would like a surgical operation where there is a 90 per cent chance of success, more will say 'yes' than if the same information is presented as a 10 per cent chance of failure! John Paling (2006) recommends that both the positive and the negative perspectives should be presented: the likelihood of the harm occurring and also the likelihood of this harm not occurring. Vivid information presented to a decision maker is likely to have greater impact than the same information presented in a dull manner. This may be understood in terms of concepts of bias considered in Chapter 5.

Words may be easily misunderstood by different listeners, but on the other hand numbers can sometimes have an unjustified air of authority about them. The presentation of information may be a particular issue in formal decision situations such as courts. There is little exploration yet in social work of communicating about probabilities with more visual means such as graphs or charts (Stevenson and Taylor, in press). One approach is to use both words and numbers, perhaps along the lines of: *Your honour, I would describe the likelihood as '...', meaning about x% based on relevant research and the evidence available in this case* (cf. Carson and Bain, 2008, p167). There are various initiatives to create a useful correspondence between numbers and words, and one example is given here. Be aware that most such correspondence scales relate to harm occurring within the environment or society in general. They may have limited use when trying to communicate, for example, higher likelihood levels (Bennett and Calman, 1999). We would emphasise that any numbers used to convey probability need to be justified by sound research evidence, and that any words used to convey probability may need some explanation to avoid misunderstanding. The following have been proposed as terms to express likelihood of re-occurrence in sexual abuse cases:

- < 5 per cent – very unlikely;
- 5–20 per cent – unlikely;
- 20–40 per cent – somewhat unlikely;
- 40–60 per cent – undetermined;
- 60–80 per cent – somewhat more likely than not;
- 80–95 per cent – likely;
- > 95 per cent – very likely

(Suggested by Wood, 1996)

RESEARCH SUMMARY *8.2*

Conceptualisations of risk amongst community dementia services professionals

Data were gathered across five focus groups (35 health and social care professionals) covering concepts and perspectives on verbal, numeric and visual forms of communicating risk. Risks were primarily conceptualised as consequences (positive and negative) rather than as likelihood, and related to a wide range of domains. Perceptions were influenced by socio-cultural factors including risk-assessment mechanisms and wider discourse relating to positive risk-taking. The language of probability was used in a non-quantified, subjective manner. While professionals routinely received quantitative information, they did not typically communicate using numeric expressions. Verbal expressions of likelihood were widely preferred to numeric. When risks were presented in numeric formats, frequency presentation was seen as more comprehensible than percentages. Several participants saw potential in visual forms of risk communication. Bar charts were generally favoured to icon arrays, as they were more easily understood. Good practice examples for risk communication were identified.

- *How is risk conceptualised in your field of social work?*

- *How could you improve your communication about risk to clients, families and other professionals?*

(Stevenson and Taylor, in press)

Rights, partnership and contested decisions

Social workers are often engaged in *contested decision making*, despite our best efforts to build commitment and partnership ways of working. Contested decisions are required where there are conflicts between rights, responsibilities and interests, such as where statutory safeguarding powers are being exercised. There are particular issues where information is given anonymously or *in confidence.* Courts are a key mechanism in society to resolve such conflicts and have increasingly clear and stringent expectations of social work judgements. *Expressions of opinion must be supported by detailed evidence and articulated reasoning* (Munby J in *Re M (Care Proceedings: Judicial Review)* [2003] 2 FLR 171, p183).

Safeguarding roles present many challenges for professionals in striving to engage clients and families in decision making and partnership working that will enable therapeutic change within relationships. It is important to be clear that such collaborative partnership working is not an end in itself. Rather, the aim is the protection of the child or vulnerable adult from abuse, neglect or self-harm, or the protection of others from crimes that might be committed by this individual. In such partnerships we should strive towards such goals as *fairness* and *openness*, recognising that as professionals with safeguarding responsibilities we have been given powers and duties by society in order to protect the most vulnerable (Morrison, 1998). It is helpful to plan the method and timing of raising issues that are anticipated to be contentious. The Department of Health (DH, 1995) outlines four levels of partnership working that focus particularly on decision making in child protection, but can be applied in other areas of social work:

- providing information;

- passive involvement (for example attending a case conference);

- participating actively, contributing to decision making;

- joint decision making based on mutual trust, listening and openness.

Court decisions and other formal settings for managing risks

The most strongly contested decision-making processes are normally conducted in a court or similar formal setting. Despite the most ardent efforts to achieve collaborative decisions it is sometimes essential to initiate legal proceedings to achieve a safeguarding decision. This is not to imply that a court setting is entirely negative. Jones (2006, p476) suggests that: *Courts can be therapeutic ... and bring reluctant parents into a setting where change becomes a reality ... The authority, thoroughness, fairness and neutrality of the court process seem to me to be ingredients that have the potential to be a foundation and driver for family change.*

As a social worker you may be in court on behalf of an organisation that is a party to the proceedings (such as a statutory authority bringing an action to protect children from abuse), or you may be in court as an expert witness (for example providing a report in a private law dispute between separated parents about custody and access to their children). However, as you are appearing in your professional capacity even in the former case, the courts will generally treat you as an expert in relation to areas within your competence. It is essential to engage your line management, professional supervisor and legal advisor appropriately.

> *You may find it surprising, in view of the emphasis on collaborative and inter-disciplinary working, that in court you are not giving evidence as a member of a team, but as an individual. As an employee, you obviously have to follow the instructions of your managers; if, for example, it is decided in a case conference to recommend the initiation of care proceedings and you are instructed to take this forward, then you must do this. However once in court your primary duty is to the court, which requires you to give evidence of your personal knowledge and opinions, not those of anyone else.... If the court wishes to hear from your team or service manager, or anyone else, then they can be called as a witness, and indeed should be if their views and decisions are important to the case.*

> (Seymour and Seymour, 2007, p101)

Evidence in a court may include facts about the client, family and context. As a professional you are expected to be knowledgeable in relevant areas, such as (in child care proceedings) attachment and bonding, child development and parenting that inform your judgement. You have to articulate the context, issues, facts, opinions, concerns and strategies. A robust argument requires that there is proper evidence, including a proper analysis for and against the proposed course of action, and that there is an adequately reasoned judgement. This must include a proper balancing exercise and an analysis of the proportionality of what is being proposed in terms of compulsory protection measures and the seriousness of the harm to be avoided (*Re B-S (Children)* [2013] EWCA Civ 1146). Quite apart from moral considerations, as an expert witness you are required by the court to provide a balanced overview of relevant research or theory, not a partisan selection of favourable studies. In such formal decision situations, you may be challenged on the facts of the case, on your credibility and on your competence. It is important to be clear on limits to your competence and to respect the competence areas of other professions. Social workers may be regarded as experts in some child protection issues (*F v Suffolk County Council* [1981] 2 FLR 208) (although it is open to the court to seek additional expert witnesses), but not in the diagnosis of sexual abuse (*Re N (Child Abuse: Evidence)* [1996] 2 FLR 214). It is often helpful to include in your report to the court or other formal decision forum a clear description of people involved and their relationship to the person at the focus of the decision, and a clear chronology of main events.

> *The fullest possible information must be given to the court. The evidence in support of the application for such an order must be full, detailed, precise and compelling. Unparticularised generalities will not suffice. The sources of hearsay evidence must be identified. Expressions of opinion must be supported by detailed evidence and articulated reasoning.*
>
> (*Re M (Care Proceedings: Judicial Review)* [2003] 2 FLR 171, p183)

The court wants to hear your opinion in order to help the magistrate, judge or jury to reach a decision. The court needs to know how you formed your opinion so that it can fairly weigh up the arguments. Courts in the UK are gradually formulating more explicitly their expectations regarding seeing essential information being weighed up in some rational manner within social work reports (*Re B-S (Children)* [2013] EWCA Civ 1146). Ensure that your opinions can be backed up by evidence.

> *A professional opinion expressed in a report should always be based on analysis of material contained in that report. Everyone who reads it should be clear on what facts your opinion is based and to what extent you have personal knowledge of those facts. You should always give the source of any facts of which you do not have personal knowledge, such as case records made before you took over the case.*
>
> (Seymour and Seymour, 2007, p73)

PRACTICE EXAMPLE *8.2*

Considering evidence for steps in a child welfare argument

A recent judgement from the Supreme Court for England in a child care case drew out three key points.

- *The child's interests are paramount, but include being brought up by his or her natural family.*

- *Statutes require courts to consider all available options when coming to a decision.*

(Continued)

(Continued)

- *The court's assessment of the parents' capacity to care for the child should include consideration of support that the public social care authorities could offer them.*

Exercise

- *What are the implications of these points for professional social work assessment of any client?*

- *How might options best be presented, including both facts and some judgement of the value and likelihood of successful and undesirable outcomes?*

- *What approaches and processes might you use to ensure that decisions are the best possible for the child or other client and the family?*

(Re B-S (Children) *[2013] EWCA Civ 1146*)

Making a rational, ethical argument

Contested decision making requires us to have rational and explicit approaches to arguing a case, often as we work through an assessment process. *Effective clinical reasoning requires skill in developing arguments, establishing the relevance of information to an argument, and evaluating the plausibility of assertions or claims* (Osmo and Landau, 2001, p489). Various frameworks might be used for the decision argument, depending on the context.

The work of Stephen Toulmin and his colleagues (1958) on ethical decision making offers a structured approach to constructing an argument. Explicit ethical argument prompts clearer engagement with values, knowledge, assumptions, feelings and experiences in arriving at the rationale for pursuing or refraining from a course of action. This model can be seen as a way to assist in guarding against arbitrariness and inflexibility in decision making when balancing the rights of the various individuals involved.

PRACTICE EXAMPLE 8.3

Establishing links in the decision argument

- *This was my starting point. I am aware of other potential starting points and I have borne these in mind as the assessment has proceeded.*

- *These were the actions I took to ensure that the child was safe while I gathered all the relevant information. I endeavoured to avoid actions that would prejudice future decisions.*

> - *I formed the judgement that the issues causing concern in the case included these elements, and my view on the available evidence was that in these circumstances there could be harm to this degree.*
>
> - *I therefore developed the following strategy to intervene, manage and reduce the risks in the case. These were the outcomes of the strategies.*
>
> - *I can therefore now say that concerns identified have changed in the following ways and the level of risk to the child is now as follows.*
>
> *(Hollows, 2008, p58)*

Table 8.1   Steps in explicit ethical argument

1   Make a **claim** about a particular matter or issue (for example, that care proceedings are the best option for a particular child).

2   Provide **grounds**, data or evidence for this claim (the particulars of this situation).

3   **Warrant** the relationship between the evidence and the claim (for example, making explicit reference to research, empirical evidence and theory in warranting and supporting the claim for care proceedings).

4   **Qualify** your claim by expressing degrees of confidence and likelihood that are associated with it (for example, the degree to which care proceedings will advance the welfare of the child based on the evidence presented).

5   Highlight the **limitations** of the claim and situations in which the claim might be weakened (for example, highlight the reasons why a Care Order is not ideal even though that is your conclusion).

6   **Justify** the warrant at stage 3 with further evidence (for example, additional research evidence, practice knowledge and theory to support the reasons for making the claim for care proceedings) to address the limitations.

(Adapted from Toulmin (1958), Osmo and Landau (2001) and Duffy *et al.* (2006))

Table 8.2   Some prompts for arguing your case

Attitude

- Be absolutely sincere and honest in arguing your case.
- Aim to be the 'honest expert' on the issues within your competence.
- Think of 'we' (i.e. including your employer) rather than 'I' as you speak.

Content

- Know the detailed facts about your client, family and context.
- Take reasonable steps to ascertain the views of the client and family, treating them with respect even where you disagree.
- Outline the decision-making processes undertaken, including engaging the client, family and other stakeholders.
- Be able to explain what your profession and organisation has done, with what authority and why.

(Continued)

Table 8.2 (Continued)

- Outline what support services your agency and others have offered and what help these have (or have not) been.
- Differentiate between fact, hearsay and opinion.
- Do not say anything that you cannot back up with evidence.
- Explain honestly and clearly the concerns of your agency, what changes are sought and how achievement towards goals will be assessed.
- Acknowledge weak points in the argument and address them before the opposition does.

Verbal aspects

- Don't repeat yourself except very sparingly.
- Keep it simple and to the point; avoid unnecessary detail.
- If you ramble, stop; apologise; say something along the lines of 'let me start again'; and say what you want to say in a more focused way.
- You can 'suggest' rather than 'tell', using words such as 'indicated that'.

Non-verbal aspects

- Observe normal dress code to avoid distracting from the decision process.
- Consider the use of possible visual aids.
- Make eye contact as appropriate (and keep eye contact with the judge or magistrate when providing answers, not the barrister for the other party).
- Use short pauses to good effect.
- Gain the empathy of the decision maker(s).
- Vary pace and tone.

(Includes some ideas from Seymour and Seymour, 2007)

Chapter summary

- Decision making in social work in more complex situations often involves collaborating with colleagues from other professions and organisations, requiring good communication skills, particularly regarding unwanted possible outcomes and their likelihood (risks).

- Inter-agency and inter-professional protocols are increasingly being created to standardise collaborative decision processes. Social workers need to develop the knowledge and skills to use these to best effect.

- Although multi-professional collaboration is very much to be encouraged, the responsibility of each profession and organisation is distinct and needs to be clear.

- Communication about complex and contentious issues such as risks needs to be timely and clear, with empathy for the perspective of someone from a different profession or organisation.

- Verbal, numeric and visual methods of communicating risk each have their place.

- Some decisions are made in contentious arenas, such as child care court hearings. Steps are outlined to assist in reflecting on the quality of your argument for a professional opinion, particularly in the context of recommendations to a court.

Bowell, T. and Kemp, G. (2010) *Critical Thinking: A Concise Guide*, 3rd edition. London: Routledge.

This well-written book focuses on the skills of constructing and analysing arguments for and against an issue. It is a useful resource for creating logical argument in contested situations.

Paling, J. (2006) *Helping Patients Understand Risks*. Gainesville, FL: Risk Communication Institute.

This very readable and visual book is one of the best available to guide professionals in clear communication about risk with their public, including the use of visual aids to communicate about the likelihoods (probabilities) of harm occurring, although the main focus is health care rather than social care.

Seymour, C. and Seymour, R. (2011) *Courtroom and Report Writing Skills for Social Workers*, 2nd edition. Exeter: Learning Matters.

This attractive textbook in the Post-Qualifying Social Work Practice series includes useful chapters on legal language and decision making, and on values and principles in law and social work.

Winton Centre for Risk and Evidence Communication (**https://wintoncentre.maths.cam.ac.uk**).

This centre, at the University of Cambridge, was founded in 2016 and aims to ensure that quantitative evidence and risk is presented to people in a fair and balanced way. The domains of interest of this new centre are not defined, and are broad across societal issues.

Chapter 9

Dynamics of practice: managing risk, re-assessing and changing your mind

He still had some doubts about the decision he had made. But he was able to understand one thing: making a decision was only the beginning of things. When someone makes a decision, he is really diving into a strong current that will carry him to places he had never dreamed of when he first made the decision.

(Coelho, 1995, pp70–2)

Introduction

Risk is a changing feature of practice, and our assessment and decision processes must be dynamic also. Do you find it hard to change your judgement when presented with new evidence? In this chapter we consider the time dimensions of decisions, assessment and risk. This includes sequences of decisions and implementing decisions through care planning and care decision pathways. Sometimes a time 'delay' is a valuable opportunity – under the helpful pressure of a timeframe – for productive problem solving. We discuss urgency and delaying decisions; contingency planning (*what if?*); planning retrievable *risk-steps*; systems for monitoring and retrieving a situation; recording; and evaluating the effectiveness of the decision. In terms of assessment and care planning, we often describe some of these activities as 'review'. We briefly consider the place of Bayes' Theorem as a model for taking account of new information to revise a judgement about the likelihood of a particular outcome. The focus is on the individual practitioner managing risk in the provision of care services and safeguarding. Risk cannot be totally removed or avoided; risk is an intrinsic component of everyday life. What we can do, and should do, is *manage risk*. Various dimensions of managing care risks with individual clients are discussed in this chapter. Legal aspects of care planning decisions and decisions where there is limited time are in Chapter 3. Prediction aspects of time (such as early intervention programmes) are considered in Chapter 6.

Time to make decisions

For some people, decisiveness is a virtue. However, taking time to reflect before 'jumping to conclusions' can also have its benefits. Most decision theory is about choice at a point in time. This is a severe limitation for application in professional decision making in social work, where a common feature is processes of decision making over time (Killick, 2008). We make decisions at various stages of the care process such as referral, initial assessment, complex assessment, specialist assessment and so on. *Risk* must be considered as part of an ongoing process of (re-)assessment rather than as something 'done and finished' although, on the other hand, delaying a decision for no justifiable reason is not good practice. Many decisions are incremental, like pruning a hedge rather than like cutting down a tree. A decision process over time gives the opportunity to learn and to adjust the course of action to suit the needs of the particular client and family as we weave a path between the challenging *brambles*. Incremental decisions over time are suited to a problem-solving approach; that is, engaging the client and appropriate others in addressing issues of concern, perhaps during the assessment process. There are often options to consider such as whether to seek more information by undertaking further interviews or by involving other professions. The scale and frequency of cycles of assessment and care planning that are appropriate to the case at hand need to be conceptualised. Decisions may be made with your line manager under pressure in order to avert a crisis by providing some practical response. Over time, several such emergency decisions may be made.

We can view the emphasis on assessment as a continuous process rather than a single event (DH and DfEE, 2000) in this context, although assessment is only meaningful as a process to inform a decision and subsequent action. There has been concern that the welfare of children in state care has been allowed to drift because of a lack of coherent longer-term decision making. Sometimes the care process is complex involving a range of professions – for example, in relation to chronic conditions. In many care contexts, it is important to have a periodic overview (review) to monitor the direction that the small decisions are leading and compare the direction with overall goals.

In effect, as social workers we operate within processes of decision making that form pathways of actions, care and intervention (Health and Social Care Change Agents Team, 2003). Each decision forms part of a larger picture encompassing many other decisions by clients, families, concerned others, professionals and organisations. Decisions need to take into account the outcome of previous decisions and the response to previous interventions. Key issues arise as to whether we have enough information to make a satisfactory decision. What prompts or requires a decision to be taken now rather than delayed?

An important feature of professional practice is that doing nothing *is* a decision! Once a referral is received, making no response is either a decision to do nothing (yet) or an administrative error. Avoiding a decision is not good decision making (Anderson, 2003), although delaying a decision for a clear, justifiable reason may be wise on occasions.

Professional risk-takers cannot escape liability simply by omitting to take decisions. Failing to detain someone with a severe mental illness, who might injure him- or herself is as much a decision, and the taking of a risk, as would be the positive act of detaining a patient.

(Carson and Bain, 2008, p97)

A delay in responding to a particular client may of course be due to competing pressure from other clients and the imperative to prioritise scarce time and resources in accordance with professional or organisational priorities. Often, time is required to build a working relationship with a client so that you can clarify your role and identify options, opportunities and objectives with clients. Some time taken and used effectively at an earlier stage may be better for longer-term care (risk and safeguarding) planning and be a more efficient use of your time and agency resources overall.

It may also be useful to delay making a major decision in order to test a hypothesis as part of the problem-solving process with the client. You might try something that should reveal desired information about the problem and a potential way forward, and evaluate what is learned, such as within some family therapy models. You could consider parallels with your general medical practitioner trying out a medicine on you for the first time and asking you to come back a short while later to see how effective it is and what the side effects are. Assessing the ability and motivation of a client and family to change in response to a planned intervention requires a time period. *Trying to identify the issues in a case too soon may have the effect of having too little information, while waiting too long may mean that opportunities for effective and swift interventions are missed* (Hollows, 2001, p14). In some situations, it is better to recognise explicitly the need for early, shared information from which hypotheses about problems may be formulated. An essential skill is to assess the urgency of making a decision. A more urgent decision may be more likely to require an *intuitive* approach, whereas a decision with serious consequences, but where there is more time, might need a more *analytic* approach and use more formal decision processes (Hammond, 1996).

Time pressure: what is 'enough' information for the decision?

Questions arise as to how far we go in gathering more information. It is always tempting to keep on *assessing*, perhaps as an avoidance of making the decision and hoping that problems will be resolved. The general principle in professional assessment is that we want to gather suitably comprehensive information in our assessment in order that an informed decision may be made.

There is a cost in terms of time and resources to gathering *comprehensive* information for a decision. Time may be the limiting factor in a crisis situation, and a decision often has to be made with less information than you would like. Gaining fuller information in order to make a *better* decision has a cost (for the client as well as for the professional), which can be weighed against the possibility of an improved decision with the fuller data that might be expected from a particular exercise in gathering further information (Baumol, 2004). These are known as *satisficing models* of cognitive judgement (Gigerenzer and Goldstein, 1996), and are an example of *heuristic models* of judgement introduced in Chapter 6.

A judgement with adequate time might be based on seeking maximum benefit, whereas a judgement under time pressure might be made to satisfy a small number of minimum criteria. When we are under time and resource pressures, we may select the first available option that meets a small number of essential criteria (*satisficing model of decision making*) so as to make a *good enough* decision (Newell and Simon, 1972). Experienced professionals usually learn to see *patterns* in situations and assess the relevance and importance of particular features more quickly than novices who have to think through more slowly the implications of each new piece of information in relation to each other factor. Indeed it may be that heuristics are widely used by those with experience in that domain of decision making (Dhami, 2003) (see Figure 9.1).

CASE STUDY 9.1

Crisis and the satisficing model of decision making

As the social worker on emergency out-of-hours duty I received a telephone call from the police at about 1 a.m. one night as they had been contacted (by a neighbour) regarding two children under eight years of age with no adult. The police officer drove me to the locality. I called with the neighbour and saw the children.

The parents were apparently out drinking. The children's names were not on the child protection register. The children suggested that they would be happy to stay with their grandparents who lived a short car drive away. The police had no concerns about the grandparents. The neighbour confirmed that the grandparents visit regularly, indicating at least some active relationship with the family.

I visited the grandparents and on the basis of the interview I was satisfied that it would be safe enough to leave the children with them overnight until the matter could be dealt with more fully in the morning. I took the children in the police car to the grandparents' home.

Practice Question: In an 'emergency' situation, under time pressure and necessarily with limited information, what criteria do you use to make a decision?

Planning care to manage risks

It is important to demonstrate that care planning, like assessment, is based on the best available professional knowledge. However, it must also be recognised within the care planning process flowing from decisions that prediction is always fallible. There will always be inaccuracy in our judgements, and this fact needs to be part of our care planning.

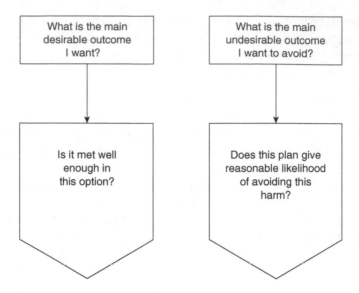

Figure 9.1   Satisficing model of decision making

CASE STUDY **9.2**

Creativity in care planning

Mrs Stevenson (68 years) has had mental health problems for many years. She was diagnosed with motor neurone disease and was subsequently admitted to hospital to have a PEG tube inserted. In planning for her discharge it was apparent that she had no family support to assist with practical tasks such as medication administration via the PEG tube. Mrs Stevenson was advised that the district nurses and home care workers were unable to administer medication. I enabled Mrs Stevenson to make a private arrangement for this part of her care needs.

- *What aspects of care planning in your role require particular creativity?*

- *How would you advise a new social worker to go about this?*

A key question in safeguarding decisions may be regarding the prospects of the parents or other family members changing their behaviour sufficiently, and sufficiently quickly, to avoid the need to take protective measures. It is important that we draw on the best available evidence about the effectiveness of interventions and typical recovery journeys. The decision process can involve setting targets and reviewing progress within an overall safeguarding plan. There are particular issues in agreeing to work on protection without allocating blame, such as issues of exaggerating the dangers and setting the standard too high. A high level of professional interpersonal skills is required for negotiating interventions in high-risk situations. Increasingly, standardised documentation is being used for care planning to:

- give structure to the implementation of decisions;

- help to ensure clarity about goals, roles, tasks and timescales; and

- assist in planning the review of decisions.

There are dilemmas in designing care planning documentation if one wishes to have standard documentation that covers a wide variety of types of intervention. Sometimes it is easier to have a care planning tool that relates to a particular service or type of intervention. One question is how flexible or loose the care planning document should be in terms of linking to an equivalent assessment tool. Greater structure does more to standardise best practice in implementing decisions. However, care planning tools need to ensure that they provide sufficient flexibility to accommodate the variation in client needs, strengths and contexts, and the variation in provision of services, systems, roles, etc.

Care plan objectives and decision outcomes

A challenge facing us as social workers is being creative in care planning, so as to use our skills effectively to engage the strengths of the client and family. One consideration in deciding on an intervention is the extent to which particular problems are likely to be responsive to intervention. This may depend on client capacity to learn, client motivation and resources for learning and growth, your own skills and the public or voluntary resources that you can harness for this client.

ACTIVITY **9.1**

Values and care plan decisions

Consider a decision making situation on your caseload

- *How well do you understand the care-related values of the client?*

- *How well do you understand the care-related values of the family or other informal carers?*

- *How well do you understand the values of other professionals or organisations in relation to the proposed care plan for this client and family?*

It is important to have clear objectives to implement the decision and, as far as possible, ones that motivate the client. The goals of the care (risk, safeguarding) plan are the justification for taking risk; they need careful thought and justification through, for example, a mutually understood agreement with the client and a basis in sound research or professionally acceptable theory. In protection decisions the safeguarding mandate needs to be clear. Clarity of care plan objectives to implement the decision is an essential and integral part of reasonable, reasoned risk-taking decision making as part of our professional role. An acronym to assist in thinking about care planning objectives is SMART.

- **Specific** – clarity about the facts and the expectations of the client, carer and professionals in plain language in relation to the care plan and its inherent risk-steps.

- **Measurable** – specifying care plan outcomes that can be measured so that you will (all) know when it has been achieved so as to minimise misunderstanding.

- **Achievable** – the care plan goals and risk-steps agreed (if possible) are designed to be successful and to build confidence amongst all parties.

- **Realistic** – the care plan goals and risk-steps are designed to relate to the key issues or problems facing the client and the reason for social work involvement.

- **Time-bounded** – any estimates of risk are put in a timeframe, and the care plan goals and risk-steps are clearly specified in terms of timescale.

Managing risk: contingency planning

In situations where the likelihood of harm is relatively high, contingency plans should be prepared in advance. In other words, consider *what if?* Having a *plan B* helps to relieve some of the pressure that the professional may feel for *plan A* to succeed. Learning to 'anticipate the unexpected' is a skill that is perhaps more easily 'caught than taught'. Identifying the 'early warning signs' that a problem is developing is an aspect of practice that requires a combination of the best knowledge of risk factors and their interactions combined with the wisdom from reflective practice.

CASE STUDY **9.3**

Planning for contingencies

Alfie Giddens is aged 12 years and has severe learning and physical disabilities. There are concerns about his parents' ability to meet his needs. Mr Giddens has periods of very low mood. The recent review of his care plan concluded that an increase in the respite care arrangement would be very beneficial in relieving pressure on the parents and on Alfie. However, due to demands on the service, this need could not be met. In order to manage the level of risk without this service in place it was agreed that I as the field social worker should visit more often.

- *Identify a recent case where a lack of resources has necessitated a change of care plan.*

- *How was this unmet need recorded and used to contribute to service planning?*

Monitoring decision implementation

In this section we consider monitoring client well-being, the equivalent to going back to the doctor to see how your new medication is working and whether your symptoms have improved or worsened. The care planning process should have considered key issues relating to managing risks, such as:

- steps to reduce the likelihood of harm occurring, i.e. removing hazards, e.g. removing the slippery mat in an older person's kitchen;

- steps to reduce the seriousness of possible harm, i.e. protective measures, e.g. the older person wearing hip protectors in case of a fall.

Once a care (or *safeguarding* or *risk*) plan has been put in place, a key issue is how it will be monitored.

Monitoring is part of implementing and reviewing decisions. Monitoring means that someone with appropriate knowledge and skills gathers information about the situation at a time after the decision has been taken and acts appropriately so that this information is used to inform a review of the care plan. The person gathering the information directly may or may not be a professional. What is important is that the person gathering the information knows what it is they are looking out for and the threshold criteria for communicating concern to the appropriate professional. The main issues to consider in monitoring are:

- **Why** *monitor? Are the objectives SMART and standards clear?*

- **Who** *will monitor?*

- **What** *will be monitored?*

- **When** *will we monitor?*

- **Where** *will we monitor? Where will it happen and be recorded?*

- **How** *will we monitor? Who will be looking out for what?*

- **Cost** *of monitoring? What level of detail is required so as to monitor efficiently?*

CASE STUDY 9.4

Monitoring and adapting a care plan

Olivia Robinson (11 years) has special educational needs and is on the child protection register due to neglect and potential emotional abuse. Her mother misuses alcohol. An initial case conference created a safeguarding plan which offered various supports

(Continued)

> *(Continued)*
>
> *to Mrs Robinson and required her not to misuse alcohol while Olivia was in her care. Unfortunately, about four weeks later another incident of Mrs Robinson misusing alcohol while caring for Olivia occurred and the child had to be taken into care.*
>
> - *Identify a recent case where you had to adapt a care plan due to changing circumstances.*
>
> - *How do you define thresholds for making a decision that such a change is required?*

Managing risk: monitoring

Monitoring a situation in order to best anticipate problems escalating and do something about this is an intangible area of practice that requires further research. The pathways to serious harm are multiple and various, so it is particularly difficult in social work to anticipate harmful sequences of events (Sidebotham *et al.*, 2016). Roles and responsibilities need to be carefully defined, proportionate to the level of risk. Often the social worker will be the person who co-ordinates the care plan and also co-ordinates the monitoring arrangements. Ensure that your co-ordination is not perceived as you doing all the monitoring! A key issue is to identify an appropriate range of people to be engaged in monitoring. Ask questions such as:

- Who else is in the house or visits regularly? E.g. family, home care worker, neighbour, community nurse, podiatrist.

- Who else might monitor the person's welfare outside the home? E.g. school, day care facility, child minder, social club.

- What arrangement could you make to improve monitoring? E.g. requiring an infant to be taken to a health centre regularly as part of a safeguarding plan.

- What technology might assist in monitoring risk? E.g. telephone call system, home security system, medicines management.

In these monitoring arrangements it needs to be clear:

- which professional is responsible for co-ordinating the arrangements;

- what is expected of other professionals, support staff and others;

- what action should be taken by anyone concerned about a deterioration;

- how deterioration or improvement will be measured;

- what evidence is required of deterioration or improvement (e.g. safeguarding);

- what the thresholds are for decisions or actions;

- when the arrangement will next be reviewed.

It is important not to place too much reliance on informal arrangements, and that non-professionals are not asked to do things beyond their job remit and training.

Managing risk: strengths perspective

In the midst of the concerns about risks of harm, do not neglect to consider a strengths perspective. Strengths may mitigate risk factors. Consider the strengths of the individual, the family, neighbours and wider contacts such as church and voluntary organisations. Various dimensions of community strengths need to be considered, such as resilience and motivation. Engaging the family in developing improved relationships and more supportive arrangements is time consuming, but extremely valuable in terms of long-term care and mutual support within society. In terms of managing risk, a focus on engaging the client and family leads to a focus on dimensions of practice, such as understanding the family context and engaging the wider family, building trust, identifying strengths to 'wrap around' the risks and discussing practical ways to communicate in crisis (e.g. 'who would you speak to if ... <a particular increasingly concerning situation arose>?').

Risk-steps

Any definition of risk has to include a timescale, and the time periods between monitoring can be thought of as *risk-steps*. What could go wrong between monitoring points, i.e. within that risk-step? These risk-steps can be thought of as retrievable time intervals for reviewing the decision. Data on critical time periods can inform risk intervals. If, for example, a mother is being required to bring her young child to the health visitor for check-ups because of child protection concerns, how are you deciding on the time intervals between check-ups?

CASE STUDY 9.5

Telephone monitoring

Mr Smith has returned home from hospital after a broken femur sustained during a fall. There are general concerns about his well-being but he is adamant that he wants to return home. He has an emergency call alarm system that he can use to alert his daughter who lives nearby. Also someone at the local Good Morning Ballytown service for vulnerable older people telephones him each day during his recovery period to check on his well-being. If they get no answer, then the daughter is called and told of this. If he were to fall and be unable to call his daughter with the emergency call system, the longest period that he would be left lying would be 24 hours before a family member was alerted.

CASE STUDY 9.6

Child welfare monitoring by a school

A 7-year-old girl, Khyra Ishaq, was kept prisoner and starved to death by her mother and her partner despite them having a (locked) kitchen stocked full of food (Tweedie, 2008; Bennett, 2009).

- *If it was an aim of the school-based social work or education welfare system to monitor such extreme neglect, at what time intervals would a child of this age typically need to be monitored in order to prevent death through starvation?*

- *What information could you use to estimate the required monitoring period for an 'average' build and ability of child who was aged (a) 14 years; and (b) 4 years?*

- *How might this monitoring best be achieved?*

Managing risk: care decision pathways

As we consider monitoring sequences of decisions and monitoring the implementation of decisions we are gradually building up a picture of a care journey for an individual, now often called a care pathway. Looked at in terms of co-ordinating a number of interventions, we might specify normal timescales for assessment and provision of specialist services such as rehabilitation. For more complex situations, we may have to consider decision points to choose between different options as well as timescales for this care journey. This then has parallels with *decision trees*, but with a time dimension added. There are various examples of care pathways, such as in relation to mental illness in the community (Goldberg and Huxley, 1979) and older people experiencing a crisis, such as a fall (Urgent Care Pathway Working Group, DH, 2007). One definition and some uses of integrated care pathways (adapted from Bandolier, 2009) are as follows.

- An integrated care pathway (ICP) is a multi-disciplinary outline of anticipated care, placed in an appropriate timeframe, to help a patient or client with a specific condition or set of symptoms move progressively through a treatment or helping experience to positive outcomes.

- Variations from the pathway may occur as professional freedom is exercised to meet the needs of the individual client.

- ICPs are important because they help to reduce unnecessary variations in client care and outcomes. They support the development of care partnerships and empower clients and their families.

- ICPs can also be used as a tool to incorporate local and national guidelines into everyday practice, manage risk and meet the requirements of clinical and social care governance.

Approaches to managing complex care pathways is something that needs to be considered in the design and use of assessment tools (Taylor, 2012b), particularly in adult social care services. Where there are several professions involved, facilitating an effective multi-professional review process can become challenging.

Re-assessment and changing your judgement

We began this chapter by considering sequences of decisions as *incremental decision making.* Sometimes, the stage of the case requires a change of decision-making perspective. For example, the early stage of a safeguarding situation may require an approach that might be conceived as *protecting this individual and others*. Once a decision has been made that the child needs to be protected (by whatever statutory means) then the mind-set may have to change to consider *balancing benefits and harms*. In other words, the decision now involves balancing options rather than considering dangers against threshold criteria.

One aspect of changing a decision that has been studied is known as *sunk costs,* which is when a decision maker continues to invest resources in a previously selected course of action even though it is now perceived not to be the best option (Chapman and Elstein, 2000, p194). It is a common human trait that we are tempted to keep to the status quo and renew our efforts to achieve the option already selected rather than write off the lost effort.

CASE STUDY **9.7**

Changing your mind in the light of new evidence

Mrs Wallace is a single mother living with her 5-year-old daughter Penny. Mrs Wallace suffers from depression and abuses alcohol. Her care of Penny gave sufficient cause for concern that the child was taken into care. A case conference has been convened to consider the advisability of Penny returning to live with her mother at this time. The factors that would influence my judgement to favour a return home include: whether there is robust evidence that Mrs Wallace no longer has an addiction problem; whether Mrs Wallace engages with a member of the community addiction team to address her addictive behaviour; whether there are reliable arrangements that can be put in place whereby family or neighbours will look after Penny when Mrs Wallace is drinking.

A reason why we may change our decision is because of new information. A key issue when we are involved in a volatile or deteriorating situation is to consider what evidence would be required for you to change your mind (for example, about safety in a protection situation or a vulnerable person living alone). As individuals, as well as in our professional roles, we like to hold on to our opinions. A change of opinion can be painful and hard work; it needs to be justified to ourselves if not to others. It is much easier emotionally and in terms of time and effort to go along with the flow. Sometimes we might make an intuitive judgement and then (subconsciously) focus on information that supports our opinion, tending to discount contradictory evidence. The integration of diverse new evidence and the management of the review (re-assessment) process is a key dimension of managing risk in terms of monitoring client welfare and risk-steps that are reasonable and achievable.

CASE STUDY **9.8**

Intensity of review depends on potential impact of the decision

The social worker had assessed a profoundly disabled young man living with his mother and two siblings in relation to public funding for social care services. The needs were considered under the provisions of the Chronically Sick and Disabled Persons Act (1970) and the regulations in England for making direct payments such that the individual (and his family) could purchase care for themselves to meet the needs. The court confirmed that the intensity of a review (re-assessment) should depend on the profundity of the impact of the decision to be made.

(R (on the application of KM) (by his mother and litigation friend JM) v Cambridgeshire County Council *[2012] UKSC 23 (1218-1236 All England Law Reports [2012] 3 All ER)* confirming the judgement of Langstaff, J in R (on the application of L) v Leeds City Council *[2010] EWHC 3324 (Admin) at [59]*)

Bayes' Theorem (**en.wikipedia.org/wiki/bayesian_probability**), named after the Revd Thomas Bayes, is a mathematical method for revising an estimate of the probability of an event (for example, a particular harm) in the light of new evidence. Bayes' Theorem allows us to start with an initial estimate of the probability of an event – for example, a person in a particular age group killing someone – based on population figures. If we have an assessment tool with known sensitivity and selectivity, then we can combine these figures to give a more accurate revised estimate of the likelihood of harm occurring. The detailed mathematics is beyond the scope of this book; the interested reader is referred to Macdonald (2001, Chapter 14) for a more detailed discussion of the application of Bayes' Theorem in social work. The essential message is that new information needs to be given due weight, irrespective of whether it confirms or contradicts our previous judgement about a situation and the mechanisms at work creating or sustaining the problem. The impact that the new information should have may be greater or lesser than one might think intuitively. Information about increased risk to a low-risk case may require a larger revision of judgement than the same increase of risk in a high-risk case.

Recording decisions and hindsight error

The ongoing recording of accurate, retrievable information and the summarising of information at intervals are the cornerstones of monitoring the quality of care (Taylor and Devine, 1993, p81). Record-keeping is essential to the social work task to improve the effectiveness of service delivery and to enable accountability for standards of practice, use of time and resources. Recording is also vital in decision making, in order to:

* record client involvement;

* record the client's understanding of the process;

* record decision processes;

* record options considered and choices made;

* provide an opportunity for reflection and evaluation; and

* provide evidence of factors taken into account in case of subsequent challenge.

The rationale for decisions needs to be retained in client records, as well as the option actually chosen. The context, options available, client views, discussion and reasoning about decisions are all an important part of the decision process that should be recorded in contentious cases. When something *goes wrong*, people and organisations may want to blame someone (or another organisation). The micro-scale interactions of interviews are rarely captured in written records. What is required is a sufficiently accurate record of critical issues that influence decisions, particularly if you are concerned that there are possible harms with serious consequences, particular contention, or interest in the decision from politicians or the media. It is worth paying close attention to how you word your records. How does it sound out of context? What impression might your words convey months or years later if a tragedy occurred?

* *It was a gamble, your honour, and it went wrong ...*

* *It is disappointing that it went wrong, your honour, but we had to take a risk ...*

* *We are sorry about the harm that occurred, your honour, but we were facing a dilemma ...*

(Cf. Carson and Bain, 2008)

It has been shown through many experiments that after an event, people think that what actually occurred was more obvious before the event than it appeared at the time or to people who do not know the real outcome. Typical experiments in this field present two groups of people with an identical decision scenario (for example, with a harm to be avoided) except that one group is told the *actual outcome* in terms of harm, and the other is not. Almost always the group that knows the *actual outcome* thinks that people should have been able to predict that outcome to a greater extent than does the other group. Recording needs to address the temptation to *hindsight error*, which faces every inquiry reporting on a tragedy.

If you have reason to believe that an event is possible, but unlikely, then you should declare and record that likelihood in an explicit form. Unless it can be shown that your estimate was inappropriate it will prove powerful in discouraging any court or other form of inquiry from utilising hindsight in order to conclude that the harm, which has now occurred, was more likely than it then seemed. The court has to try to avoid hindsight; why not help it?

(Carson, 1996, p10)

There are many problems with relying on memory for the detail of events, decisions and sequences of these, hence the need for contemporaneous records.

The sooner after the event a record is made, the more accurate it is likely to be, which is why your case records are so important. If they are detailed, objective and compiled promptly, there is a good chance that a court will regard them as accurate accounts of the events concerned. In cases with a significant amount of contemporaneous documentary material, courts are likely to accept as accurate evidence which matches the documents.

(Seymour and Seymour, 2007, p128)

ACTIVITY **9.2**

Memory and recall of events

- *Try to remember what you were doing this time last week.*

- *What time did you leave work this day last week?*

- *If you think you know, is that because you remember or because you usually or always leave at that time?*

- *What time did your last journey by car or public transport begin and end?*

- *Where did you last park your car other than at home or work?*

- *Describe the people sitting near you the last time you were on public transport.*

Records assist in evaluating progress with implementing decisions. They also support reflective practice so that you can learn from each situation and transfer learning to other similar situations.

Chapter summary

- Individual decisions are sometimes part of a sequence of decisions that can be viewed as a *care decision pathway*. Unnoticed incremental decisions may result in drift, where the care plan direction is not clear.

- It is always worth considering the degree of urgency that attaches to a decision. Delaying a decision for a sound, rational reason may be wise on some occasions.

- When a decision is being made, it is valuable to consider *what if* and to plan for the most likely or most serious contingencies.

- A series of short, retrievable risk-steps may be better than larger steps so that professionals are more likely to be aware and able to respond.

- Systems for monitoring (and retrieving) a situation and recording are key elements of decision processes.

- Re-assessment (review) should include reconsideration of the facts as well as the response to the intervention. The intensity of the review should be proportionate to the complexity of the case.

- The effectiveness of decisions should be evaluated, but avoid the error of assuming that a good outcome demonstrates a sound decision process or that a harmful outcome demonstrates a poor decision process.

- Inquiries into tragedies often fall prey to this *hindsight bias*. Key implications are that contemporary recording must take account of the range of contextual factors, and that the quality of decisions must be judged on the quality of decision processes, not outcomes.

FURTHER READING

De Luc, K. (2000) *Developing Care Pathways: The Handbook Vol. 2 – The Toolkit.* London: Radcliffe Publishing for National Pathways Association.

A handbook giving valuable practical guidance on developing integrated (multi-professional) care pathways to support improvements in care where clarity about timescales and decision points is helpful.

French, S. (1989) *Readings in Decision Analysis: Chapman & Hall Statistics Text Series.* London: Chapman & Hall/CRC.

This book contains a section on the application of Bayes' Theorem to decision making for the enthusiast who wishes to know more.

Middleton, S., Barnett, J. and Reeves, D. (2001) What is an integrated care pathway? *Evidence Based Medicine*, 3: 1–8. **www.bandolier.org.uk/Conflicts%20Folder/What_is_an_ICP.pdf**

A clear, well-written article outlining key elements of integrated care pathways in health and social care.

Chapter 10

Managing decisions, assessment and risk: support, blame and learning

Some people are very decisive when it comes to avoiding decisions.

(Francis, quoted in Chang, 2006, p201)

Introduction

Employing organisations are both the strength and the bane of social workers. The vast majority of social workers are employed in organisations rather than being in solo private practice, and the organisational dimension is an essential component of practice. Although the focus of this book is on practice, it is essential that the practice focus is linked to a positive approach to managing the integration of practice with the organisational context and that social work managers recognise their role (and develop their knowledge and skills) in relation to the subject matter of this book. This chapter considers the effective management of decision making and risk, including the demand to 'account for resources and priorities' (cf. Taylor, 2006b). Tragedies and inquiries are considered in relation to the lessons of studies of hindsight bias, and the implications for practice including recording. We emphasise the need for managers and senior professionals to provide effective support for reasoned, reasonable decision making by front-line professionals that empowers clients to achieve care (risk, safety) plan goals. This includes the use of supervision in managing decision making. This chapter discusses issues facing organisations in developing decision support systems, policies, training, strategies, and appropriate engagement in inter-organisational working. The management of decisions by the organisation is viewed within the framework of social care governance, creating a learning organisation, and managing effective risk-taking decision making through learning from safeguarding incidents, including near misses as well as tragedies. The responsibility of all professional staff to evaluate decision quality and contribute within their own role to sound decision making and risk management as an aspect of social care governance is emphasised.

Accountability to society

It is quite proper in a democratic society that as social workers, just as members of any other profession, we are held to account for our actions. Inquiries, courts, questions by politicians and the activities of the media are all valuable, when used appropriately, in playing their part in providing checks and balances that ensure as far as possible that the activities of professionals and organisations are carried out responsibly, justifiably and fairly. As professionals, we have a responsibility to manage decisions:

* in accordance with the values and standards of the profession;

* to the best of our knowledge and skills, within available resources;

* in good faith and in the best interests of the client;

* in partnership with clients, families and other professionals as far as possible;

* utilising sound principles and processes; and

* using robust professional knowledge to inform our decisions.

The challenge for society is to have effective accountability mechanisms in a complex arena of rights, risks, needs, resources, knowledge, skills and values yet also support professionals to carry out an effective job. Many decisions involve a measure of risk-taking, just as in everyday life. This cannot be avoided. Even if it could be avoided, taking risks is essential to both children and adults for growing and learning by tackling new challenges and enjoying the richness of life.

Safeguarding and service prioritisation decisions sometimes take place in a context of conflict. This conflict may be through a challenge to professional and organisational decision making at a case conference or through a judicial process. Aggrieved parties may express their anger through various legitimate and illegitimate means. In a democratic society, the rights of citizens are enshrined in law which is enforced through the courts. Decisions by social workers and other professionals are open to challenge by those regarded as having a legitimate right. These mechanisms have a valuable place when used properly. This context of conflict is part of the price we pay for democratic accountability, but it can be stressful for those workers and managers who are the unwilling focus of attention. For the practitioner, there is a clear message that if you believe that a politician or the media have an interest in a particular case or that a complaint may be forthcoming, you should inform your line manager as soon as possible (DHSS, 1998). Politicians and the media have a proper role, but their involvement challenging decisions in an individual case can waste valuable public resources when we have to respond to issues raised on the basis of limited and misleading information. In a few countries (but fortunately only a very few) there is an unhealthy style of reporting among some of the prominent media which seems to seek to undermine the profession and ultimately provides little benefit to clients. It is essential that members of the profession, as well as those in management roles, seek to support each other so as to best provide a confident and competent service to clients and families, whilst at the same time recognising the need for appropriate accountability to society.

Tragedies and hindsight

When a tragedy occurs – such as a child homicide or homicide by a person with a mental illness or learning disability, or a potentially preventable death of an older person – an inquiry may be held and a detailed report produced. Inquiry reports can be useful learning tools. The narrative (story) approach is accessible; professional readers can empathise with the misfortune of victims and the professionals who might possibly have been able to protect them. *The narrative approach can prove effective for students since it portrays the 'real' world of practice with its resource constraints, movements of personnel, difficulties in communication and general realignment of services, policies and imperatives* (Stanley and Manthorpe, 2004, p10).

There are also limitations to learning from inquiry reports. Professions and organisations need to learn from good decisions and near misses as well as extreme situations of tragedy. Because of the frequent unrealistic expectations about predicting harm, inquiries can fuel the exaggerated allocation of blame. It is difficult after the event to appreciate the challenges that were faced at the time, including limitations of information, time and resources. *Hindsight bias* has been well researched, and occurs when, after the event, decision makers inflate the probability that they would have got the answer correct if they had been making the decision at the time (Chapman and Elstein, 2000). *Some of the more reflective inquiry reports acknowledge the distinction between hindsight vision and the viewpoint available at the time to professionals under scrutiny* (Stanley and Manthorpe, 2004, p3). An inquiry report that avoids hindsight bias more than most is Perry and Sheldon (1995). What seems *obvious* in hindsight often did not seem so obvious to many sensible people at the time! With hindsight, the influence of other important factors at the time, such as the feared reaction of family, politicians and media if a stronger safeguarding intervention was used, fades into the shadows in the light of the knowledge that the outcome is tragic.

> *If a decision involves risk, then even when one can demonstrate that one has chosen the unarguably optimal course of action, some proportion of the time the outcome will be suboptimal. It follows that a bad outcome in and of itself does not constitute evidence that the decision was mistaken. The hindsight fallacy is to assume it does.*
>
> (Macdonald and Macdonald, 1999, p22)

A good decision makes effective use of the available information and of the context of systems, legal, policy and procedural aspects. Even this will not prevent harm from occurring on every occasion given the inherent unpredictability of human behaviour and the limitations of the knowledge we have available. Blame should not ensue if a sound decision-making process has been used, regardless of the outcome. We can only do our best to reduce the likelihood and consequences of citizens harming each other; we will never be able to prevent all harm whilst respecting basic human rights.

Decision making in social work is inherently complex, and the potential for predicting emotive human behaviour is limited. We must accept that there are limitations to predicting human behaviour, even with the best actuarial tools and the most experienced professional opinion. We need to establish realistic expectations of ourselves as a profession so that we can be confident in the face of adverse publicity that might seek to convey the impression that a social worker should be some sort of fortune-teller.

We have limited control over the situations that we address compared to a hospital or a school environment. It is no more reasonable to blame a Director of Social Services for the homicide of a child by his or her parents than to blame a Chief Constable for failing to prevent all crime or a Chief Education Officer for failing to prevent any child leaving school without a string of academic qualifications! Organisations and professionals can only take reasonable, reasoned decisions based on the information and resources that they have available at the time. Of course, the relevant senior managers of organisations need to be held to account for their particular responsibilities, such as having in place robust systems, policies and procedures, how they have used resources or the way that staff recruitment and retention issues are being addressed. However, that is a far cry from believing that we can predict with precision the behaviour of each individual in society, especially when they are experiencing distress or anger, or struggling with addiction or mental health problems.

The real strength of inquiries is to inform improvements to future decision-making systems and services (Cambridge, 2004). For a valuable summary of reviews of child abuse inquiries, see Reder and Duncan (2004), and for useful summaries of inquiries into homicides by people with mental illness, see Sheppard (2004). We need to learn from tragedies. But to learn best from inquiries, we must not fall into a blame culture where some politicians or some of the media turn their (understandable) distress into anger at social workers or other professionals because of their own inadequate understanding of the limitations to predicting individual human behaviour.

Organisation culture and defensive practice

The experience of a *blame culture* in society and organisations does not promote good practice. We cannot predict accurately, although we could improve our estimates with the use of sound statistical approaches and more rigorous research as discussed earlier.

> *Social work decisions are often problematic balancing acts, based on incomplete information, within time constraints, under pressure from different sources, with uncertainty as to the likely outcome of the different options, and the constant fear that something will go wrong and the social worker will be blamed.*

(O'Sullivan, 1999, p3)

It is estimated that there are approximately 80 child homicides each year in England and Wales (Creighton and Tissier, 2003; see also Creighton, 2004a, 2004b). If there are very approximately 160 local authorities responsible for child protection work in the same geographical area, then they should each expect on average to have one child homicide every two years. Given the variation in risk factors, some authorities can expect to have more than that and some less. This is (sadly) what our society is like at the present time. To suggest that professionals have necessarily failed in their responsibilities because someone in our society kills someone or commits suicide is nonsense. Predicting individual human behaviour using actuarial and clinical risk factors is better than guesswork or tossing a coin, but is a long way from being precise.

ACTIVITY **10.1**

The culture of society and your organisation

- *Do you feel that you are working in a 'blame culture'?*

- *What are the main sources of pressure that you think would influence you to feel 'blamed' if a tragedy ensued after a decision?*

- *What do you think are appropriate mechanisms for accountability of professional and organisational decision making in your ideal society?*

- *What might be done by the social work profession to support you more in professional judgements and decision making?*

- *What might be done by your employer to support you more in judgements and decision making?*

- *What might you do so that if a tragedy were to ensue, your judgements and decision-making processes would still be regarded as sound?*

There is a major challenge to managing risk and decisions in organisations because uncertainty is, by definition, unpredictable, and particularly so for complex systems such as health and social care. In complex systems there are many variables (factors) that come into play in any situation that we wish to consider, and these factors are inter-dependent on each other. The state of the factors is not readily transparent and they change with time due to other factors, so it is hard to measure the 'state' of the organisational system even when we limit our interest to just one part of it.

In relation to professional social work decisions the amount of information to be considered in relation to the client, family, community, society and the employing organisation is vast. The human brain uses heuristics to process and deal with this array of data efficiently. Not only are different heuristics used for different situations, the heuristic decision processes themselves are adapted to improve the progress of the decision making, with new information. Whilst the focus is on cognitive aspects of decision making, the emotional and motivational aspects must be considered also.

To be effective in decision making in this complex arena a good decision maker needs to undertake broad planning for anticipated decision situations that considers the multiple aspects that may be relevant, as well as both short-term and long-term effects. Policies introduced to manage one aspect of risk and decision making will have implications for other aspects of the functioning of the organisation. To be effective in managing decisions and risk, managers need to consider the causal factors and dynamics in the organisation that have led to 'poor decisions', as well as the resulting situations themselves. The difficulty is that it is impossible to isolate one element of the organisation and act on that alone. There will always be an effect on some other aspects of the service and its support systems.

Managers seeking to fulfil their responsibilities for managing risk and decision making – whether or not conceptualised as social care governance – face some of the same challenges as practitioners. The information available for making the decision (about managing decisions and risks) will never be complete. When assumptions are made, as they will have to be in order to act, it has to be recognised that the assumptions may not be correct. In seeking to change – improve – the organisation in terms of its management of risks, you face the difficulty that a large complex organisation is mostly inert and sluggish in responding. The effects of an intervention through a new policy are seen only after a delay, and it is difficult to monitor the effects of the policy change in terms of success and failure.

Organisations and the managers in them have a particular responsibility to create a working environment that is supportive to front-line professionals in managing risk and decisions. The profession needs to develop an inclusive culture that respects all members of the profession, whether they are in practice, management, regulation or education and training. The challenges of the external world are so pressing that it is essential that members of the profession in diverse aspects of the work pull together rather than criticise each other publicly. An appropriate and helpful knowledge base on risks and effectiveness should be made available to managers and practitioners. Best practice ideas and models should be disseminated to encourage innovation. Assessment tools should be selected on the basis of supporting the professional task rather than primarily for the needs of central data gathering to monitor service outputs. The relationship between the completion of any assessments that are mandatory in the organisation and thresholds for decisions (for example about provision of particular services) needs to be clarified as part of the responsibility of the organisation.

Principles for managing risk and decisions

It has been argued that weaknesses in understanding and analysis of risk taking are a cause of poor decision making in conditions of uncertainty and lead to professional risk-aversion (Carson and Bain, 2008, pp227–32; Carson, 2012a). Effective risk management requires the leadership necessary to support appropriate risk-taking. One step forward was the recent approval of ten *Principles of Risk-Taking* by the Association of Chief Police Officers for England, Wales and Northern Ireland (ACPO, 2011) (see Figure 10.1). These principles were cited favourably by the *Munro Review of Child Protection* (Munro, 2011) in England and Wales and by the government in its response to that review. These principles emphasise the impropriety of judging a risk decision by its outcome and are suitable for adaptation to a variety of social work contexts. Whilst the management of risk has become more common in social work (Taylor and Campbell, 2011), the conceptualisation of managing decisions is still in its infancy. In England, the material generated for learning from serious case reviews, serious adverse incident reports and equivalents has grown to the extent that the volume of material has itself become almost unmanageable (Devaney *et al.*, 2013). The principles developed by David Carson (2012b; summarised in Figure 10.1) provide a distillation of wisdom from practice viewed in a legal context, providing a framework for taking a holistic view of proactive management of risks and decisions that will support front-line practitioners.

---

1. Inaction, as well as action, can cause harm; professionals have a duty to take apt risk decisions relating to their clients.

2. If it is a 'risk' then harm will sometimes result irrespective of how well the decision was made and managed.

3. Professional risk-taking requires an assessment and comparison of the possible outcomes – both the benefits and the harms, their degrees and their likelihoods – and the ability to manage the resulting decision.

4. Risk-taking involves relative values, including competent clients' wishes, as well as an imperfect science.

5. Professionals' risk decisions, and risk management, must satisfy the requirements of the civil law of negligence (i.e. they must be supportable by a responsible body of co-professional opinion).

6. When judging risk-taking, any difficulties (e.g. emergencies or dilemmas) must be accounted for and hindsight must not be allowed to influence assessments or infer conclusions about blame.

7. We can learn more from good than from poor practice so professional risk-taking, which achieves goals or prevents losses, deserves to be recognised and accounted for.

8. We need to identify and learn from all the significant causes of our successful and unsuccessful risk decision making and risk management, including systemic and cultural factors, as well as the sufficiency of resources and support.

9. It is improper to draw conclusions about blame and responsibility merely from findings about cause. Causation concerns science; responsibility involves moral or legal attribution.

10. To promote an open, supportive and learning work culture, professionals should be entitled to cite and rely upon these principles in any proceedings.

   • How applicable are these principles to social work in your organisation?

   • Would adoption of a comparable set of principles support good practice?

   • Which principles present the greatest challenge in your working environment?

   • What steps might be taken towards your organisation adopting a set of risk principles?

Figure 10.1   Ten principles for risk management

(Adapted from Carson, 2012b)

Evaluating decision processes

When evaluating decisions the focus must be on understanding the information available at the time; the knowledge and skills of the individuals involved; the context of systems and culture within which the decision was taken; and the purpose of the decision. If a crisis occurs, organisations may be under pressure to blame someone even though practice and decisions may have been sound in the circumstances. A poor outcome does not necessarily mean that a poor decision has been made; conversely, a good outcome does not necessarily mean that a good decision has been made. What professionals and organisations should be held to account for is the quality of the decision process. Overall, better decision processes based on what is learned through integration into practice of research, theory and lessons from near misses and tragedies will result in better outcomes. But even then, a safe outcome is *not* guaranteed on every occasion just because the process is reasonably robust (i.e. meeting the minimum standards expected by society through the law and professional standards at the time) or even if it is exemplary. The quality of decisions attempting to predict human behaviour cannot be judged by their outcome; they should be judged on the way they were reached – that is the decision processes.

A decision to take a risk must be justified against likely benefits, recognising that sometimes harm will occur. If the chance of *success* (for example in successfully returning children home or some independence step for people with a disability) is 99 per cent, then on average harm will occur in one in 100 decisions, or ten in 1,000 decisions. Would you never take a decision with a 99 per cent probability of success? How high a probability would you require, given that absolute certainty is not possible? The potential benefits to the client in terms of the opportunities for growth, change and development needs to be one part of the equation in making a decision.

The danger is that the intense blame culture will lead to defensive practice (Carson, 2012a). It is noteworthy that after a public outcry when a child homicide inquiry report is published the rate of admission of children to state care often increases markedly. Organisations need to take a firm stand against such a blame culture in order to support sound professional decision making that balances rights and risks, needs and available resources in a reasoned and reasonable decision process. *If people are entrusted to take difficult decisions regarding risk taking, it must be accepted that they cannot later be blamed if the outcome leads to tragedy* (Norman, 1980, p27).

ACTIVITY 10.2

Prompts for reflection on judgement and decision processes

- *What are the main aspects of the context that are driving this decision?*
- *What additional information would I like to have?*
- *Is this a crisis and would it help to delay a decision?*

(Continued)

(Continued)

- *What legal issues are important including capacity, human rights and health and safety?*

- *How can I most effectively engage with key stakeholders?*

- *How are the values of the client, family and society (through you and your organisation) influencing the decision making?*

- *What responsibilities are there for safeguarding, informing and respecting rights of various parties to the decision?*

- *What knowledge base is informing my judgement and what more could I usefully know?*

- *What biases might be influencing me, and how can I counter these?*

- *What assessment tools, guidelines and other decision aids might help?*

- *Are coherent plans evolving from the decision processes over time?*

- *Is the decision process being managed effectively?*

- *What am I learning from this judgement and decision process?*

- *What can the organisation learn from this decision process?*

Policies and systems for managing decisions and risks

For the organisation, the challenge is to take steps to avoid a blame culture and to provide systems and processes that support sound decision making and which provide opportunities for learning from good practice, near-misses and tragedies. Social workers who undertake management roles have a particular responsibility for articulating the nature of risks in social work, and the professional response. Whereas *risks* in such domains as flight safety, machine construction or health care are essentially about the side effects of a planned activity or intervention, the *risks* considered in social work are primarily those posed by family members or citizens to each other. The risks of concern are not normally attributable to the side effects of social work intervention as they are, for example, in terms of the side effects of medicines (Taylor and Moorhead, in press). In the types of safeguarding (protecting) functions carried out by social workers, the fundamental pathways to harm are beyond the control and detailed knowledge of the professionals involved.

> *The pathway of harm thus consists of the interaction between the child's [or adult client's] vulnerability and any risks posed by the parents, carers or others; this interaction takes place within the context of the wider social, physical and cultural environment within which the child and family live. Such interactions may result in*

harmful actions or omissions by perpetrators or carers, which, in turn, may lead to the child [or vulnerable adult] being seriously or fatally harmed.

(Sidebotham *et al.*, 2016, p24)

The dangers of over-proceduralising professional activity in an attempt to 'minimise risk' are slowly becoming apparent (Munro, 2011). Excessive mandatory procedures de-skill staff; stifle creative, therapeutic problem solving with clients; are time consuming; and sap morale. There are problems created by imposing a heavy bureaucracy in order to try to prevent error. A corporate approach will influence the practice of staff. The board or authority with its non-executive representatives of the public, and senior managers, have a key role in establishing a culture that supports professional staff in good decision making. The organisation culture can be changed by establishing sound overarching policies to support professional decision making, which in turn support reasonable risk-taking by clients.

Decision management policies help to give a consistent approach for clients, staff and managers. Policies exist in most organisations that assist in certain aspects of decision making, such as:

- health and safety;
- child and adult protection procedures;
- assessment and care planning in complex cases;
- communication and recording;
- administration of medicines;
- lone working; and
- violence at work.

What is required is an overarching approach that supports reasoned and reasonable risk-taking decision making, recognising that this is intrinsic to human life – including that of our clients – and is hence intrinsic to social work. Elements of a comprehensive decision support policy might include the following.

- Service mandate, mission and objectives – the legal mandate, mission and objectives of the organisation, including the main clientele and services, what is (not) permitted by law and mentioning the (varying) limitations of resources.

- Service principles and values – principles to support staff that can be made available to the media, including the right of clients to take risks and potentially controversial issues such as criminality, integration in society, sexuality and alcohol.

- Decision support policy and procedures – standards and support for practitioners and managers in making decisions to use to justify decisions if criticised, particularly when there are pressures of time and resources.

- Knowledge base to inform decisions – the provision of a professional knowledge base (for example, through training and computerised library resources) that can be used to inform decision making.

- Risk strategy context – the location of the policy in relation to governance, management support, supervision, communication, integration across the organisation, training, organisation development, monitoring of services and unmet need, recording and accountability.

- Endorsement – by the appropriate professions and commissioning bodies and a statement about protocols for decision making with other organisations.

Such policies need to seek to do justice to the professional task of supporting prudent risk-taking as the essence of decision making with and on behalf of clients. Where there is dispute over appropriate support, a conflict resolution mechanism is required, such as referral to senior management or a multi-professional decision-making body.

> *We propose that arrangements be put in place to manage more complex situations where there are different views held between the individual, the family carers or the professionals to seek agreed solutions ... Such arrangements will enable all those involved to explore the issues and set arrangements which go as far as possible in meeting the individual's aspirations whilst balancing the needs and risks to themselves and others.*

> (DH, 2007, p4, para. 7)

ACTIVITY **10.3**

Decision support policies

- *Identify policies in your organisation that contribute to supporting professional decision making where the possibility of harm must be weighed against potential gains for clients and families.*

- *What are the strengths of the decision support policies?*

- *What are the gaps where policies would be helpful?*

Decision policies and allocating scarce resources

Resources for health and social care are finite; the demand for services is potentially infinite. Decisions about one client may need to be taken in the light of a decision about the needs of another client when resources are scarce. Social workers and their managers have to *account for resources and priorities* (Taylor, 2006b). Scarce resources, whether funded from the public purse or charitable funding, must be allocated between clients in a manner that can be demonstrated to be fair and meet other legal standards.

Decision policies can assist in meeting the challenge of allocating scarce resources by giving greater consistency of decision making. They help to ensure fairness between different clients. The use of decision policies assists individuals and organisations to make decisions efficiently and consistently, and is a valuable defence against challenge, complaint or litigation. A decision maker may reduce anxiety and stress by identifying the features of this decision that are common to previous decisions, including decisions by others, and hence normalise the activity. A decision policy regarding rationing of services would normally include an explicit system for prioritising services, usually by date order of application, and an explicit system for dealing with high priority, urgent cases that jump the date-order queue.

Such decision policies enable organisations and individuals to be more consistent in their decisions, and thereby have greater credibility. Credibility and staff morale can plummet if decision policies are overridden by managers in the face of irrational external pressures. A major challenge is managers giving in to 'squeaky wheels' regarding service prioritisation, thereby allowing people to jump the waiting list by applying political or media pressure. The people who suffer most in this situation are the *hidden clients* who are on the waiting list for services and who have to wait even longer when someone queue-jumps by soliciting external advocates who exert pressure to change the decision on the basis of emotive or political pressure rather than new evidence, logic or justice. Quite apart from the moral considerations of the needs of the 'unseen' people on the waiting list, this reinforces staff fears that their manager will not back them up when a tragedy occurs (as it will inevitably, someday, for someone!).

Inter-agency protocols for decision and risk management

Various government documents emphasise the importance of co-ordinated decision making across organisations, sometimes expressed in terms of co-ordinated assessment processes (e.g. Social Exclusion Task Force, 2008). Co-ordinated decision making requires clarity about roles and responsibilities and a common language.

> To change the culture around the provision of services and address the fear of blame among staff, we propose that organisations and their partners consider establishing a joint choice, empowerment and risk policy that promotes more open and transparent practices. It will need to be supported by senior leadership and shared across the organisation and their partners. There need to be clear lines of accountability and support within the professional team and the respective responsibilities of the council, primary care trust, independent and voluntary sector organisations, the member of staff and the individual using services. The policy would best be supported by appropriate working arrangements and systems.

(DH, 2007, p6, para. 16)

Where organisations seek to collaborate, each must be clear about its own function. Collaboration provides a valuable opportunity to learn about the roles of other organisations and to clarify language so as to reduce misunderstanding.

Agreements between agencies need to cover the following key areas:

- *clear procedures and protocols for joint working;*

- *clear roles and responsibilities;*

- *a clear management structure for accountability;*

- *a commitment to good quality supervision which includes professional development;*

- *agreed policies and procedures for delivering the service that everyone uses, including responses in crisis;*

- *agreed documentation for the needs assessment process, care planning, risk assessment, monitoring and review, and recording;*

- *information-sharing policies with partner agencies;*

- *timely process for resolving complex funding issues – panel with senior decision making/ budget holder;*

- *processes for managing complex cases;*

- *processes for conflict resolution.*

(DH, 2007, p41, box 3.9)

Governance: risk and quality of decisions

Organisations have governance systems in order to carry out their corporate responsibilities for managing risks and quality improvement. Professionally, we have clinical and social care governance, which is about *organisations being accountable for continuously improving the quality of their services and safeguarding high standards of care and treatment* (DHSSPS, 2002, p3, section 6; cf. DH, 1996). Social care governance incorporates both risk and quality dimensions as integral components (Flynn, 2002; Alaszewski, 2003; DHSSPS, 2003). Ensuring the quality of decision and risk management is part of the organisation's governance responsibilities (Taylor *et al.*, 2015). Every individual member of staff has a role in contributing to the governance processes in the organisation; for professionals, supervisors and managers this particularly includes decision management and risk management (Taylor and Campbell, 2011).

Professional supervision, support and training

A key mechanism for support and accountability of practice decisions is professional supervision (British Association of Social Workers, 2011). Social workers in all grades and roles need effective supervision so as to:

- have access to a professional relationship that will provide support, challenge practice, enhance learning and demand accountability as appropriate;

- create a *sounding board* for complex professional decisions as a prompt to consider other perspectives and knowledge to inform the decision;

- provide effective direction and monitoring of work, with clear accountability for levels of decision making;

- benefit from a wider range of relevant research and theory through the knowledge and experience of the supervisor to challenge bias;

- ensure that practice is in accord with professional and organisational standards;

- enable communication and gate-keeping to supports (such as legal advice) and some aspects of multi-professional and multi-agency working and management decision making;

- improve practice with insights from a broader knowledge of legislation, policies, procedures, systems and work cultures; and

- provide an opportunity for professional growth and learning for supervisee, supervisor and the organisation through the application of professional knowledge to critical practice issues.

To make the best use of supervision you should go prepared, not just with a list of issues but with a list of proposed responses and decisions in relation to those issues. You should have in mind some rationale for these proposed decisions, even if this is mental rather than in writing for less substantial issues. Supervision needs to attend to what has been observed and experienced by the social worker, and the emotion inherent in the helping processes. These are an essential forerunner to exploring the worker's intuitions and reasoning processes about the risks and decisions about proposed next steps.

As well as accountability and support for ongoing case management, some key issues to raise in a timely fashion at supervision might include:

- critical decisions;

- thinking through factors and issues;

- feeling over-involved with client and situation;

- client's issue is too close to a personal one;

- a stressful abuse situation;

- growing sense of vicarious traumatisation; and

- before stress and burn-out, ideally (see McFadden *et al.*, 2015)!

It is important to remember that as an employee you are acting on behalf of your employer. You must, therefore, stay within the functions, policies, procedures and direction from line management. You should, of course, express your own opinion and rationale for your judgements and debate these with your professional supervisor and line manager; you are not expected to be a passive dummy! You would normally expect to face disciplinary issues if you refused to follow your line manager's instructions, but it is possible that you could be criticised for failing to challenge the decision of a line manager (British Association of Social Workers, 2008, p5). If there is a difference of opinion, ensure that accurate records are kept.

ACTIVITY **10.4**

Plan your use of supervision

- *Write a list of points to discuss at your next supervision session.*

- *Make arrangements to meet if these are not made by your supervisor.*

- *What will you do if supervision does not happen as planned?*

- *What is the threshold for involving your supervisor in decisions (Carpenter et al., 2015)?*

As you have worked your way through this book you will probably have become aware of the many aspects of professional practice that interface with decision making. Ongoing training for various aspects of decision making is essential for social workers in all types of roles. From the perspective of a professional supervisor or manager it is important to note that, quite apart from higher moral considerations, an employer can be liable for failing to provide adequate supervision or support, thereby endangering the employee's health or safety (*Walker v Northumberland County Council* [1995] 1 All ER 737).

ACTIVITY **10.5**

Training and learning needs

- *How does your training and learning plan (for example, as part of re-registration requirements) need to incorporate topics related to decision making?*

- *What in-service and post-qualifying training courses are available in relation to aspects of professional judgement and decision making relevant to your work?*

- *What is the system in your organisation for identifying and analysing training needs, and how do your training needs get fed into this process?*

Communicating about risk and decisions in organisations

There are immense societal pressures to address risk issues and, sometimes, impossible expectations. Some politicians and media may pounce on care decisions where a complaint occurs. In this complex arena of conflicting demands and considerations – from the public, the client, the family, the organisation – the professional needs a robust and yet flexible framework to inform practice decisions such as we are developing in this book. Empowerment of patients and clients to make decisions is more effective if professionals are knowledgeable in their field and can communicate effectively about their judgements and their decision-making knowledge, skills and systems (Stevenson *et al.*, in press). As an individual professional, you should abide by the protocols of your organisation regarding public communication for your own protection as well as the need to support your employer in maintaining public confidence so that the organisation can function most effectively in serving society.

In the interests of justice and confidentiality there are proper limitations on the freedom of organisations and professionals to discuss publicly details of individual cases. The more general challenge is to communicate the nature of the professional task with its possibilities and limitations, and the complexity of information that must be *taken into account* in the critical types of decisions that we make. The challenges in predicting harm to individuals are little understood by the public, as is the interplay between rights and intervening to safeguard (Kitzinger and Reilly, 1997). Effective public communication and education by employers, government and the profession needs concerted attention. Perhaps as a profession we need to be ready to provide *bite-sized* information to the media in a form that the public can readily understand when a relevant issue arises. Many topics – such as the apparent expectation of being able to predict when a parent is going to kill their child – are so recurrent that materials could be ready prepared.

The learning organisation and evaluating decisions

Both individual practitioners and organisations need to create a culture of learning from decisions (Senge, 1990). We need to learn from good outcomes, near misses, staff insights and regular feedback from the public and other stakeholders, as well as tragedies (see Table 10.1). Whistle-blowing schemes assist employers in their responsibilities for developing safe systems of work. For practitioners, the opportunity to learn from the outcomes of their interventions is often neglected. Evaluating the decision process and the decision outcomes may be called *review* in relation to individual clients and families. Schön (1996, p26) describes reflective practice as *thoughtfully considering one's own experiences in applying knowledge to practice while being coached by professionals in the discipline.* There are organisational as well as individual professional responsibilities in seeking to base practice decisions on best evidence (Taylor *et al.*, 2015). This includes looking for creative ways to promote good practice as well as responsibilities to work with clients to evaluate outcomes of service provision (Sidebotham *et al.*, 2016). In a culture where 'evidence-based practice' is not only an ideal but is expected, organisations need to become more savvy about learning from their processes, including 'double-loop' learning (Argyris, 2005), where there is a growing shared understanding of the dynamic service delivery environment. What front-line professionals need from their managers is good management conducted with the same professional integrity, sensitivity, robustness and recognition of complexity that is expected in practice.

Table 10.1 Criteria for evaluating and reflecting on decisions

---

- What helped and what hindered the decision making?
- What might have gone better?
- Was the decision context appropriately taken into account?
- Did the client and family participate effectively in the decision making including explicit discussion of values and probabilities of desirable and undesirable possible outcomes?
- Was there client consent and ownership of the decision?
- Was effective use made of accurate client and family information?
- Was there appropriate consideration and management of the time dimension such as delaying a decision, care (risk) planning and decision pathways?
- Was a purposeful and effective decision process created?
- Were other professions engaged appropriately?
- Was the decision in accordance with requirements of the law and the social work role (including health and safety, human rights and safeguarding functions)?
- Was there effective use of professional knowledge and models of decision making?
- Was bias avoided through reflective practice and appropriately incorporating best evidence in judgements?
- Was there appropriate use of risk factors, assessment tools and other decision aids?
- Was information presented as well as possible for the decision making?
- Were facts, opinions and knowledge brought together into a cohesive argument?
- Was there a systematic appraisal of the options available?
- Was there clarity about possible benefits and possible harms?
- Were decision outcomes monitored so as to adapt decisions appropriately?

(Adapted from Dowie, 1999; O'Sullivan, 1999; and other sources)

Chapter summary

- Sound decision making by front-line professionals requires support by managers and supervisors for reasonable, reasoned decision-making processes. That is the standard by which quality should be judged. No one can foresee the outcomes, but we can use the information that we have to best effect.

- Professional supervision is a central element in managing sound decision making and empowering social workers in supporting clients to achieve care (risk, safety) plan goals.

- Organisations need to have decision support systems, policies, training and strategies as well as appropriate engagement in inter-agency working.

- A decision role for managers even more than for practitioners is to *account for resources and priorities* particularly in the allocation of scarce public or charitable resources across clients.

- The management of decisions may be viewed within the framework of social care governance, creating a learning organisation (including the evaluation of decision quality), and managing effective risk-taking decision making through learning from good outcomes as well as safeguarding incidents, and including near misses as well as tragedies.

- Principles are presented which summarise from a legal perspective key points to guide future development derived from inquiries into tragedies and other untoward incidents.

- All professionals have a responsibility to contribute within their own role to sound decision making as an aspect of social care governance.

- Individual professionals have a responsibility for ensuring that their judgements are based on the best possible knowledge of research, theory, policy and standards as well as of the client, context and services.

- Organisations have a responsibility for developing a culture of evidence-based practice and supporting staff with the best available knowledge from research, theory, policy and standards to inform their decisions.

FURTHER READING

Hawkins, P. and Shohet, R. (2000) *Supervision in the Helping Professions.* Buckingham: Open University Press.

This is a well-written book on the essentials of social work supervision.

Kline, R. and Preston-Shoot, M. (2012) *Professional Accountability in Social Care and Health: Challenging Unacceptable Practice and Its Management.* London: Sage/Learning Matters.

This attractively presented book explores the nature and meaning of accountability in the context of legal rules and codes of practice, and relates this to the knowledge and skills required to address dilemmas and tricky '*what if?*' issues.

Simmons, L. (2007) *Social Care Governance: A Practice Workbook.* Belfast: Department of Health, Social Services and Public Safety (Clinical and Social Care Governance Support Team) and London: Social Care Institute for Excellence.

This attractive workbook provides a helpful structure for teams, departments and organisations in developing social care governance arrangements.

Stanley, N. and Manthorpe, J. (eds) (2004) *The Age of the Inquiry: Learning and Blaming in Health and Social Care.* London: Routledge.

This book provides some interesting and useful perspectives on the place of inquiries in social work practice and management.

Taylor, B.J., Killick, C. and McGlade, A. (2015) *Understanding and Using Research in Social Work*. London: Sage.

This readable textbook is unique in focusing responsibility as much on organisations and their managers as on practitioners for developing practice that is based on the most robust knowledge. It contains much practical wisdom gleaned from experience as well as useful general principles.

Conclusion

Two things fill the mind with ever new and increasing wonder and awe: the starry heavens above me, and the moral law within me.

(Kant, quoted in Peter, 1980, p173)

The journey so far

This book has been about competent social work assessment, judgement, decision making, and working with risk. Decisions must be sound from the perspective of our profession and employers who may have statutory safeguarding functions, and roles as custodians of funding for services provided by the taxpayer or those who give to charitable causes. Many factors need to be considered in undertaking assessment and making decisions: systems; legislation and case law; regulations and guidance; policy and procedures; standards and principles; professional guidance and ethical codes; opinions of other professions; client perspectives and choice; family views; neighbours; voluntary and statutory resources; and professional knowledge based on research, theory and many varieties of learning from experience including inquiries, audits and governance systems. The pressures of the threat of legal action for negligence, sanction by a commission or inquiry, or interest by the media or a politician can create a *wariness of lurking conflict* (Taylor, 2006b).

Social workers have to manage complex ethical issues, dilemmas and conflicts. Probabilities, values, choices, law, knowledge and skills have to be combined in a complex dynamic interplay in making judgements. Evidence must be incorporated into practice judgements to inform safeguarding decisions, the selection of objectives for social work intervention, the choice of practice method, and advice to clients and families to inform their decision making. Nonetheless, risk-taking decisions are an everyday, inevitable part of being human, and hence are an everyday, inevitable aspect of social work decision making. The professional task includes supporting clients and promoting their well-being through reasonable, reasoned risk-taking. This creates tensions that are inherent in the professional task. Reasoned, reasonable professional judgement entails support for reasonable, informed client risk-taking, unless safeguarding duties and powers override or the client lacks decisional capacity or competence.

Theoretical sources and models

This book has drawn on a wide variety of theoretical and knowledge sources, selected as showing promise for informing social work practice. The diverse and growing study

213

of risk and uncertainty has led to concrete application, such as in terms of risk factors and our understanding of appropriate professional risk-taking. We have drawn on and developed understandings of assessment in social work incorporating both actuarial and professional discretion elements, and the social work role in relation to both specialist and holistic assessment tools, and collaborative assessment processes. Our discussion of judgement and decision making has focused on concepts and models that are most readily applied in social work (Taylor, 2012c). This has included the main branches of decision study (Bekker *et al.*, 1999; Beresford and Sloper, 2008).

- *Normative decision study* (such as *subjective expected utility theory*), which focuses on how rational human beings *ought* to make decisions, provides the basis for our thinking about *balancing benefits and harms* such as visualised in a *decision tree* (Chapter 7) and in making care (or safeguarding or risk) plans (Chapter 9) to assist in clarifying options, roles, values and responsibilities.

- Our discussion of supporting client decision making (Chapter 2) has encompassed the *naturalistic decision making* school of thought with the *envisioning the future* model to assist in clarifying the voice of the client.

- *Satisficing and decision policy models* have been incorporated into our discussion of safeguarding decisions (Chapter 6) and making decisions on limited information (Chapter 9) due to time and resource pressures.

- Our discussion of heuristics and biases within professional judgement (Chapters 5 and 6) has drawn on the school of *descriptive decision study* of real-world decision making as a model to support reflective practice and the use of professional knowledge. The use of multiple cues within professional judgement has drawn on *Brunswick's lens model* and the concepts of learning from experience have parallels in *recognition primed decision making*.

- We have used *prescriptive decision study* (aiming to improve decision making even if we do not use a specified rational model) in our discussion of assessment tools and the gradual growth of decision support systems in Chapter 4.

Overall, we have conceptualised our theoretical domain as *psycho-social rationality*, lying between strict actuarial prediction and the unstructured narrative explanation. This encompasses *heuristic* models and *fuzzy logic* models such as those developed by Brearley.

The professional needs to select an appropriate model, taking into account the type of decision and the types of factors that are important. Rather than risk getting lost in the detail, our general approach has been to focus on those aspects of theoretical models that are most likely to be useful for social work practice – for *doin' the stuff*, in the memorable words of John Wimber (2009)! In time, we may develop a unified model of decision making in social work such that these models come to be seen as simplifications (special cases) of the general theory in situations where fewer aspects need to be considered.

Practice issues

The task of engaging and supporting clients and families in working with risk and in making decisions is central to effective practice. Clients and families may be in a state of crisis when a social worker enters their lives and value a supportive sense of security as they engage in assessment processes that support problem solving. There are varying emotions for clients and workers facing uncertain situations and engaging in far-reaching decisions about family and life issues. We support clients and families in their decision-making processes using knowledge (perhaps embodied within assessment tools) that assists in understanding issues and clarifying options.

The law provides accountability in a democracy, supporting reasoned, reasonable decision making by professionals. We require an evidence base of professional knowledge to justify our judgements in critical situations. Statutory human rights need to be taken into account explicitly in decision-making processes and in the decision itself. Each professional needs to be sure that a client consents and has capacity to consent to whatever intervention is proposed unless explicit, justifiable safeguarding powers apply. The touchstone is to ask oneself: *what would a competent professional do?*

Assessment tools and other decision support systems are developing steadily to support gathering, collating and analysing information to assist in making a judgement. Assessment tools have become more sophisticated and are beginning to be integrated across professions and organisations, and to integrate specialist assessments into a holistic whole. Perhaps the areas where professional decision making in social work could be most obviously improved are in greater clarity about the purposes of assessment tools, and through the increased use of appropriate validated assessment tools in specialist areas. These then contribute to the holistic assessment process. During the past two decades, the use of computer systems has become more widespread, providing information to inform decisions. Information systems to manage client data are common even if they lack integration across settings and professions. Passive decision support systems are available in a few places; expert systems are rare. I anticipate that we will see increasing computerised support for our judgements and decision making.

Heuristics, or short-cuts, to deal with the complex and varying decisions are an intrinsic component of human judgement but can also lead to bias. Social work practice involves processing large amounts of information, some of it of questionable truth and authority. Reflecting on practice issues in the light of knowledge based on the best available research and theory, individually and through good professional supervision, is central to avoiding bias. We must face the challenges in using the best evidence to inform decisions. When there are limitations of time or resources, professional judgements may be based on information relating to a limited number of key criteria rather than on a comprehensive appraisal of all the factors. Detailed analytic decision making is not possible in every situation.

Trying to predict possible harm on the basis of experience (*clinical prediction*) is prone to more error than using *actuarial* risk factors based on rigorous research. However, even *actuarial* methods are weak at predicting the behaviour of individuals, although they are useful at a population level for planning services. With rigorous research, improved risk factors will become available to better inform our decision making. While actuarial and clinical risk factors should be used where available, their limitations should be recognised and acknowledged. Safeguarding decisions must be taken in the honest recognition that predicting human behaviour will always be prone to error, even though we could improve accuracy by using *actuarial* tools. Clarity about thresholds for interventions is required as we make these *criterion-based judgements*.

All of life involves taking risks. Supporting client decision making will involve risk-taking for the client, family, professional and organisation. We have to support clients to take reasoned, reasonable risks as part of our role in helping them to achieve worthwhile care-related life goals. We need to be able to justify risk-taking in relation to potential benefits and strengths that mitigate the likelihood or seriousness of harm as we *balance benefits and harms*. We also need to fulfil our legal and moral responsibilities to take reasonable care of our own and other people's health and safety.

Collaborative decision-making processes with other professionals and organisations (as well as with clients and families) are a feature of more important decisions. The distinct competence and responsibilities of each profession and organisation must be recognised within a general framework of seeking consensus and thus sharing risk. For *contested decision making*, models can support robust argument in contexts such as child care court proceedings. Timely, focused communication with your line management and professional supervisor are essential in these situations.

In social work we are well used to the time dimension in terms of taking time to engage clients and families in assessment processes; re-assessing situations; monitoring well-being and risk; and (increasingly) care pathways for clients. Sometimes, delaying a decision may be justifiable, but this is in itself also a decision. There are often options at a decision point in social work practice to seek further information or undertake some sort of trial run. Social work practice often involves multiple decisions over time, building up care (risk, decision) pathways. It is salutary to consider what evidence is required to change your mind about a situation! In some social work decisions, not only are we lacking full information but also there are time pressures so that *intuitive* models of decision making have their place as well as the *analytic* models that can be applied to weighing options in decisions involving fuller deliberation. Decisions need to be monitored and adapted over time, with appropriate processes for reviewing the implementation of decisions. Monitoring and review points can helpfully be considered as risk-steps and consideration can be given to contingency plans and how the situation might be retrieved if it starts to deteriorate.

Organisations have a responsibility to manage more serious decisions in a way that supports front-line professionals in their challenging tasks of supporting reasoned, reasonable, client risk-taking decision making and taking safeguarding decisions in emotional, contested situations. Organisations need to take positive steps to counter the blame culture that threatens to undermine professional practice and public confidence in the organisation. *No one* can guarantee good decision outcomes, but we *can* set standards for robust, justifiable decision processes which form the proper basis for accountability. There is a pressing challenge in communicating risk and educating the public about the strengths and limitations of predicting harm in a human service field such as social work.

Further learning

The aim of this book is to aid the professional social worker with a robust general framework of concepts to support continuing professional development. You should attend courses or otherwise learn about specific aspects of decision making, assessment and risk relevant to your role, in particular:

- child and adult protection knowledge, skills, policies and procedures;

- other protective frameworks for your area of work such as guardianship, enduring power of attorney, etc;

- human rights legislation and recent case law on negligence;

- risk factors, needs and effective helping processes for your own client group;

- decisional capacity and consent to care and treatment;

- your responsibility for health and safety at work, including personal safety for yourself and responsibilities to other staff;

- specialist assessment tools embodying sound research and theory; and

- clinical and social care governance and related policies and procedures (including professional supervision) for the management of decisions.

As you develop your career through post-qualifying studies you could, in relation to the topic of this book:

- explore more detailed aspects of the decision models presented here;

- consider the application of these decision models in more specialised settings;

- explore other decision models;

- develop skills in enabling others in judgement and decision making;

- contribute to organisation development activities such as working groups to develop systems, policies and procedures to support aspects of professional decision making; and

- contribute to developing professional knowledge to inform decision making, through research, audit, service evaluation, and by retrieving, appraising, synthesising and disseminating research by others.

Further research and development

A recent UK government report highlighted the lack of knowledge of what works that is available to social workers in making critical professional judgement

(Kirkman and Melrose, 2014). There is generally very limited investment in social work research by comparison, for example, with our colleagues in the health professions. Much further research is required on judgement and decision making in social work so as to explore potentially useful models and develop them to the stage of being tools for practice (Carroll and Johnson, 1990; Beach and Connolly, 1997; Taylor, 2006a; Taylor, 2012c). Some key issues for further research and development are:

- developing the application of models of judgement, decision, assessment and risk in social work; and developing a curriculum for qualifying and post-qualifying social work education and training;

- studying the impact of the typical crises encountered in social work referrals for client and family decision making;

- exploring the interplay between health and safety regulation, common law standards of care in relation to negligence, and social care decisions in areas such as provision of home care services;

- developing assessment tools with rigorous tests of validity and reliability, and with increased support for analysis of information to inform decisions, and exploring the potential of various decision support systems (Gillingham, 2015);

- looking at how types of knowledge such as research, theory, law, service availability and client context are used in various types of social work decisions and understanding better how experienced professionals recognise patterns and identify the most important factors for making a decision;

- undertaking robust studies of risk factors (including effect size), particularly dynamic risk factors that might be amenable to social work intervention, and strengths (mitigating factors); exploring the effective use risk factors; and making up-to-date best data on risk factors available to the profession to inform practice, management and teaching, such as through a web-hub;

- developing our knowledge and skills in synthesising knowledge (Taylor *et al.*, 2015) and undertaking systematic reviews of the best research on the effectiveness of social work interventions for identifiable types of client problems and on client, family and professional perspectives on care processes;

- studying multi-professional decision making in a way that will inform the development of professional knowledge and skills amongst social workers for this;

- exploring the time dimension of decisions, in particular the connection with care (risk) planning and care pathways, so as to avoid the over-simplification often inherent in decision models that consider options only at a single point in time;

- creating organisation policies that support reasoned, reasonable decision making by practitioners and managers in supporting reasoned, reasonable risk-taking decision making by clients.

Reflection: from novice to expert

Professionals increasingly need to articulate their reasoning in judgements and decision making. Our aim is reasoned and reasonable support for client decision making and sound professional decisions about safeguarding vulnerable people, based on facts considered in the context of values, principles, law, theory, research, policy and procedures. As professionals, we are on a journey where we learn from the interplay between experience and our professional knowledge base. There are encouraging signs that the expertise of social workers as a professional group is being better recognised, but at the same time there are challenges from some of the media and politicians in some countries. By reflecting on our practice in the light of professional knowledge – individually, with colleagues, on training courses and in supervision – we will improve our professional judgement and decision making in situations of risk (uncertainty) for the ultimate benefit of our clients, their families and our society.

Take-home messages

- Be clear about your role and responsibilities in relation to decisions, assessment and risk, and clarify this with your professional supervisor, line manager, other professionals, clients and families.

- Make yourself familiar with the relevant statutes, standards, regulations, guidance, policies and procedures relevant to the risk-decision situation and assessment task.

- Know how to use the decision processes in your organisation, including, in particular, professional supervision, and be proactive in your role in using them to foster engagement and mutual support.

- Maintain good communication with your professional supervisor and other professionals as well as the client and family.

- Consider the decision situation from the perspective of the various stakeholders, and the potential benefits, harms, mitigating factors and issues for each person.

- Maintain a reflective attitude within decision processes, aware of your own feelings, potential biases, pressures and influences.

- Evaluate the diverse sources of information relating to the risks and decisions within assessment processes, and use specialist assessment tools where appropriate.

- Work to base your judgements on as good a knowledge base as possible, including knowledge of risk factors combined effectively with professional wisdom from experience.

- Ensure that your judgements are reasoned and reasonable, bearing in mind legal and ethical dimensions, and not severely out of line with what experienced professionals might do.

- There is much creative thinking, ready for development by managers into applications, about how organisations can best support front-line professionals in their challenging task of making reasonable, reasoned risk-taking decisions in the best interests of clients and families.

Krogerus, M. and Tschäppeler, R. (2011) *The Decision Book: Fifty Models for Strategic Thinking*. London: Profile Books.

This concise book will appeal to anyone who would enjoy having two-page summaries of models of decision making to spark their imagination, covering categories such as understanding yourself and understanding others as well as models applicable to organisational and business contexts.

Appendix 1

Pointers in designing or completing an assessment to inform a decision in uncertainty

- Who is the client?

- Who are the key family members and other stakeholders?

- Is it a risk? From others? To others? To self?

- What is the issue for decision?

- How will the assessment process be managed?

- What are the main dangers (the undesirable outcomes to be avoided) for this individual, family, neighbours, other clients, other citizens, care workers, volunteers and the organisation?

- What are the options being considered?

- What are your statutory responsibilities and powers?

- What is the timeframe and degree of urgency, and what is the impact of delaying a decision?

- Clarify the role of the client in the assessment and decision process and how this will be supported, including issues of consent and capacity.

- Clarify your role as the social worker in relation to your supervisor, the client, family, other professionals and organisations.

- What are the main vulnerabilities (background hazards, factors that predispose the harm to occur)?

- What are the main trigger factors (situational hazards that might induce the harm to occur)?

- What are the main strengths in the client, family and neighbourhood?

- What are the mitigating factors that might reduce the likelihood or seriousness of harm (perhaps in relation to services that might be provided under each option)?

- What were the outcomes of relevant previous interventions and what has changed since then?

- What value (appreciation, benefit, dread, fear) does the client place on the various options?

- What value does society, the organisation and the profession place on the various options?

- What professional knowledge from research and theory is most useful and what conclusions do you reach?

- What is the likelihood of the benefit being achieved and harm being avoided based on your analysis?

- What are the views of the client and family on the options?

- How will you engage other professionals in the assessment process, and what are their opinions?

- What are the relevant organisational policies and procedures?

- What are the resource implications of each option?

- What is the contingency plan and how will this be initiated?

- What is the proposed monitoring and review arrangement?

(Developed by the author during teaching over the past
decade; uses ideas published in Brearley, 1982;
Kelly, 1996; Baron, 2008)

Appendix 2

Supported decision tool (Department of Health, 2007, pp50–1)

1. What is important to you in your life?

2. What is working well?

3. What isn't working so well?

4. What could make it better?

5. What things are difficult for you?

6. Describe how they affect you living your life.

7. What would make things better for you?

8. What is stopping you from doing what you want to do?

9. Do you think there are any risks?

10. Could things be done in a different way, which might reduce the risks?

11. Would you do things differently?

12. Is the risk present wherever you live?

13. What do you need to do?

14. What do staff/organisation need to change?

15. What could family/carers do?

16. Who is important to you?

17. What do people important to you think?

18. Are there any differences of opinion between you and the people you said are important to you?

19. What would help to resolve this?

20. Who might be able to help?

21. What could we do (practitioner) to support you?

Agreed next steps – who will do what

How would you like your care plan to be changed to meet your outcomes?

Record of any disagreements between people involved

Date agreed to review how you are managing

Signatures

When using the tool with the individual, consider carefully the following aspects of the person's life and wishes:

- dignity;

- diversity, race and culture, gender, sexual orientation, age;

- religious and spiritual needs;

- personal strengths;

- ability/willingness to be supported to self-care;

- opportunities to learn new skills;

- support networks;

- environment – can it be improved by means of specialist equipment or assistive technology?

- information needs;

- communication needs – tool can be adapted (Braille, photographs, simplified language);

- ability to identify own risks;

- ability to find solutions;

- least restrictive options;

- social isolation, inclusion, exclusion;

- quality of life outcomes and the risk to independence of 'not supporting choice'.

(Crown Copyright material is reproduced with
the permission of HMSO)

Appendix 3
Professional Capabilities Framework

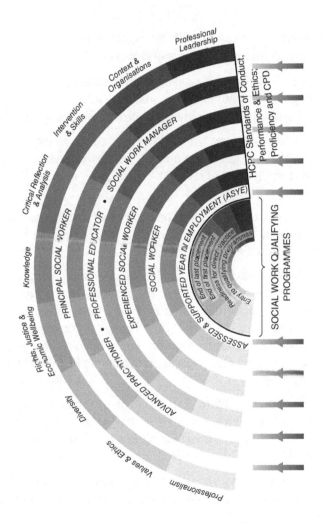

Professional Capabilities Framework diagram reproduced with permission of the College of Social Work.

Glossary of terms

Actuarial assessment Involves an algorithmic, objective procedure to inform a decision by combining measured risk factors (Grove and Meehl, 1996, p293).

Assessing risk The professional task, working with the client, family and others as far as possible and appropriate, in gathering and analysing information relevant to the possibility of harm and desired goals in order to inform a risk-taking decision about care.

Assessment The professional task, working with the client, family and others as far as possible and appropriate, in gathering and analysing information – about the client problem and context in the light of relevant knowledge – in order to address problem and plan care.

Assessment tool The written document that shapes what information is gathered for an assessment. The term 'instrument' is used for a comparable document research rather than practice purposes.

Care plan (Case plan) This term is used to include plans to safeguard individuals and to support clients to take reasonable, reasoned risks as well as other forms of planning care such as where the focus is deciding about long-term care or provision of public resources such as home care. The term is used here as a generic term to include local and contextual variations such as 'protection plan', 'hospital discharge plan', 'prison discharge plan', 'safeguarding plan', 'home care services plan', 'individual risk management plan', 'case plan', etc.

Clinical factors in prediction Factors about a client, family or situation widely recognised by professionals through experience as having an impact on the likelihood of the undesirable harm occurring in similar situations but which have not been tested or measured, and which are therefore not established risk factors.

Clinical social work Professional social work with individuals, particularly where there is a therapeutic or counselling focus rather than, for example, community development, group care or care management.

Dangerousness The seriousness and likelihood of harm being caused by an individual or group to others or to property.

Decision frame The psycho-social factors and events that give the decision and risk situation its meaning, limitations and possibilities.

Decision making A conscious process (individually or as a corporate exercise with one or more others) leading to the selection of a course of action from among two or more alternatives.

Decision management The systems and process of the organisation (including professional, risk-taking, policy, procedural, strategic, communication, resource, legal and financial aspects) that support accountable professional judgement and decision making for the benefits of clients and society, and that enable continuing learning as a means to improve the quality of decision making.

Decision outcome What happens as a result of a decision, whether intended or not.

Decision policy A rule created by an individual or an organisation so as to standardise the response to future decisions that have similar features.

Decision tree A visual aid to illustrate the component parts or sequence of questions (or tests) which comprise a judgement or decision-making process. A simplified form of *decision tree* without a time element is a way of visualising or calculating the probability and value of different options (such as for care or intervention alternatives). A *fast and frugal tree* is a particular type of *decision tree*, using the least number of steps in a sequence for an efficient decision.

Descriptive approaches to studying human judgement Studying how people make judgements in the 'real world', without assuming any prior model of how decisions would be made if 'rational'. See also *Normative* and *Prescriptive* approaches.

Direct care risks This includes all types of risks that relate to the direct care of clients including those relating to:

1. standards of care (including provision of appropriately trained staff and skill mix);

2. ascertaining the facts (including ensuring that care plans and interventions are appropriate, and confidentiality);

3. consent to treatment (including ascertaining capacity to consent);

4. injury arising from failure in communication with clients and internally; and

5. working beyond one's competence (including provision of supervision, training and support) (cf. DH, 1993).

Expected utility see *Subjective expected utility*.

Fast and frugal heuristics Rules of thumb for judgements that exploit structures of information in the environment and which are simple enough to work effectively when time, knowledge and computational ability are limited (Goldstein and Gigerenzer, 2002).

Fast and frugal tree A *decision tree* that uses the least number of steps to reach a robust judgement or decision, based on principles of *fast and frugal heuristics*.

Framework for decisions, assessment and risk This book outlines a framework for the main considerations and component parts of the professional tasks involved in undertaking assessment leading to decisions in a context of risk or uncertainty. The main parts of the framework correspond to the chapters of this book.

Fuzzy logic When risks are brought together in a model that considers the relationship between predisposing factors (vulnerabilities), precipitating factors (triggers) and strengths (mitigating factors) but without quantifying either values or probabilities.

Hazard Something that may cause harm (HSE, 2016).

Health and safety risks This includes all types of risks that relate to health and safety requirements including:

1. provision of a safe place of work;

2. having safe systems of work (including in relation to personal safety);

3. control of substances hazardous to health; and

4. provision of information, instruction, training and supervision (cf. DH, 1993).

Heuristic *A heuristic is a strategy that ignores part of the information with the goal of making decisions more accurately, quickly and frugally (i.e. with fewer pieces of information) compared to more complex methods* (Gigerenzer and Gaissmaier, 2015, p913). This may be contrasted with the use of 'actuarial' tools based on statistical weighting of factors (such as risks of harm) relevant to the decision (Taylor, in press). See also *Psycho-social rationality*.

Hindsight error Assuming that because there is an undesirable outcome then the decision process must have been flawed, without taking due account of the information available at the time and the context of the decision.

Image theory A theory of decision making that proposes that individuals use three successive stages or images (values; life goals; tactics) as frames of reference through which to make a judgement, using successive stages only if the judgement is not made at an earlier stage (Beach and Connolly, 1997).

Indirect care risks This includes all types of risks that relate to indirect aspects of care such as:

1. security risks (including risks to personal safety of staff, clients and others);

2. fire risks;

3. risks arising from buildings, plant and equipment;

4. risks arising from waste; and

5. control of infection risks (cf. DH, 1993).

Integrated assessment system A system of assessment whereby there is more than one level of assessment, according to complexity of need and risk, and which co-ordinates specialist assessments into a holistic overview for analysis and decision making (cf. Taylor, 2012b).

Judgement The considered evaluation of evidence by an individual using their cognitive faculties so as to reach an opinion on a situation, event or proposed course of action based on values, knowledge and available information.

Likelihood see *Probability*.

Managing risk The professional task, working with the client, family and others as far as possible and appropriate, in reaching a judgement and participating in a decision-making process and its implementation, monitoring and review to support a client or act to protect a client in care planning that involves risk taking. See also *Risk management.*

Monitoring Gathering information about the situation at regular time periods after the decision has been taken so as to initiate revision of the care plan if appropriate.

Normative approaches to studying human judgement Starting from a model of how people ought to make judgements if they are 'rational' and then studying ways in which they follow or deviate from this model. See also *Descriptive* and *Prescriptive* approaches.

Organisational risks This includes all types of risks that relate to the organisation being able to fulfil its purpose or mandate including:

1. the exercise of statutory functions;

2. internal communications within and between teams and departments;

3. communications with external bodies;

4. legal liability and maintaining public credibility;

5. provision of goods and services to other organisations;

6. financial risks; and

7. information systems (cf. DH, 1993)

Planning risk see *Taking risk*.

Prescriptive approaches to studying human judgement Exploring ways to improve decision making without seeking to use any particular model or understand how the decisions are made. See also *Normative* and *Descriptive* approaches.

Probability A numerical measure of the strength of a belief that a certain event will occur (adapted from Baron, 2008, p104). Normally the term 'probability' is used where there is data available about how frequently this type of event has occurred in the past and the term 'likelihood' is used when this event has not occurred before. This distinction depends on the definition of what is a similar event.

Problem solving Inventing, finding and creating options between which to select as part of the decision process.

Professional judgement When a professional considers the evidence about a client or family situation in the light of professional knowledge to reach a conclusion or recommendation.

Protective factor By contrast with a risk factor (q.v.) this is a factor that correlates with less probability of harm occurring. The terms 'mitigating factor' and 'desistance factor' (in criminal justice) are also used.

Psycho-social rationality A way of conceptualising the domain of being 'rational' that lies between an exclusive reliance on quantified *risk factors* and exclusive reliance on a descriptive, narrative approach by researching and developing ways in which professionals can use *risk factors* in practice. See also *Heuristic* and *Structured professional judgement*.

Review When an *assessment* is repeated, this is often called review. One difference from an *assessment* is that the effects of the planned intervention also need to be evaluated.

Risk A time-bounded decision-making situation where the outcomes are not known and where benefits are sought but undesirable outcomes are possible. Sometimes contrasted with *uncertainty*.

Risk assessment see *Assessing risk*.

Risk cluster The consideration of clusters of risk types as a way that the human brain processes multiple risks. This may be considered as a dimension of psycho-social rationality, that is, a rational approach to human judgement that is not based on the balancing of the utilities and likelihoods of every potential benefit and harmful outcome (Taylor, in press). See also *Psycho-social rationality*.

Risk communication The exchange of information between individuals receiving services, family members and professionals about possible harm and potential benefits of a course of action, usually in relation to a decision about a possible health and social care intervention. The term *risk-benefit communication* is also used.

Risk-benefit communication The exchange of information between individuals receiving services, family members and professionals about possible harms and possible benefits of a course of action, usually in relation to a decision about a possible health and social care intervention. Compare the more familiar term *risk communication*.

Risk factor Factors about a client, family or situation that have been shown through thorough research to correlate with the undesirable harm occurring to a significant extent.

Risk management The systems and processes of the organisation (including professional, decision-making, policy, procedural, strategic, communication, resource, legal and financial aspects) that support accountable professional judgement and reasonable risk-taking for the benefit of clients and society, and that enable continuing learning from mistakes and near misses as a means to improve safety and performance. See also *Managing risk*.

Risk planning see *Taking risk*.

Risks The situations of uncertainty that face an organisation providing social care services, including professional social work services. See *Direct care risks*; *Health and safety risks*; *Indirect care risks*; and *Organisational risks*.

Satisficing A model of cognitive judgement based on identifying the first option or factor that satisfies the essential criterion to be met. This is in contrast to *expected utility* models, which premise that a judgement is based on weighing up the values and likelihoods of every factor for and against the option.

Social construction of risk The ways in which the seriousness or likelihood of undesirable events is understood by people when it does not correspond in some way with established factual measures of the likelihood of that harmful outcome (Stevenson *et al.*, in press).

Structured professional judgement An approach to conceptualising professional judgement that uses (statistical, actuarial) risk factors but also incorporates the (clinical, intuitive, learned by experience) judgement of the professional (Bouch and Marshall, 2005). See also *Psycho-social rationality*.

Subjective expected utility A model of human judgement which posits that a rational person weighs up the options in terms of the benefit (utility) that is expected from each course of action. The attractiveness of the options is normally calculated by multiplying the value (utility) placed on that option (often calculated in monetary terms) by the probability of that outcome coming to pass (Savage, 1954).

Sunk cost bias When a decision maker continues to invest resources in a previously selected course of action even though it is now perceived not to be the best option (Chapman and Elstein, 2000, p194).

Taking risk A positive activity working with the client and others as far as possible to weigh the values and likelihoods of possible harms and benefits of a decision, within professional principles and the frameworks of society and the organisation, to achieve reasoned and reasonable care goals where harm may occur, taking reasonable steps to identify and minimise harm.

Threshold judgement A dichotomous (two-option) judgement about whether a situation is one side or the other of a 'line' or threshold. The threshold may relate, for example, to an aspect of compulsory intervention on behalf of society or to eligibility for services.

Trigger factor A situation that may precipitate the occurrence of an identified undesirable event.

Uncertainty Where the probability of an event (usually the outcome of a decision) cannot be calculated. Sometimes contrasted with *risk*, used in the sense of meaning the probability of an unwanted decision outcome.

Vulnerability The susceptibility of an individual to suffer from an identified, undesirable event.

References

ACPO (Association of Chief Police Officers) (2011) *Appendix A: ACPO's statement of risk principles* (pp97–8), in Munro, E. *The Munro Review of Child Protection Interim Report: The Child's Journey*. London: Department for Education. **www.gov.uk/government/uploads/system/uploads/attachment_data/file/206993/DFE-00010-2011.pdf**

Agathanos-Georgopolou, H. and Browne, K. (1997) The prediction of child maltreatment in Greek families. *Child Abuse and Neglect*, 21 (8): 721–35.

Alaszewski, A. (2003) Editorial: Risk, trust and health. *Health, Risk & Society*, 5 (3): 235–9.

Alberg, C., Hatfield, B. and Huxley, P. (1996) *Learning Materials on Mental Health Risk Assessment*. Manchester: Manchester University and the Department of Health.

American Psychiatric Association (2003) *Practice Guideline for the Assessment and Treatment of Patients with Suicidal Behaviours*. Arlington, VA: APA.

Anderson, C.J. (2003) The psychology of doing nothing: forms of decision avoidance result from reason and emotion. *Psychological Bulletin*, 129 (1): 139–66.

Andrews, R. and Gibson, R. (2005) *Hamlet by William Shakespeare*. Cambridge: Cambridge University Press.

Argyris, C. (2005) Double-loop learning in organizations: a theory of action perspective (pp261–79), in Smith, K.G. and Hitt, M.A. *Great Minds in Management: The Process of Theory Development*. New York: Oxford University Press.

Austin, C.D. and Seidl, F.W. (1981) Validating professional judgment in a home care agency. *Health and Social Work*, 6: 50–6.

Ball, D. (2007) Risk and the demise of children's play (pp57–76), in Thom, B., Sales, R. and Pearce, J.J. (eds) *Growing Up with Risk*. Bristol: Policy Press.

Baltes, P.B. and Baltes, M.M. (1990) Psychological perspectives on successful aging: the model of selective optimisation with compensation (pp1–34), in Baltes, P.B. and Baltes, M.M. (eds) *Successful Aging: Perspectives from Behavioural Sciences*. Cambridge: Cambridge University Press.

Bandolier (2009) *Integrated Care Pathway*. **www.bandolier.org.uk/booth/glossary/ICP.html**

Banks, S. (2001) *Ethics and Values in Social Work*, 2nd edition. Hampshire: Palgrave.

Barlow, J. and Calam, R. (2011) A public health approach to safeguarding in the 21st century. *Child Abuse Review*, 20: 238–55.

Barlow, J., Fisher, J.D. and Jones, D. (2012) *Systematic Review of Models of Analysing Significant Harm*. London: Department for Education and Oxford: Oxford University Press.

Baron, J. (2008) *Thinking and Deciding*, 4th edition. Cambridge: Cambridge University Press.

Baron, J. and Ritov, I. (2004) Omission bias, individual differences, and normality. *Organizational Behavior and Human Decision Processes*, 94 (2): 74–85.

Baumann, D., Dalgleish, L., Fluke, J. and Kern, H. (2011) *The Decision-Making Ecology*. Washington, DC: American Humane Association.

Baumol, W.J. (2004) On rational satisficing, in Augier, M. and March, J.G. (eds) *Models of a Man: Essays in Memory of Herbert A. Simon.* Cambridge, MA: MIT Press.

Beach, L.R. and Connolly, T. (1997) *The Psychology of Decision Making: People in Organisations.* Thousand Oaks, CA: Sage.

Beaumont, B. (1999) Risk assessment and prediction research (pp69–106), in Parsloe, P. (ed) *Risk Assessment in Social Care and Social Work.* Research Highlights 36. London: Jessica Kingsley.

Beck, U. (1992) *Risk Society* (trans. M. Ritter). London: Sage.

Beckett, C. (2008) Risk, uncertainty and thresholds (p46), in Calder, M.C. (ed) *Contemporary Risk Assessment in Safeguarding Children.* Lyme Regis: Russell House.

Begley, E., O'Brien, M., Carter-Anand, J., Killick, C. and Taylor, B. (2012) Older people's views of support services in response to elder abuse in communities across Ireland. *Quality in Ageing,* 13 (1): 48–59.

Bekker, H., Thornton, J.G., Airey, CM., Connelly, J.B., Hewison, J., Robinson, M.B., Lilleyman, J., Macintosh, M., Maule, A.J., Michie, S. and Pearman, A. (1999) Informed decision making: an annotated bibliography and systematic review. *Health Technology Assessment* 3 (1).

Benbenishty, R., Segev, D., Surkis, T. and Elias, T. (2002) Information-search and decision-making by professionals and non-professionals in cases of alleged child-abuse and maltreatment. *Journal of Social Service Research,* 28 (3): 1–18.

Benner, P. (1984) *From Novice to Expert: Excellence and Power in Clinical Nursing Practice.* Menlo Park, CA: Addison-Wesley (also Commemorative edition published 2001: Upper Saddle River, NJ: Prentice Hall).

Bennett, P. and Calman, K. (eds) (1999) *Risk Communication and Public Health.* Oxford: Oxford University Press.

Bennett, R. (2009) Khyra Ishaq held captive and starved by her mother and stepfather, *The Times.* **www.timesonline. co.uk/tol/news/uk/crime/article6440362.ece**

Beresford, B. and Sloper, T. (2008) *Understanding the Dynamics of Decision-Making and Choice. A Scoping Study of Key Psychological Theories to Inform the Design and Analysis of the Panel Study.* York: Social Policy Research Unit, University of York.

Best, P., Gil-Rodriguez, E., Manktelow, R. and Taylor, B.J. (in press) Seeking help from everyone and no-one: conceptualising the online help-seeking process among adolescent males. *Qualitative Health Research.*

Best, P., Manktelow, R. and Taylor, B.J. (2014) Online communication, social networking and adolescent wellbeing: a systematic narrative review. *Children and Youth Services Review,* 41: 27–36.

Best, P., Manktelow, R. and Taylor, B.J. (2016) Social work and social media: online help-seeking and the mental well-being of adolescent males. *British Journal of Social Work,* 46 (1): 257–76.

Best, P., Taylor, B.J. and Manktelow, R. (2015) 'I've 500 friends, but who are my mates?': investigating the influence of online friend networks on adolescent wellbeing. *Journal of Public Mental Health,* 14 (3): 136–48.

Best, P.A., Foye, U., Taylor, B.J., Hazlett, D. and Manktelow, R. (2013) Online interactive suicide support services: quality and accessibility. *Mental Health Review Journal,* 18 (4): 226–39.

Bingham, T. (2011) *The Rule of Law.* London: Penguin.

Boeije, H.R., Janssens, A. and Cecile, J.W. (2004) It might happen or it might not: how patients with multiple sclerosis explain their perception of prognostic risk. *Social Science & Medicine,* 59 (4): 861–8.

Bostock, L., Bairstow, S., Fish, S. and Macleod, F. (2005) *Managing Risk and Minimising Mistakes in Services to Children and Families. Children and Families' Services Report 6.* London: Social Care Institute for Excellence.

Bouch, J. and Marshall, J.J. (2005) Suicide risk: structured professional judgement. *Advances in Psychiatric Treatment Feb 2005,* 11 (2): 84–91.

Boyd, W. (Chairman) (1996) *Report of the Confidential Inquiry into Homicides and Suicides by Mentally Ill People.* London: Royal College of Psychiatrists.

Brearley, P. (1982) *Risk in Social Work.* London: Routledge & Kegan Paul.

Breckon, J. (2016) *Using Research Evidence: A Practice Guide.* London: Alliance for Useful Evidence.

Bridge Child Care Consultancy (1995) *Paul: Death through Neglect.* London: Bridge Child Care Consultancy.

British Association of Social Workers (2008, November) BASW secures first GSCC appeal win. *Professional Social Work,* p5.

British Association of Social Workers (2011) *UK Supervision Policy.* London: BASW.

Brown, K. and Rutter, L. (2006) *Critical Thinking for Social Work.* Exeter: Learning Matters.

Brown, R. and Barber, P. (2008) *The Social Worker's Guide to the Mental Capacity Act 2005.* Exeter: Learning Matters.

Brown, R., Barber, P. and Martin, D. (2015) *The Mental Capacity Act 2005: A Guide for Practice,* 3rd edition. London: Sage.

Bryan, C. and Rudd, M. (2006) Advances in the assessment of suicide risk. *Journal of Clinical Psychology,* 62 (2): 185–200.

Bunyan, N. (2001) Doctors 'let off hook' in report over ex-Beatle's attacker. *Daily Telegraph,* 24 Oct.

Buri, H. and Dawson, P. (2000) Caring for a relative with dementia: a theoretical model of coping with fall risk. *Health, Risk and Society,* 2 (3): 283–93.

Byrne, R. (2005) *The Rational Imagination: How People Create Alternatives to Reality.* Cambridge, MA: MIT Press.

Calman, K.C., Bennett, P.G. and Coles, D.G. (1999) Risks to health: some issues in management, regulation and communication. *Health, Risk and Society,* 1: 107–16.

Cambridge, P. (2004) Abuse inquiries as learning tools for social care organisations (pp231–54), in Stanley, N. and Manthorpe, J. (eds) *The Age of the Inquiry: Learning and Blaming in Health and Social Care.* London: Routledge.

Campbell, A., Taylor, B.J. and McGlade, A. (2016) *Research Design in Social Work: Qualitative, Quantitative and Mixed Methods.* London: Sage.

Carpenter, J.S.W., Shardlow, S., Patsios, D. and Wood, M.J.E. (2015) Developing the confidence and competence of newly-qualified child and family social workers in England: outcomes of a national programme. *British Journal of Social Work,* 45 (1): 153–76.

Carrère, S. and Gottman, J. (1999) Predicting divorce among newlyweds from the first three minutes of a marital conflict discussion. *Family Process,* 38 (3): 293–301.

Carroll, J.S. and Johnson, E.J. (1990) *Decision Research: A Field Guide.* London: Sage.

Carson, D. (1988) Risk-taking policies. *Journal of Social Welfare Law,* 5: 328–32.

Carson, D. (1996) Risking legal repercussions (pp3–12), in Kemshall, H. and Pritchard, J. (eds) *Good Practice in Risk Assessment and Risk Management 1.* London: Jessica Kingsley.

Carson, D. (2012a, July) *Reviewing Reviews: Learning Lessons about Learning Lessons.* Presentation at Decisions, Assessment, Risk and Evidence in Social Work (DARE II) Conference hosted by University of Ulster, Templepatrick, Northern Ireland. **www.ulster.ac.uk/dare**

Carson, D. (2012b) Reviewing reviews of professionals' risk-taking decisions. *Journal of Social Welfare and Family Law,* 34 (4): 395–409.

Carson, D. and Bain, A. (2008) *Professional Risk and Working with People: Decision-Making in Health, Social Care and Criminal Justice.* London: Jessica Kingsley.

Chang, L. (2006) *Wisdom for the Soul: Five Millennia of Prescriptions for Spiritual Healing.* Washington, DC: Gnosophia.

Chapman, G.B. and Elstein, A.S. (2000) Cognitive processes and biases in medical decision making (pp183–210), in Chapman, G.B. and Sonnenberg, F.A. (eds) *Decision Making in Health Care: Theory, Psychology and Applications.* Cambridge: Cambridge University Press.

Cocker, C. and Allain, L. (2011) *Advanced Social Work with Children and Families.* Exeter: Learning Matters.

Coelho, P. (1995) *The Alchemist.* London: HarperCollins.

College of Social Work (2012) *Professional Capabilities Framework.* London: CSW. **www.basw.co.uk/pcf**

Cooksey, R.W. (1996) *Judgment Analysis: Theory, Methods and Applications.* New York: Academic Press.

Corby, B. (2003) Supporting families and protecting children: assisting child care professionals in initial decision-making and review of cases. *Journal of Social Work,* 3 (2), 195–210.

Coren, E. and Fisher, M. (2006) *The Conduct of Systematic Research Reviews for SCIE Knowledge Reviews.* London: Social Care Institute for Excellence.

Covell, N.H., McCorkle, B.H., Weissman, E.M., Summerfelt, T. and Essock, S.M. (2007) What's in a name? Terms preferred by service recipients. *Administration and Policy in Mental Health,* 34: 443–7.

Creighton, S.J. (2004a) *Child Protection Statistics 1: Child Protection in the Community.* London: National Society for the Prevention of Cruelty to Children.

Creighton, S.J. (2004b) *Prevalence and Incidence of Child Abuse: International Comparisons.* London: National Society for the Prevention of Cruelty to Children.

Creighton, S.J. and Tissier, G. (2003) *Child Killings in England and Wales.* London: National Society for the Prevention of Cruelty to Children.

Dalgleish, L.I. and Drew, E.C. (1989) The relationship of child abuse indicators to the assessment of perceived risk and to the court's decision to separate. *Child Abuse and Neglect,* 13: 491–506.

Darragh, E. and Taylor, B.J. (2009) Research and reflective practice (pp148–60), in Higham, P. (ed) *Post Qualifying Social Work: From Competence to Expertise.* London: Sage.

Dasgupta, N. and Greenwald, A.G. (2001) On the malleability of automatic attitudes: combating automatic prejudice with images of admired and disliked individuals. *Journal of Personality and Social Psychology,* 81 (5): 800–14.

Davidson, G., Kelly, B., Macdonald, G., Risso, M., Lombard., L., Abogunrin, O., Clift-Matthews, V. and Martin, A. (2015) Supported decision making: a review of the international literature. *International Journal of Law and Psychiatry,* 38: 61–7.

Dawes, R.M., Faust, D. and Meelh, P.E. (1989) Clinical versus actuarial judgment. *Science,* 243: 1668–74.

DCSF (Department for Children, Schools and Families) (2009) *Common Assessment Framework: Managers' and Practitioners' Guides.* London: Department for Children, Schools and Families.

DH (Department of Health) (1993) *Risk Management in the NHS (Merrett Report)* London: Department of Health, National Health Service Management Executive.

DH (1995) *The Challenge of Partnership in Child Protection.* London: HMSO.

DH (1996) *Building Bridges: A Guide to Arrangements for Inter-Agency Working for the Care and Protection of Severely Mentally Ill People.* London: HMSO.

DH (1998) *Modernising Mental Health Services: Safe, Sound and Supportive.* London: Department of Health.

DH (2001) *Valuing People: A New Strategy for Learning Disability for the 21st Century.* London: Department of Health.

DH (2002) LAC (2002) 13: *Fair Access to Care Services: Guidance on Eligibility Criteria for Adult Social Care.* London: Department of Health.

DH (2007) *Independence, Choice and Risk: A Guide to Best Practice in Supported Decision Making.* London: Department of Health.

DH (2009) *Valuing People Now: A New Three Year Strategy for Learning Disability: Making It Happen Now.* London: Department of Health.

DH and DfEE (Department for Education and Employment) (2000) *Framework for the Assessment of Children in Need and Their Families.* London: Home Office.

DHSS (Department of Health and Social Security) (1998) *Community Care – From Policy to Practice – The Case of Mr Fredrick Joseph McLernon (Deceased)*. Belfast: The Stationery Office.

DHSSPS (Department of Health, Social Services and Public Safety) (2002) Departmental Guidance HSS(PPM) 10/2002 *Governance in the HPSS – Clinical and Social Care Governance: Guidelines for Implementation*. Belfast: Department of Health, Social Services and Public Safety for Northern Ireland.

DHSSPS (2003) *Risk Management: Core Standard*. Belfast: Department of Health, Social Services and Public Safety.

Devaney, J., Bunting, L., Hayes, D. and Lazenblatt, A. (2013) *Translating Learning into Action: An Overview of Learning from Case Management Reviews in Northern Ireland 2003–2008*. Belfast: DHSSPS, NSPCC and Queen's University.

Dhami, M.K. (2003) Psychological models of professional decision making. *Psychological Science*, 14: 175–80.

Dimond, B. (1997) *Legal Aspects of Care in the Community*. London: Macmillan Press.

Dodds, P., Rae, B. and Brown, S. (2012) Perhaps unidimensional is not unidimensional, *Cognitive Science*, 36 (8): 1542–55.

Doel, M. and Marsh, P. (1992) *Task-Centred Social Work*. Aldershot: Ashgate.

Doueck, H.J. and English, D.J. (1993) Decision making in child protective services: a comparison of selected risk assessment systems. *Child Welfare*, 72 (5): 441–53.

Dowding, D. and Thompson, C. (2002) Decision analysis (pp131–46), in Thompson, C. and Dowding, D. (eds) *Clinical Decision Making and Judgement in Nursing*. Edinburgh: Churchill Livingstone.

Dowie, J. (1993) Clinical decision analysis: background and introduction, in Llewelyn, H. and Hopkins, A. (eds) *Analysing How We Reach Clinical Decisions*. London: Royal College of Physicians.

Dowie, J. (1999) Communication for better decisions: not about 'risk'. *Health, Risk and Society*, 1 (1): 41–53.

Doyal, L. and Gough, I. (1991) *The Theory of Human Need*. London: Macmillan Press.

Duffy, J., Taylor, B.J. and McCall, S. (2006) Human rights and decision making in child protection through explicit argumentation. *Child Care in Practice*, 12 (2): 81–95.

Dyckman, K.M. and Carroll, S.J. (1981) *Inviting the Mystic, Supporting the Prophet: An Introduction to Spiritual Direction*. New Jersey: Paulist Press.

Eddy, D.M. (1996) *Clinical Decision Making From Theory to Practice: A Collection of Essays from the Journal of the American Medical Association*. Sudbury, MA: Jones and Bartlett.

Egan, G. (2010) *The Skilled Helper: A Problem Management and Opportunity Development Approach to Helping*. Belmont, CA: Brooks-Cole.

Egan, M., Wells, J., Byrne, K., Jaglal, S., Stolee, P., Chesworth, B.M. and Hillier, L.M. (2009) The process of decision-making in home-care case management: implications for the introduction of universal assessment and information technology. *Health and Social Care in the Community*, 17 (4): 371–8.

English, D. and Pecora, P. (1994) Risk assessment as a practice method in child protective services. *Child Welfare*, LXXIII (5): 451–73.

Enosh, G. and Bayer-Topilsky, T. (2015) Reasoning and bias: heuristics in safety assessment and placement decisions for children at risk. *British Journal of Social Work*, 45: 1771–87.

Farmer, E. and Owen, M. (1995) *Child Protection Practice: Private Risks and Public Remedies*. London: HMSO.

Fazel, S., Langstrom, N., Hjern, A., Grann, M. and Lichtenstein, P. (2009) Schizophrenia, substance abuse, and violent crime. *Journal of the American Medical Association*, 301 (19): 2016–23.

Ferguson, H. (2010) Walks, home visits and atmospheres: risk and the everyday practices and mobilities of social work and child protection. *British Journal of Social Work*, 40 (4): 1100–17.

Fiedler, K. (2017) Illusory correlation, in Pohl, R.F. (ed) *Cognitive Illusions: Intriguing Phenomena in Thinking, Judgement and Memory,* 2nd edition. London: Routledge.

Fish, S., Munro, E. and Bairstow, S. (2008) *Learning Together to Safeguard Children: Developing a Multi-Agency Systems Approach for Case Reviews.* London: Social Care Institute for Excellence.

Fisher, M., Qureshi, H., Hardyman, W. and Homewood, J. (2006) *Using Qualitative Research in Systematic Reviews: Older People's Views of Hospital Discharge: SCIE Report 09.* London: Social Care Institute for Excellence. **www.scie.org.uk/ publications/reports/report09.asp**

Flynn, R. (2002) Clinical governance and governmentality. *Health, Risk & Society,* 4 (2): 155–73.

Foster, C. (1998) Bolam: consolidation and clarification. *Health Care Risk Report,* 4 (5): 5–7.

Freel, K.A. (1995) The guardians of childhood safety: the role of parents in injury prevention. *Dissertation Abstracts International: Section B: The Sciences and Engineering,* 55 (8-B): 3607.

Friedman, D., Isaac, R.M., James, D. and Sunder, S. (2014) *Risky Curves: On the Empirical Failure of Expected Utility.* London: Routledge.

Gambrill, E. (1995) Behavioral social work: past, present, and future. *Research on Social Work Practice,* 5 (4): 460–84.

Gambrill, E. (2008) Decision making in child welfare: constraints and potentials (pp 175–93), in Lindsey, D. and Shlonsky, A. (eds) *Child Welfare Research: Advances for Policy and Practice.* Oxford: Oxford University Press.

Garson, G.C. (1998) *Neural Networks: An Introductory Guide for Social Scientists.* Thousand Oaks, CA: Sage.

Gigerenzer, G. (2014) *Risk Savvy: How to Make Good Decisions.* New York: Penguin.

Gigerenzer, G. (2015) *Simply Rational: Decision Making in the Real World.* Oxford: Oxford University Press.

Gigerenzer, G. and Gaissmaier, W. (2015) Decision making: non-rational theories (pp 911–16), in Smelser, N.J. and Baltes, P.B. (eds) *International Encyclopedia of the Social and Behavioural Sciences, Volume 5, 2nd edition.* Amsterdam: Elsevier.

Gigerenzer, G. and Goldstein, D.G. (1996) Reasoning the fast and frugal way: models of bounded rationality. *Psychological Review,* 103 (4): 650–69.

Gigerenzer, G., Todd, P. and the ABC Research Group (1999) *Simple Heuristics That Make Us Smart.* New York: Oxford University Press.

Gillingham, P. (2015) Predictive risk modelling to prevent child maltreatment and other adverse outcomes for service users: inside the 'black box' of machine learning. *British Journal of Social Work,* 46 (4): 1044–58.

Gillingham, P. and Humphreys, C. (2010) Child protection practitioners and decision-making tools: observations and reflections from the front line. *British Journal of Social Work,* 40 (8): 2598–616.

Gilovich, T., Griffin, D. and Kahneman, D. (eds) (2002) *Heuristics and Biases: The Psychology of Intuitive Judgement.* Cambridge: Cambridge University Press.

Gladwell, M. (2006) *Blink: The Power of Thinking without Thinking.* London: Penguin.

Godefroy, S. (2015) *Mental Health and Mental Capacity Law for Social Workers.* London: Sage.

Goldberg, D. and Huxley, P. (1979) *Mental Illness in the Community: The Pathway to Psychiatric Care.* London: Routledge.

Goldstein, D.G. and Gigerenzer, G. (2002) Models of ecological rationality: the recognition heuristic. *Psychological Review,* 109 (1): 75–90.

Gottman, J. (2000) *The Mathematics of Marriage.* Cambridge, MA: MIT Press.

Graybeal, C.T. and Konrad, S.C. (2008) Strengths-based child assessment: locating possibility and transforming the paradigm (pp185–97), in Calder, M.C. (ed) *Contemporary Risk Assessment in Safeguarding Children.* Lyme Regis: Russell House.

Green, E., Mitchell, W. and Bunton, R. (2000) Contextualising risk and danger: an analysis of young people's perceptions of risk. *Journal of Youth Studies,* 3 (2): 109–26.

Grice, E. (2008) Hannah Jones: I have been in hospital too much. *The Telegraph*, 12 Nov. **www.telegraph.co.uk/news/ health/3444840/Hannah-Jones-I-have-been-in-hospital-too-much.html**

Grove, W. and Meehl, P. (1996) Comparative efficiency of informal (subjective, impressionistic) and formal (mechanical, algorithmic) prediction procedures. *Psychology, Public Policy and Law*, 2: 293–323.

Gunnell, D. (1994) *The Potential for Preventing Suicide: A Review of the Literature on the Effectiveness of Interventions Aimed at Preventing Suicide*. Bristol: University of Bristol Health Care Evaluation Unit.

Hackett, S. (1999) Towards a resilience-based intervention model for young people with harmful sexual behaviours, in Erooga, M. and Masson, H. (eds) *Children and Young People Who Sexually Abuse Others: Challenges and Responses*. London: Routledge.

Hagell, A. (1998) *Dangerous Care: Reviewing the Risks to Children from their Carers*. London: Bridge Child Care Consultancy.

Hammond, K.R. (1996) *Human Judgment and Social Policy: Irreducible Uncertainty, Inevitable Error, Unavoidable Injustice*. New York: Oxford University Press.

Hardman, D. (2009) *Judgment and Decision Making*. London: Oxford University Press.

Hardy, B., Young, R. and Wistow, G. (1999) Dimensions of choice in the assessment and care management process: the views of older people, carers and care managers. *Health and Social Care in the Community*, 7 (6): 483–91.

Haynes, P. (2003) *Managing Complexity in the Public Services*. Maidenhead: Open University Press.

Health and Social Care Change Agents Team (2003) *Discharge from Hospital: Pathway, Process and Practice*. London: Department of Health.

Heffernan, K. (2006) Social work, new public management and the language of service user. *British Journal of Social Work*, 36: 139–47.

Heyman, A., Shaw, M., Alaszewski, A. and Titterton, M. (2010) *Risk, Safety and Clinical Practice: Health Care through the Lens of Risk*. Oxford: Oxford University Press.

Hindley, N., Ramchandani, P. and Jones, D.P.H. (2006) Risk factors for recurrence of maltreatment: a systematic review. *Archives of Diseases in Childhood*, 91 (9): 744–52.

Hirokawa, R.Y., Erbert, L. and Hurst, A. (1996) Communication and group decision-making effectiveness (pp269–300), in Hirokawa, R.Y. and Poole, M.S. *Communication and Group Decision Making*. Thousand Oaks, CA: Sage.

Hitzler, S. and Messmer, H. (2010) Group decision-making in child welfare and the pursuit of participation. *Qualitative Social Work*, 9 (2): 205–26.

Hollows, A. (2001) The challenges to social work. *Child Psychology & Psychiatry Review*, 6 (1): 11–15.

Hollows, A. (2003) Making professional judgements in the framework for the assessment of children in need and their families (pp61–74), in Calder, M.C. and Hackett, S. (eds) *Assessment in Child Care*. Lyme Regis: Russell House.

Hollows, A. (2008) Professional judgement and the risk assessment process (pp52–60), in Calder, M.C. (ed) *Contemporary Risk Assessment in Safeguarding Children*. Lyme Regis: Russell House Publishers.

Hood, R. (2014) Complexity and integrated working in children's services. *British Journal of Social Work*, 44 (1): 27–43.

Hood, R. and Shute, S. (2000) *The Parole System at Work: A Study of Risk Based Decision-Making, Home Office Research Study 202*. London: Home Office.

Howarth, J. (2007) *Child Neglect: Identification and Assessment*. Hampshire: Palgrave Macmillan.

Høybye-Mortensen, M. (2015) Decision-making tools and their influence on caseworkers' room for discretion. *British Journal of Social Work*, 45 (2): 600–15.

HSE (Health and Safety Executive) (2008) *Myth: Children Need to be Wrapped in Cotton Wool to Keep Them Safe*. London: Health and Safety Executive. **www.hse.gov.uk/myth/nov08.htm**

HSE (2009a) *About the Health and Safety Executive.* London: Health and Safety Executive. **www.hse.gov.uk/aboutus/index.htm**

HSE (2009b) *Health and Safety Law: What You Need to Know.* London: Health and Safety Executive. **www.hse.gov.uk/pubns/law.pdf**

HSE (2009c) *Violence at Work.* London: Health and Safety Executive.

HSE (2009d) *The Five Steps to Risk Assessment.* London: Health and Safety Executive. **www.hse.gov.uk/risk/fivesteps.htm**

HSE (2009e) *Evaluate the Risks and Decide on Precautions.* London: Health and Safety Executive.

HSE (2009f) *Principles of Sensible Risk Management,* Speech 9 May 2006 by Tony Bandle, Strategy Division. London: Health and Safety Executive. **www.hse.gov.uk/aboutus/speeches/tbrospacongress.pdf**

HSE (2009g) *Myth: Health and Safety Rules Take the Adventure Out of Playgrounds.* London: Health and Safety Executive. **www.hse.gov.uk/myth/mar09.htm**

HSE (2016) *Controlling the Risks in the Workplace.* London: Health and Safety Executive.

Hughes, G.W. (2008) *God of Surprises,* 3rd edition. London: Darton, Longman and Todd.

Hughes, S. (2005) *Spoken from the Heart.* Farnham, Surrey: CWR.

Human Rights Act (1998) London: The Office of Public Sector Information. **www.opsi.gov.uk**

IASSW and IFSW (2001) *International Definition of the Social Work Profession* (Supplement to *International Social Work*), International Association of Schools of Social Work and International Federation of Social Workers [ISSN 0020-8728].

Janis, I.L. (1982) *Groupthink: Psychological Studies of Policy Decisions and Fiascoes.* New York: Houghton Mifflin.

Janis, I.L. and Mann, L. (1977) *Decision Making: A Psychological Analysis of Conflict, Choice and Commitment.* New York: The Free Press.

Johnson, W., Clancy, T. and Bastian, P. (2015) Child abuse/neglect risk assessment under field practice conditions: Tests of external and temporal validity and comparison with heart disease prediction. *Children and Youth Services Review,* 56 (C): 76–85.

Jones, D. (2006) Assessments: a child mental health perspective. *Family Law in Practice,* 36 (6): 471–7.

Jones, D.P.H. (1998) The effectiveness of intervention (pp91–120), in Adcock, M. and White, R. (eds) *Significant Harm: Its Management and Outcome,* 2nd edition. Croydon: Significant Publications.

Jones, E.E. and Harris, V.A. (1967) The attribution of attitudes. *Journal of Experimental Social Psychology,* 3 (1): 1–24.

Jones, N.J., Brown, S.L. and Zamble, E. (2010) Predicting criminal recidivism in adult male offenders: researcher versus parole officer assessment of dynamic risk. *Criminal Justice and Behaviour,* 37 (8): 860–82.

Juby, H. and Farrington, D.P. (2001) Disentangling the link between disrupted families and delinquency: sociodemography, ethnicity and risk behaviours. *British Journal of Criminology,* 41 (1): 22–40.

Kahnemann, D., Slovic, P. and Tversky, P. (1982) *Judgement under Uncertainty: Heuristics and Biases.* Cambridge: Cambridge University Press.

Kahneman, D. and Tversky, A. (eds) (2000) *Choices, Values and Frames.* New York: Cambridge University Press.

Kane, R.A., Degenholtz, H. and Kane, R.L. (1999) Adding values: an experiment in systematic attention to values and preferences of community long-term care clients. *Journal of Gerontology,* 54B (2): S109–S119.

Kane, R.L., Kane, R.A. and Ells, M. (2002) *Assessing Older Persons: Measures, Meaning, and Practical Applications.* New York: Oxford University Press.

Karpman, S.B. (1968) Fairy tales and script drama analysis. *Transactional Analysis Bulletin,* 7 (26): 39–43.

Keaney, F., Strang, J., Martinez-Raga, J., Spektor, D., Manning, V., Kelleher, M., Wilson-Jones, C., Wanagaratne, S. and Sabater, A. (2004) Does anyone care about names? How attendees at substance misuse services like to be addressed by professionals. *European Addiction Research,* 10: 75–9.

Kelly, G. (1996) Competence in risk analysis (pp108–23), in O'Hagan, K. (ed) *Competence in Social Work Practice*. London: Jessica Kingsley.

Kelly, N. and Milner, J. (1996) Child protection decision-making. *Child Abuse Review*, 5: 91–102.

Kemshall, H. (2008) Actuarial and clinical risk assessment: contrasts, comparisons and collective usages (pp198–205), in Calder, M.C. (ed) *Contemporary Risk Assessment in Safeguarding Children*. Lyme Regis: Russell House Publishing.

Killick, C. and Taylor, B.J. (2012) Judgments of social care professionals on elder abuse referrals: a factorial survey. *British Journal of Social Work*, 42 (5): 814–32.

Killick, C., Taylor, B.J., Begley, E., Anand, J.C. and O'Brien, M. (2015) Older people's conceptualization of abuse: a systematic narrative review. *Journal of Elder Abuse and Neglect*, 27 (2): 100–20.

Killick, J.C. (2008) *Factors Influencing Judgments of Social Care Professionals on Adult Protection Referrals*. Thesis (PhD). Coleraine, Northern Ireland: University of Ulster.

Kirkman, E. and Melrose, K. (2014) *Clinical Judgement and Decision-Making in Children's Social Work: An Analysis of the 'Front Door' System (Research Report DFE 323)*. London: The Behavioural Insights Team, Department for Education. **http://bit.ly/QTOkOZ**

Kitzinger, J. and Reilly, J. (1997) The rise and fall of risk reporting: media coverage of human genetics research, 'false memory syndrome' and 'mad cow disease'. *European Journal of Communication*, 12 (3): 319–50.

Klein, G. (2000) *Sources of Power: How People Make Decisions*. Cambridge, MA: MIT Press.

Kopels, S. and Kagle, J.D. (1993) Do social workers have a duty to warn? *Social Service Review*, 67 (1): 101–26.

Koprowska, J. (2010) *Communication and Interpersonal Skills in Social Work*. London: Sage.

Kühlberger, A. (2017) Framing, in Pohl, R.F. (ed) *Cognitive Illusions: Intriguing Phenomena in Thinking, Judgement and Memory*, 2nd edition. London: Routledge.

Laming, H. (2003) *The Victoria Climbie Inquiry Report*. London: HMSO.

Lawhead, S. (1989) *Arthur*. London: Lion Publishing.

Leventhal, T. and Brooks-Gunn, J. (2000) The neighbourhoods they live in: the effects of neighbourhood residence on child and adolescent outcomes. *Psychological Bulletin*, 126 (2): 309.

Lewis, L.F. (2010) Group support systems: overview and guided tour (pp249–68), in Kilgour, D.M. and Eden, C. (eds) *Handbook of Group Decision and Negotiation*. Heidelberg: Springer.

Lipsky, M. (1980) *Street-Level Bureaucracy: Dilemmas of the Individual in Public Services*. New York: Sage.

Littlechild, B. and Reid, J. (2007) Assessment (pp149–64), in Tovey, W. (ed) *The Post-Qualifying Handbook for Social Workers*. London: Jessica Kingsley.

Lloyd, C., King, R., Bassett, H., Sandland, S. and Saviage, G. (2001) Patient, client or consumer: a survey of preferred terms. *Australasian Psychiatry*, 9: 321–4.

Lockett, G. and Naudé, P. (1998) The stability of judgemental modelling: an application in the social services. *Group Decision and Negotiation*, 7: 41–53.

Luft, J. (1969) *Of Human Interaction*. Palo Alto, CA: National Press.

Macdonald, G. (2001) *Effective Interventions for Child Abuse and Neglect: An Evidence-Based Approach to Planning and Evaluating Interventions*. Chichester: Wiley.

Macdonald, G. and Sheldon, B. (1998) Changing one's mind: the final frontier? *Issues in Social Work Education*, 18 (1): 3–25.

Macdonald, K.I. and Macdonald, G.M. (1999) Risk perception, in Parsloe, P. (ed) *Risk Assessment in Social Care and Social Work*. Aberdeen: Research Highlights.

Maguire, M. (2009) *Law and Youth Work.* Exeter: Learning Matters.

Manthorpe, J. and Moriarty, J. (2010) *Nothing Ventured, Nothing Gained: Risk Guidance for People with Dementia.* London: Department of Health. **www.gov.uk/government/publications/nothing-ventured-nothing-gained-risk-guidance-for-people-with-dementia**

Manthorpe, J., Walsh, M., Alaszewski, A. and Harrison, L. (1997) Issues of risk practice and welfare in learning disability services. *Disability & Society*, 12 (1): 69–82.

Marsh, J. and Soulsby, J. (1994) *Outlines of English Law.* Cheltenham: Stanley Thornes.

Marsh, P. and Fisher, M. in collaboration with Mathers, N. and Fish, S. (2005) *Developing the Evidence Base for Social Work and Social Care Practice: Using Knowledge in Social Care, Report 10.* London: Social Care Institute for Excellence.

Maslow, A. (1943) A theory of human motivation. *Psychological Review*, 50: 370–96.

Mathew, R., Davies, N., Manthorpe, J. and Iliffe, S. (2016) Making decisions at the end of life when caring for a person with dementia: a literature review to explore the potential use of heuristics in difficult decision-making. *British Medical Journal*, 6 (7): e010416.

Matthews, I. (2009) *Social Work and Spirituality.* London: Sage.

Maung, N.A. and Hammond, N. (2000) *Risk of Re-offending and Needs Assessments: The Users' Perspective, Home Office Research Study 216.* London: Home Office.

May, R. (1969) *Love and Will.* London: Fontana.

McCormack, B.G., Taylor, B.J., McConville, J.E., Slater, P.F. and Murray, B.J. (2007a) *The Validity of the Core Component of the Northern Ireland Single Assessment Tool (NISAT) for the Health and Social Care of Older People.* Belfast: Department of Health, Social Services and Public Safety.

McCormack, B.G., Taylor, B.J., McConville, J.E., Slater, P.F. and Murray, B.J. (2007b) *The Reliability of the Core Component of the Northern Ireland Single Assessment Tool (NISAT) for the Health and Social Care of Older People.* Belfast: Department of Health, Social Services and Public Safety.

McCormack, B.G., Taylor, B.J., McConville, J.E., Slater, P.F. and Murray, B.J. (2008a) *The Northern Ireland Single Assessment Tool (NISAT) for the Health and Social Care of Older People.* Belfast: Department of Health, Social Services and Public Safety.

McCormack, B.G., Taylor, B.J., McConville, J.E., Slater, P.F. and Murray, B.J. (2008b) *Guidance Document for the Northern Ireland Single Assessment Tool (NISAT) for the Health and Social Care of Older People.* Belfast: Department of Health, Social Services and Public Safety.

McCormack, B.G., Taylor, B.J., McConville, J.E., Slater, P.F. and Murray, B.J. (2008c) *The Usability of the Northern Ireland Single Assessment Tool (NISAT) for the Health and Social Care of Older People.* Belfast: Department of Health, Social Services and Public Safety.

McCormack, B.G., Taylor, B.J., McConville, J.E., Slater, P.F. and Murray, B.J. (2008d) *The Reliability of the Complex Component of the Northern Ireland Single Assessment Tool (NISAT) for the Health and Social Care of Older People.* Belfast: Department of Health, Social Services and Public Safety.

McDonald, G. and McDonald, K. (2010) Safeguarding: a case for intelligent risk management. *British Journal of Social Work*, 40: 1174–91.

McFadden, P., Campbell, A. and Taylor, B.J. (2015) Resilience and burnout in child protection social work: individual and organizational themes from a systematic literature review. *British Journal of Social Work*, 45 (5): 1546–63.

McFadden, P., Taylor, B.J., Campbell, A. and McQuilkin, J. (2012) Systematically identifying relevant research: case study on child protection social workers' resilience. *Research on Social Work Practice*, 22 (6): 626–36.

McGinn, A.H., Taylor, B.J. and McColgan, M. (in press) Survivor perspectives of change processes in their domestically-violent partner: systematic narrative review. *Trauma, Violence & Abuse.*

McKillop, C. (2007) *Assessing Child Neglect: An Exploration into the Usefulness of the Graded Care Profile (GCP) for the Assessment of Child Neglect by Social Work Staff Directly Involved in the Assessment Process.* Report (Application of Research Methods in Social Work Programme). Coleraine, Northern Ireland: University of Ulster.

Meehl, P.E. (1954) *Clinical Versus Statistical Prediction: A Theoretical Analysis and a Review of the Evidence.* Minneapolis: University of Minnesota Press.

Miller, G.A. (1956) The magical number seven, plus or minus two: some limits on our memory for processing information. *Psychological Review,* 63 (2): 81–97.

Milner, J.S. (1995) Physical child abuse assessment: perpetrator evaluation, in Campbell, J.C. (ed) *Assessing Dangerousness: Violence by Sexual Offenders, Batterers and Child Abusers.* Thousand Oaks, CA: Sage.

Monahan, J. (1981) *Predicting Violent Behaviour: An Assessment of Clinical Techniques.* Beverley Hills, CA: Sage.

Monahan, J. (1993) Limiting therapist exposure to Tarasoff liability: guidelines for risk containment. *American Psychologist,* 48 (3): 242–50.

Monahan, J., Steadman, H.J., Silver, E., Appelbaum, P.S., Robbins, P.C., Mulvey, E.P., Roth, L.H., Grisso, T. and Banks, S. (2001) *Rethinking Risk Assessment: The MacArthur Study of Mental Disorder and Violence.* Oxford: Oxford University Press.

Monahan, J., Steadman, H., Robbins, P., Appelbaum, P., Banks, S., Grisso, T., Heilbrun, K., Mulvey, E., Roth, L. and Silver, E. (2005) An actuarial model of violence risk assessment for persons with mental disorders. *Psychiatric Services,* 56: 810–15.

Montgomery, L., Anand, J.C., McKay, K., Taylor, B.J., Pearson, K. and Harper, C. (2016) Implications of divergences in adult protection legislation. *Journal of Adult Protection,* 18 (3): 149–60.

Morgan, S. (2000) *Clinical Risk Management: A Clinical Tool and Practitioner Manual.* London: The Sainsbury Centre for Mental Health.

Moriarty, J., Rapaport, P., Beresford, P., Branfield, F., Forrest, V., Manthorpe, J., Martineau, S., Cornes, M., Butt, J., Iliffe, S., Taylor, B. and Keady, J. (2007) *Practice Guide 11: The Participation of Adult Service Users, Including Older People, in Developing Social Care.* London: Social Care Institute for Excellence.

Morrison, T. (1998) Partnership, collaboration and change under the Children Act (pp121–48), in Adcock, M. and White, R. (eds) *Significant Harm: Its Managementand Outcome,* 2nd edition. Croydon: Significant Publications.

Morrison, T. and Henniker, J. (2006) Building a comprehensive interagency assessment and intervention system for young people who sexually harm, in Erooga, M. and Masson, H. (eds) *Children and Young People Who Sexually Harm Others: Current Developments and Practice Responses.* London: Routledge.

Munby, Sir James (2013, June) *View from the President's Chambers: The Process of Reform: Expert Evidence.* London: Office of the President of the Family Division. **www.judiciary.gov.uk/wp-content/uploads/JCO/Documents/FJC/Publications/VIEW+President+Expert(3).pdf**

Munro, E. (1996) Avoidable and unavoidable mistakes in child protection work. *British Journal of Social Work,* 26 (6): 793–808.

Munro, E. (1999) Common errors of reasoning in child protection work. *Child Abuse and Neglect,* 23 (8): 745–58.

Munro, E. (2008) *Effective Child Protection,* 2nd edition. London: Sage.

Munro, E. (2011) *Munro Review of Child Protection.* London: Department for Education (Cm 8062).

National Audit Office (2016) *Children in Need of Help or Protection.* London: NAO.

Nelson-Jones, R. (1989) *Effective Thinking Skills: Preventing and Managing Personal Problems.* London: Cassell Educational.

Newell, A. and Simon, H.A. (1972) *Human Problem Solving.* Englewood Cliffs, NJ: Prentice Hall.

Newhill, C.E. (1996) Prevalence and risk factors for client violence toward social workers. *Families in Society,* 77 (8): 488–95.

Norman, A.J. (1980) *Rights and Risk.* London: Centre for Policy on Ageing.

Northern Ireland Social Care Council (2016) *Professional in Practice: Continuing Professional Development Framework.* Belfast: Northern Ireland Social Care Council. **www.niscc.info/storage/resources/20160419_aboutpip_your-cpd-framework.pptx**

Northern Ireland Statistics and Research Agency (2007) *Statistical Bulletin: Deaths in Northern Ireland.* Belfast: Northern Ireland Statistics and Research Agency.

Nouwen, H. (2001) *Turn My Mourning Into Dancing.* Nashville, TN: Nelson.

Novaco, R.W. (1994) *Novaco Anger Scale and Provocation Inventory (NAS-PI).* Los Angeles, CA: Western Psychological Services.

O'Brien, M., Begley, E., Anand, J.C., Killick, C., Taylor, B.J., McCarthy, M., McCrossan, S., Moran, E. and Doyle, E. (2011) *A Total Indifference to Our Dignity: Older People's Understandings of Elder Abuse.* Dublin: Age Action Ireland.

O'Hagan, K. (1991) Crisis intervention in social work (pp138–56), in Lishman, J. (ed) *Handbook of Theory for Practice Teachers in Social Work.* London: Jessica Kingsley.

O'Sullivan, T. (1999) *Decision Making in Social Work.* London: Macmillan.

Osmo, R. and Landau, R. (2001) The need for explicit argumentation in ethical decision-making in social work. *Social Work Education,* 20 (4): 483–92.

Paling, J. (2006) *Helping Patients Understand Risks.* Gainesville, FL: Risk Communication Institute.

Parton, N., Thorpe, D. and Wattam, C. (1997) *Child Protection: Risk and the Moral Order.* London: Macmillan.

Pascoe-Watson, G. and Wilson, G. (2008) Baby P gets the justice you demanded. *The Sun,* London (1 December 2008).

Pattison, S. (2006) *Medical Law and Ethics,* 2nd edition. London: Sweet and Maxwell.

Pennycook, G. and Thompson, V.A. (2017) Base-rate neglect, in Pohl, R.F. (ed) *Cognitive Illusions: Intriguing Phenomena in Thinking, Judgement and Memory,* 2nd edition. London: Routledge.

Perry, J. and Sheldon, B. (1995) *Richard Phillips Inquiry Report.* London: City of Westminster, and Kensington and Chelsea and Westminster District Health Authority.

Peter, L. (1980) *Quotations for Our Time.* London: Methuen.

Pfister, H.-R. and Bohm, G. (2008) The multiplicity of emotions: a framework of emotional functions in decision making. *Judgment and Decision Making,* 3 (1): 5–17.

Porter, D. (1986) *Children at Risk.* Sussex: Kingsway.

Pritchard, C., Davey, J. and Williams, R. (2013) Who kill children? Re-examining the evidence. *British Journal of Social Work,* 43: 1403–38.

Raynor, P., Kynch, J., Roberts, C. and Merrington, S. (2000) *Risk and Need Assessment in Probation Services: An Evaluation, Home Office Research Study 211.* London: Home Office.

Re B-S (Children) [2013] EWCA Civ 1146. **www.familylawweek.co.uk/site.aspx?i=ed117048**

Reason, J. (1991) *Human Error.* Cambridge: Cambridge University Press.

Reder, P. and Duncan, S. (2004) From Colwell to Climbie: inquiring into fatal child abuse (pp92–115), in Stanley, N. and Manthorpe, J. (eds) *The Age of the Inquiry: Learning and Blaming in Health and Social Care.* London: Routledge.

Reeves, A., McKee, M., Gunnell, D., Chang, S.S., Basu, S., Barr, B. and Stuckler, D. (2015) Economic shocks, resilience and male suicides in the Great Recession: cross-national analysis of 20 EU countries. *European Journal of Public Health,* 25 (3): 404–9.

Reinhard, M.-A., Marksteiner, T., Schindel, R. and Dickhäuser, O. (2014) Detecting lies and truths in social work: how suspicion level and familiarity affect detection accuracy. *British Journal of Social Work,* 44 (2): 328–47.

Reith, M. (1998) *Community Care Tragedies: A Practice Guide to Mental Health Inquiries.* Birmingham: Venture Press.

Reynolds, B.C. (1942) *Learning and Teaching in the Practice of Social Work.* New York: National Association of Social Workers.

Righthand, S., Kerr, B. and Drach, K. (2003) *Child Maltreatment Risk Assessments: An Evaluation Guide.* New York: The Hawthorne Maltreatment and Trauma Press.

Roberts, A.R. (2000) *Crisis Intervention Handbook.* New York: Oxford University Press.

Roberts, A.R. and Greene, G.J. (2002) *The Social Workers' Desk Reference.* Oxford: Oxford University Press.

Robertson, C. (ed) (1996) *The Wordsworth Dictionary of Quotations*. Ware, Hertfordshire: Wordsworth Editions.

Rogers, W.V.H. (2006) *Winfield and Jolowicz on Tort*. London: Sweet & Maxwell.

Ross, L. and Waterson, J. (1996) Risk for whom? Social work and people with physical disabilities (pp80–92), in Kemshall, H. and Pritchard, J. (eds) *Good Practice in Risk Assessment and Risk Management 1*. London: Jessica Kingsley.

Russell, T. and Reimer, T. (2015) Risk communication in groups (pp272–87), in Cho, H., Reimer, T. and McComas, K.A. (eds) *The Sage Handbook of Risk Communication*. Thousand Oaks, CA: Sage.

Ryan, M., Scott, D.A., Reeves, C., Bate, A., van Teijlingen, E.R., Russell, E.M., Napper, M. and Robb, C.M. (2001) Eliciting public preferences for healthcare: a systematic review of techniques. *Health Technology Assessment*, 5 (5).

Ryan, R., Nolan, M., Reid, D. and Enderby, P. (2008) Using the senses framework to achieve relationship-centred dementia care services: a case example. *Dementia*, 7 (1): 71–93.

Saleebey, D. (2001). *Practicing the Strengths Perspective: Everyday Tools and Resources*. Boston, MA: Pearson Education.

Savage, L.J. (1954) *The Foundations of Statistics*. New York: Wiley.

Schön, D.A. (1983) *The Reflective Practitioner: How Professionals Think in Action*. London: Temple Smith.

Schön, D.A. (1996) *Educating the Reflective Practitioner: Toward a New Design for Teaching and Learning in the Professions*. San Francisco, CA: Jossey Bass.

Schwartz, J., Chapman, G., Brewer, N. and Bergus, G. (2004) The effects of accountability on bias in physician decision making: going from bad to worse. *Psychonomic Bulletin & Review*, 11 (1): 173–78.

Scott-Jones, J. and Raisborough, J. (eds) (2007) *Risk, Identities and the Everyday*. Hampshire: Ashgate.

Seal, M. (2008) *Not About Us Without Us: Client Involvement in Supported Housing*. Dorset: Russell House.

Sellnow, T.L. (2015) Crisis communication (Chapter 20), in Cho, H., Reimer, T. and McComas, K.A. (eds) *The Sage Handbook of Risk Communication*. Thousand Oaks, CA: Sage.

Senge, P. (1990) *The Fifth Discipline*. New York: Doubleday.

Seymour, C. and Seymour, R. (2007) *Courtroom Skills for Social Workers*. Exeter: Learning Matters.

Sheppard, D. (2004) Mental health inquiries 1985–2003 (pp165–212), in Stanley, N. and Manthorpe, J. (eds) *The Age of the Inquiry: Learning and Blaming in Health and Social Care*. London: Routledge.

Shlonsky, A. (2007) Initial construction of an actuarial risk assessment measure using the national survey of child and adolescent well-being (pp62–80), in Haskins, R., Wulczyn, F. and Webb, M.B. (eds) *Child Protection: Using Research to Improve Policy and Practice*. Washington, DC: Brookings Institution.

Shlonsky, A. and Wagner, D. (2005) The next step: integrating actuarial risk assessment and clinical judgment into an evidence-based practice framework in child protection service case management. *Children and Youth Services Review*, 27 (3): 409–27.

Shulman, L. (2011) *The Skills of Helping Individuals, Families, Groups and Communities*. Belmont, CA: Brooks/Cole Cengage Learning.

Sidebotham, P., Brandon, M., Bailey, S., Belderson, P., Dodsworth, J., Garstang, J., Harrison, E., Retzer, A. and Sorensen, P. (2016) *Pathways to Harm, Pathways to Protection: A Triennial Analysis of Serious Case Reviews 2011 to 2014: Final Report*. London: Department for Education.

Simmonds, J. (1998) Making decisions in social work: persecuting, rescuing or being a victim (pp175–96), in Adcock, M. and White, R. (eds) *Significant Harm: Its Management and Outcome*, 2nd edition. Croydon: Significant Publications.

Simmons, L. (2007) *Social Care Governance: A Practice Workbook*. Belfast: Department of Health, Social Services and Public Safety (Clinical and Social Care Governance Support Team) and London: Social Care Institute for Excellence.

Simon, H. (1957) *Models of Man: Social and Rational*. New York: Wiley.

Slovic, P. (1999) Trust, emotion, sex, politics, and science: surveying the risk-assessment battlefield. *Risk Analysis*, 19 (4): 689–701.

Social Exclusion Task Force (2008) *Think Family: Improving the Life Chances of Families at Risk.* London: Cabinet Office.

Social Services Inspectorate (1993) *Evaluating Performance in Child Protection: A Framework for the Inspection of Local Authority Social Services Practice and Systems.* London: Department of Health.

Spratt, T. (2001) The influence of child protection orientation on child welfare practice. *British Journal of Social Work*, 31 (6): 933–54.

Srivastava, O.P., Fountain, R., Ayre, P. and Stewart, J. (2003) The Graded Care Profile: a measure of care, in Calder, M. and Hackett, S. (eds) *Assessment in Child Care.* Lyme Regis: Russell House.

Stacey, R.D. (2000) *Strategic Management and Organisational Dynamics: The Challenge of Complexity,* 3rd edition. Harlow: Pearson.

Stanley, N. and Manthorpe, J. (2004) Introduction: the inquiry as Janus (pp1–16), in Stanley, N. and Manthorpe, J. (eds) *The Age of the Inquiry: Learning and Blaming in Health and Social Care.* London: Routledge.

Stevenson, M., McDowell, M.E. and Taylor, B.J. (in press) Concepts for communication about risk in dementia care: a review of the literature. *Dementia: The International Journal of Social Research and Practice.*

Stevenson, M. and Taylor, B.J. (2016) Risk communication in dementia care: family perspectives. *Journal of Risk Research*, 18 (1–2): 1–20.

Stevenson, M. and Taylor, B.J. (in press) Risk communication in dementia care: Professional perspectives on consequences, likelihood, words and numbers. *British Journal of Social Work.*

Stoner, J. (1968) Risky and cautious shifts in group decision: the influence of widely-held values. *Journal of Experimental Social Psychology*, 4: 442–59.

Straus, M.A. (2009) Violence between parents reported by male and female university students: prevalence, severity, chronicity and mutuality. *Journal of Aggression, Conflict and Peace Research*, 1 (1): 4–12.

Taylor, B.J. (1999) Developing partnership between professions in implementing new children's legislation in Northern Ireland. *Journal of Inter-Professional Care*, 13 (3): 249–59.

Taylor, B.J. (2003) Literature searching (pp171–6), in Miller, R. and Brewer, J. (eds) *The A to Z of Social Research.* London: Sage.

Taylor, B.J. (2006a) Factorial surveys: Using vignettes to study professional judgement. *British Journal of Social Work*, 36 (7): 1187–207.

Taylor, B.J. (2006b) Risk management paradigms in health and social services for professional decision making on the long-term care of older people. *British Journal of Social Work*, 36 (8): 1411–29.

Taylor B.J. (ed) (2011) *Working with Aggression and Resistance in Social Work.* London: Sage.

Taylor, B.J. (2012a) Intervention research (Chapter 27, pp424–39), in Gray, M., Midgley, J. and Webb, S. (eds) *Social Work Handbook.* New York: Sage.

Taylor, B.J. (2012b) Developing an integrated assessment tool for the health and social care of older people. *British Journal of Social Work*, 42 (7): 1293–1314.

Taylor, B.J. (2012c) Models for professional judgement in social work. *European Journal of Social Work*, 15 (4): 546–62.

Taylor B.J. (in press) Heuristics in professional judgement: a psycho-social rationality model. *British Journal of Social Work.*

Taylor, B.J. and Campbell, B. (2011) Quality, risk and governance: social workers' perspectives. *International Journal of Leadership in Public Services*, 7 (4): 256–72.

Taylor, B.J., Dempster, M. and Donnelly, M. (2003) Hidden gems: systematically searching electronic databases for research publications for social work and social care. *British Journal of Social Work*, 33 (4): 423–39.

Taylor, B.J., Dempster, M. and Donnelly, M. (2007) Grading gems: appraising the quality of research for social work and social care. *British Journal of Social Work*, 37 (2): 335–54.

Taylor, B.J. and Devine, T. (1993; latest reprint 2005) *Assessing Needs and Planning Care in Social Work.* Aldershot: Ashgate.

Taylor, B.J. and Donnelly, M. (2006a) Risks to home care workers: professional perspectives. *Health, Risk & Society*, 8 (3): 239–56.

Taylor, B.J. and Donnelly, M. (2006b) Professional perspectives on decision making about the long-term care of older people. *British Journal Social Work*, 36 (5): 807–26.

Taylor B.J. and Killick C.J. (2013) Threshold decisions in child protection: systematic narrative review of theoretical models used in empirical studies (conference abstract). *Medical Decision Making*, 33 (2): E145–E203.

Taylor, B.J., Killick, C. and McGlade, A. (2015) *Understanding and Using Research in Social Work.* London: Sage.

Taylor, B.J., Killick, C., O'Brien, M., Begley, E. and Carter-Anand, J. (2014) Older people's conceptualisation of elder abuse and neglect. *Journal of Elder Abuse and Neglect*, 26 (3): 223–43.

Taylor, B.J. and McKeown, C. (2013) Assessing and managing risk with people with physical disabilities: development of a safety checklist. *Health, Risk and Society*, 15 (2): 162–75.

Taylor, B.J. and Moorhead, A. (in press) Social science research approaches to risk communication about medicines, in Bahri, P. (ed) *Communicating about Risks and Safe Use of Medicines: Real Life and Applied Research.* Heidelberg: Springer.

Taylor, B.J., Mullineux, J.C. and Fleming, G. (2010) Partnership, service needs and assessing competence in post qualifying education and training. *Social Work Education: The International Journal*, 29 (5): 475–89.

Taylor, B.J., Wylie, E., Dempster, M. and Donnelly, M. (2007) Systematically retrieving research: a case study evaluating seven databases. *Research on Social Work Practice*, 17 (6): 697–706.

Taylor, B.J. and Zeller, R.A. (2007) Getting robust and valid data on decision policies: the factorial survey. *Irish Journal of Psychology*, 28 (1–2): 27–42.

Thom, B., Sales, R. and Pearce, J. (eds) (2007) *Growing Up with Risk.* Bristol: Policy Press.

Thompson, C. (2002) Human error, bias, decision making and judgement in nursing: the need for a systematic approach (pp21–46), in Thompson, C. and Dowding, D. (eds) *Clinical Decision Making and Judgement in Nursing.* Edinburgh: Churchill Livingstone.

Thornton, D. (2007) Risk Matrix 2000 (Revised): Assessment and Management of Sex Offenders, *Probation Circular PC17/2007*, 1 July.

Tooth, G. (2009) Decision-making (pp66–83), in Mantell, A. (ed) *Social Work Skills with Adults.* Exeter: Learning Matters.

TOPSS (2005) *National Occupational Standards for Social Work in England.* London: Training Organisation for Personal Social Services.

Toulmin, S.E. (1958) *The Uses of Argument.* Cambridge: Cambridge University Press.

Turnell, A. and Edwards, S. (1999) *Signs of Safety: A Safety and Solution-Oriented Approach to Child Protection Casework.* New York: WW Norton.

Turney, D., Platt, D. and Selwyn, J. (2011) *Improving Child and Family Assessments: Turning Research into Practice.* London: Jessica Kingsley.

Turnpenny, A. and Beadle-Brown, J. (2015) Use of quality information in decision-making about health and social care services: a systematic review. *Health & Social Care in the Community*, 23: 349–61.

Tweedie, N. (2008) Why did Khyra Ishaq's neighbours not come to her aid? *Daily Telegraph*, 24 May. **www.telegraph. co.uk/news/uknews/2017378/Khyra-Ishaq-Why-did-her-neighbours-not-come-to-her-aid.html**

Urgent Care Pathway Working Group, Department of Health (2007) *Urgent Care Pathways for Older People with Complex Needs (Guidance)*. Gateway reference: 7817. London: Department of Health.

Vale of Glamorgan Council (2009) *Report of the Case Management Enquiry*. Glamorgan: Vale of Glamorgan Council. **www.scie-socialcareonline.org.uk/report-of-the-case-management-enquiry/r/a11G00000017zMOIAY**

Volavka, J. and Swanson, J. (2010) Violent behavior in mental illness: the role of substance abuse. *Journal of the American Medical Association*, 304 (5): 563–4.

von Kleist, H. (1962 ed.) *Amphytryon: A Comedy, translated by Marion Sonnenfeld*. New York: Frederick Ungar.

Wallander, L. and Molander, A. (2014) Disentangling professional discretion: a conceptual and methodological approach. *Professions and Professionalism*, 4 (3): 1–19.

Walter, I., Nutley, S., Percy-Smith, J., McNeish, D. and Frost, S. (2004) *Improving the Use of Research in Social Care Practice (Knowledge Review 7)*. London: Social Care Institute for Excellence.

Walters, H. (2008) *Gillick Competency or Fraser Guidelines: An Overview*. London: National Society for the Prevention of Cruelty to Children, Library and Information Service.

Weld, N. (2008) The three houses tool: building safety and positive change, in Calder, M. (ed) *Contemporary Risk Assessment in Safeguarding Children*. Lyme Regis: Russell House Publishing.

White, C. (2008) *Northern Ireland Social Work Law*. West Sussex: Tottel Publishing.

White, R., Broadbent, G. and Brown, K. (2009) *Law and the Social Work Practitioner*, 2nd edition. London: Sage.

Wimber, J. (2009) *Everyone Gets to Play*. Boise, ID: Ampelon.

Wood, J., Ashman, M., Davies, C., Lloyd, H. and Lockett, K. (1966) *Report of the Independent Inquiry into the Care of Anthony Smith*. Derbyshire: Southern Derbyshire Health Authority and Derbyshire County Council.

Wood, J.M. (1996) Weighing evidence in sexual abuse evaluations: an introduction to Bayes Theorem. *Child Maltreatment*, 1 (1): 25–36.

World Health Organisation (2002) *Active Aging: A Policy Framework*. Noncommunicable Disease and Mental Health Cluster, Noncommunicable Disease Prevention and Health Promotion Department, Aging and Life Course. Geneva: World Health Organisation (Noncommunicable Disease Prevention and Health Promotion Department, Aging and Life Course).

Wynne-Harley, D. (1991) *Living Dangerously: Risk-Taking, Safety and Older People*. London: Centre for Policy on Ageing.

Young, W.P. (2008) *The Shack*. London: Hodder & Stoughton.

Index

Note: Page numbers in **bold** refer to the Glossary.

A and others v East Sussex County Council and another [2003] 143
abuse 35
accountability to society 195–6, 215
ACPO (Association of Chief Police Officers) 199
active decision support 88
actuarial approaches 114, 115–18, 120–1, 215–16
actuarial assessment 45, **226**
Agathanos-Georgopolou, H. 119
analytic decision making 85, 92, 180, 215, 216
Anger Scale and Provocation Inventory 81
Argyris, C. 210
assess, plan, implement, evaluate 16–17, 19
Assessed and Supported Year in Employment 4
Assessed Year in Employment (NI) 4
assessing risk 73–4, 74f, 86, 221–2, **226**
assessment 17, 37, 70, 72, **226**
  collaborative assessment 38–9
  co-ordinating and communicating about care 79–80
  decision support systems 87–9
  engaging client, family and other professionals 11–12, 17–18, 39–43, 72–4
  information requirements for decision making 89, 180–1
  integrated assessment 80, 80f, **228**
  multi-professional assessment 161–3
  of needs, risk and strengths 54, 73–4, 74f
  processes and information gathering 71–2
  proportionate assessment 80
  purposes and theories 77–9, 79f
  reassessment 189–90
  safeguarding and thresholds 86–7
  social work role 14–15, 16
  values and risk-taking decisions 149–51
assessment analysis 81–5
  analytic hierarchy process 85, 216
  assessment tools 82–4, 85
  child protection 83
  classification trees 84–5
  heuristic models of judgement 85
  linear regression 84
  multi-attribute decision modelling 85
  perpendicular scales 85

assessment and care planning cycle 17f
assessment tools 71–2, 75–7, 215, **226**
  computerised systems 89
  principles 78, 78t, 79
  quality of 79–80, 87
  risk assessment tools 86
  specialist tools 77, 80–1, 83, 86
  supporting analysis 82–4, 85
Associated Provincial Picture Houses v Wednesbury Corporation [1948] 51
Association of Chief Police Officers (ACPO) 199
Austin, C.D. 166
autonomy 7

background hazards *see* vulnerabilities
Bain, A. 53, 55, 56, 62, 145, 170, 180, 191
balancing benefits and harms (care planning) 18, 19f, 22, 45, 128, 147–8, 155, 216
  see also risk-taking decisions
Ball, D. 145
Banks, S. 1
Barber, P. 61, 63
Barlow, J. *et al.* 122
Baron, J. 152
Barrett v Enfield London Borough Council [2001] 56
Bayes' Theorem 190
Beaumont, B. 126
Beckett, C. 123, 124
Benbenishty, R. *et al.* 102–3
beneficence 152
benefit, defined 13
  see also balancing benefits and harms
Bennett, P. 170
Bennett, R. 188
bias 22
  avoiding potential bias 99, 101
  cognitive biases 97, 98–9t
  in group decision making 165
  and heuristics 98–9t, 104, 215
  in professional judgement 37, 97–9
  reluctance to make decisions 30
Bingham, T. 52, 56
blame and risk-taking 112–13, 144–5
blame culture 197, 201, 202, 205

Boeije, H.R. *et al.* 149
Bolam test (*Bolam v Friern Hospital Management Committee* [1957]) 57, 64
Bolitho v City & Hackney Health Authority [1998] 57, 64, 152
bounded rationality 22, 100
Brearley, P. 112
British Association of Social Workers 68
Brown, R. *et al.* 48, 61, 63
Browne, K. 119
Brunswick, E. 93, 214
Bunyan, N. 113
Byrne, R. 34

Calman, K. 170
Campbell, A. *et al.* 108
capacity to consent 61–2, 70, 215
   see also decisional capacity
care: duty of care 53, 55–6
care management 16
care pathways 88
   integrated care pathways 188
   managing risk 188–9
care planning 71
   assessment and care planning cycle 17*f*
   balancing benefits and harms 18, 19*f*, 22, 45, 128, 147–8, 155, 216
   decisions 18
   to manage risk 181–3, 186–7
   monitoring 185–7
   objectives 183–4
care plans **226**
Carrère, S. 104
Carroll, S.J. 30–1
Carson, D. 20, 53, 55, 56, 62, 145, 170, 180, 191, 192, 200, 200*f*
case law 49, 51, 55
case plans *see* care plans
CC v KK and another [2012] 52
Chang, L. 194
chaos theory 10
child abuse 54, 59
   court decisions 173
   inquiries 20, 52, 65, 197, 201
   risk factors 115, 116–17*t*, 119, 120*t*
child care 2
child care aftercare 2
child homicide 198, 201
   risk factors 117–18
child protection 15
   assessment tools 79, 81, 83, 86
   case conferences 167
   court decisions 173
   decision making 171
   information search 102–3
   judgements 95
   monitoring by a school 188
   reassessment 189
   risk factors 125
   Signs of Safety approach 75

children
   admittance to care 43
   decisional capacity 63–4
   development and risk-taking 145–6, 147*t*
   parents' perceptions of risks 150
children with disability 3
Chronically Sick and Disabled Persons Act (1970) 93, 190
civil law 49
client decision making
   confidentiality, values and resilience 28–30
   emotion in assessment and decisions 30–4
   envisioning the future 43–5, 44*t*
   needs and decisions in crisis 26–8
   ownership of the decision 45–6
   supported decision tool 41, 223–4
   supporting clients 17–18, 39–43
client well-being, monitoring 185–7
clients
   defined 8
   engagement in assessment/decision processes 11–12, 17–18, 39–43, 72–4
   engagement in decision outcomes 42–3
   hidden clients 205
   relationships and risk in engaging with 35–7
   risk-taking 35
clinical factors in prediction 45, 113–14, 120–1, 215–16, **226**
clinical social work **226**
Cochrane Collaboration 105–6
Coelho, P. 178
Coles v Reading and District Hospital Management Committee and Another [1963] 64, 65
collaborative assessment 38–9
collaborative decision making 37–8, 159–61, 216
   communicating information 167–71
   contested decision making 171–5
   in groups 163–7
   integrated care pathways (ICP) 188
   inter-agency protocols 205–6
   key tasks 160
   levels of partnership working 171
   liability for decisions 66, 160–1
   multi-professional assessment 161–3
College of Social Work 4
Common Assessment Framework 79
common law 49
communicating information for decisions 79–80
   communicating risk: likelihoods 169–71
   conceptualising and communicating risk 168–9
   co-ordinating and communicating about care 79–80
   language 167–8
   in organisations 209
competence 4, 173
   of individual professionals 80, 160, 172, 173
   of professions 66, 160–1
   see also decisional capacity; Gillick competence

complexity theory 10
concerns 130
confidentiality 28
    and duty to communicate risk 65–6
conflict in decision making 67–8, 195–6
contested decision making 171, 216
    court decisions 172–4
    rational, ethical arguments 174–5
contingency planning 184
continuing professional development 6–7
Cooksey, R.W. 93
Council of Civil Service Unions v Minister for the Civil Service [1985] 50
court decisions 172–4
Creighton, S.J. 198
criminal law 49, 53

D v Bury Metropolitan Borough Council [2006] 52
Dalgleish, L.J. 124
dangerousness 13, **226**
Darragh, E. 105
Davidson, G. *et al.* 39
decision frames 34, **226**
decision making 11*f*, 21, **226**
    analytic decision making 85, 92, 180, 215, 216
    in assessment and care planning cycle 16, 17*f*
    engaging clients, families and stakeholders 11–13
    ethical decision-making process 18, 174–5, 175–6*t*
    evaluating decision processes 200–2
    in groups and teams 66, 160–1, 163–4
    incremental decision making 179, 180, 189
    intuitive judgements 92, 100, 109, 113, 180, 190, 216
    key elements 12
    law and reasonable decision making 50–3
    naturalistic decision making 43, 214
    place of in social work 1–3
    rational decision making 15, 50–1, 52
    recording decisions 191–2
    social work role 14–15, 16
    sunk costs 189
    and time 67, 179–81, 216
decision management 194, **227**
    accountability to society 195–6, 215
    decision policies and scarce resources 204–5
    evaluating decision processes 200–2
    inter-agency protocols 205–6
    organisation culture and defensive practice 197–9, 205
    policies and systems 202–4
    principles 199–200
    tragedies and hindsight 196–7
decision outcomes **227**
decision policies 127, 204–5, **227**
decision support systems 87–9

decision trees 133*f*, 134, 155–7, 156*f*, 188, **227**
    dynamic decision trees 156
    fast and frugal trees 22, 134, **227**
    static decision trees 156
decisional capacity 62–3
    of children 63–4
    consenting to take risks 61–2, 70
    and learning disability 37
    and mental health 46, 61
decisions
    defined 21
    everyday decisions 9–10
    holding decisions 27, 86
    important decisions 11–12
    social work decisions 17–18, 19*f*
    see also client decision making
Decisions, Assessment, Risk and Evidence in Social Work symposium 1
defensive practice 197–9
dementia
    conceptualisations of risk 170–1
    interventions 106
    risk-taking decisions 132, 149, 155
    vulnerability and trigger factors 132
Department of Health 36, 41, 60, 62, 127, 143, 144, 146–7, 171, 204, 205, 206, 223–4
descriptive approaches to studying human judgement 21, 22, 214, **227**
desistance 130
Devine, T. 16, 54, 72, 74, 151
dilemmas 67
Dimond, B. 62
direct care risks **227**
discretion 93–4
Donnelly, M. 27–8, 116
Donoghue v Stevenson [1932] 55, 59
'double-loop' learning 210
Doueck, H.J. 83
Dowding, D. 157
Dowie, J. 21, 157
Drew, E.C. 124
Duncan, S. 197
duties 49
duty of care 53, 55–6
duty to communicate risk 64–6
    and confidentiality 65–6
Dyckman, K.M. 30–1
dynamic risk factors 114, 115, 119
    acute dynamic factors 115
    stable dynamic response mechanisms 115

ECHR *see* European Convention on Human Rights (1950)
Eddy, D.M. 127
Egan, G. 39
Egan, M. *et al.* 89
Eisai Limited v the National Institute for Health and Clinical Excellence (NICE) [2007] 51
elder abuse 42, 62–3

emotion in assessment and decisions 30–4
empowerment 35, 127, 209
English, D. 79
English, D.J. 83
envisioning the future 18, 19f, 43–5, 44t
ethical decision-making 18, 174–5, 175–6t
European Convention on Human Rights (1950) (ECHR) 53, 54–5
European Social Work Research Association 1
evidence-based practice 57, 210
evidence, defined 21
expected utility see subjective expected utility theory
expert systems 88, 89
expert witnesses 84, 172–3

F v Suffolk County Council [1981] 173
family and child care 2
Family Division 2
family engagement in assessment/decision processes 11–12
Farmer, E. 167
fast and frugal decision trees 22, 134, **227**
fast and frugal heuristics **227**
Fazel, S. et al. 115
Foster, C. 57
framework for risk, assessment and decisions 23, 24f, **227**
framing the decision 34, 95–6
framing the risks 95
Francis, B. 194
Fraser Guideines 63
Freel, K.A. 150
fuzzy logic 130, 214, **227**

'gambling' 153
game theory 38
Gigerenzer, G. et al. 14, 100, 138, 181
Gillick competence 63–4
Gillick v West Norfolk and Wisbech Area Health Authority [1985] 63–4
Gladwell, M. 100
Goldstein, D.G. 181
Gottman, J. 104
governance 206
Graded Care Profile (GCP) 81
Green, E. et al. 35
Grice, E. 64
gross negligence 53
groups and teams
    decision making 163–4
    decision processes 164–7
    liability for decisions 66, 160–1
    risk-averse group decisions 167
groupthink 165
Grove, W. 121
guidelines 128
Gunnell, D. 118

Hardman, D. 152
harm 35
    defined 13
    forseeability of 59–60
    protective factors 130
    see also balancing benefits and harms; health and safety at work; predicting harm; risk-taking decisions
hazards 13, 131, 139–41, **228**
health and safety at work 139, 139t
    justifying risks 144–5, 145f
    minimising situational hazards 139–41
    personal safety 141–2
    reasonably practicable steps 142–3
    rights and risk-taking 143
Health and Safety at Work Act (1974) 15–16, 139
Health and Safety at Work (NI) Order (1978) 15–16, 139
Health and Safety Executive (2009) 139–40, 139t, 142, 143, 146, 147t
health and safety risks **228**
healthy scepticism 67
helping process 16–17, 17f, 19
Henniker, J. 85
heuristic models 22, 23, 85, 133–4, 135f, 181, 214
heuristics 99, 133, **228**
    and biases 98–9t, 104, 215
    fast and frugal heuristics **227**
    in professional judgement 99–101
Heyman, A. et al. 169
hindsight
    bias 196
    error 191–2, **228**
    and tragedies 196–7
Hirokawa, R.Y. et al. 165
historical determinants see vulnerabilities
HL v UK [2004] 54
holding decisions/judgements 27, 86
Hollows, A. 95, 174–5, 180
hospital social work 3
Howarth, J. 86
Høybye-Mortensen, M. 84
Hughes, G.W. 31
Hughes, S. 30, 97
Human Rights Act (1998) (HRA) 2, 49, 51, 53–5, 215
Hunter v Hanley [1955] 57

ICP (integrated care pathways) 188
image theory 43–5, 44t, **228**
incremental decision making 179, 180, 189
indirect care risks **228**
information search 102–3
inquiries
    child abuse 20, 52, 65, 197, 201
    inquiry reports 162–3, 196–7
integrated assessment system 80, 80f, **228**
integrated care pathways (ICP) 188
inter-agency protocols 205–6

interactionist model of social work 71
Interim Care Orders 52
International Professional Development
    Programme 4
internet 28
interpreters 36
interventions 71
    knowledge of application 107–8
    knowledge of effectiveness 104–7
intuitive judgements 92, 100, 109, 113, 180,
    190, 216

Janis, I.L. 30, 33, 36, 165
Jones, D. 172
Jones, D.P.H. 128
Jones, N.J. *et al.* 115
judgement 21, **228**
    in assessment and care planning cycle 16, 17*f*
    descriptive approaches 21, 22, 214, **227**
    everyday judgements 9–10
    holding judgements 27, 86
    normative approaches 21, 22, 214, **229**
    prescriptive approaches 21, 22, 214, **229**
    see also professional judgement

Kagle, J.D. 66
Kane, R.A. *et al.* 29
Kant, I. 213
Karpman, S.B. 38
Killick, C. 94
Klein, G. 92, 100
knowledge
    anchors of knowledge 99
    of application of interventions 107–8
    of effectiveness of interventions 104–7
    professional knowledge 2, 21, 101–4, 108–9
    of risk 96–7
    and skills for professional practice 3–5
Kopels, S. 66
Koprowska, J. 73
Kühlberger, A. 34

Laming, H. 162, 167
Landau, R. 174
lasting power of attorney 62
Lawhead, S. 70
learning disability 3
    assessment tools 81
    balancing benefits and harms 57–8, 146,
        153–4
    contingency planning 184
    decisional capacity 37
learning organisations 209–10, 210*t*, 217
legal aspects 7, 48
    basis of law 49
    case law 49, 51, 55
    civil law 49
    common law 49
    conflict, confidence and being sued 67–8
    consenting to take risks 61–2

legal aspects *cont.*
    court decisions 172–4
    criminal law 49, 53
    decisional capacity 62–4
    decisions under time pressure 67
    duty to communicate risk 64–6
    gross negligence in criminal law 53
    health and safety 15–16, 139
    health and safety at work 139*t*
    Human Rights Act 2, 49, 51, 53–5, 215
    legislation 49
    liability for decisions in teams and groups 66,
        160–1
    liability for risk-taking decisions 60–1, 67–8
    negligence 52–3, 55–60
    power of attorney 62
    precedents 49
    and reasonable decision making 50–3
    regulation of professionals 49–50
    vicarious liability 55
legal persons 66
legality of decisions 50
legislation 49
legitimate aim 54
lens of risk 93, 169, 214
liability
    for decisions in teams and groups 66, 160–1
    for risk-taking decisions 60–1, 67–8
    vicarious liability 55
likelihood of benefits and harms
    risk communication 169–71
    risk-taking decisions 154–5
    see also probability
Lockett, G. 134

M (Minor) v Newham London Borough Council 56
McCormack, B.G. *et al.* 80
Macdonald, G. 190
Macdonald, G.M. 196
Macdonald, K.I. 196
McFadden, P. *et al.* 97
McKeown, C. 31–2
McKillop, C. 81
Maguire, M. 64
managing decision making *see* decision
    management
managing risk **228–9**
    see also risk management
Mann, L. 30, 33, 36
Manthorpe, J. 196
Marsh, J. 55
Marsh, P. *et al.* 102
Maslow, A. 26
Matthews, I. 31
May, R. xi
Meehl, P. 121
Mental Capacity Act (2005) 46, 54, 61, 62, 63
mental health 3
    assessment analysis 84, 162
    balancing benefits and harm 147–8

mental health *cont.*
  decisional capacity 46, 61
  risk factors for violence 115, 197
Merrett Report (1993) 74
mitigating factors 130, 131–2
Monahan, J. *et al.* 66, 84, 114, 115
monitoring decision implementation 185–7, **229**
  monitoring by a school 188
  telephone monitoring 187
Montgomery (Appellant) v Lanarkshire Health
    Board (Respondent) (Scotland) [2015] 64
Morrison, T. 85
multi-attribute decision modelling 85
multi-professional assessment 161–3
Munby, Sir James 2, 84, 171
Munro, E. 95, 112, 113, 199, 203

narrative approach 196
National Audit Office 138
National Occupational Standards for Social Work 5
National Survey of Child and Adolescent
    Wellbeing (NSCAW) 125
naturalistic decision making 43, 214
Naudé, P. 134
needs 26–7, 54, 73–5
negligence 55
  causation 58
  defined 55
  duty of care 53, 55–6
  foreseeability of losses 59 60
  gross negligence in criminal law 53
  recognised losses 58–9
  standards of care 56–8
Nelson-Jones, R. 39
non-maleficence 152
Norman, A.J. 200
normative approaches to studying human
    judgement 21, 22, 214, **229**
Northern Ireland
  Assessed Year in Employment (NI) 4
  Health and Safety at Work (NI) Order (1978)
    15–16, 139
  Single Assessment Tool for the Health and
    Social Care of Older People 80*f*
Nouwen, H. 26
Novaco, R.W. 81
NSCAW (National Survey of Child and
    Adolescent Wellbeing) 125

older people 3
  assessment tool 80*f*
  balancing benefits and harms 147–8, 155
  elder abuse 42, 62–3
  long-term care 27–8
  risk factors for admission to care 116, 163
  telephone monitoring 187
organisational context 19–21, 20*f*, 194, 216–17
  communicating risk and decisions 209
  culture and defensive practice 197–9, 205
  governance 206

organisational context *cont.*
  learning organisations 209–10, 210*t*, 217
  see also decision management
organisational risks **229**
Osman v UK (23452/94) [1998] 53
Osmo, R. 174
O'Sullivan, T. 197
Owen, M. 167

Paling, J. 169
Partington v London Borough of Wandsworth
    [1990] 59–60
passive decision support 88
Pecora, P. 79
Perry, J. 128, 130, 196
person-centred approaches 37
personal safety 141–2
Peter, L. 48, 213
physical disability 3
  enabling discussion of risk issues 31–2
Pippin and Wife v Sheppard [1822] 55
place of work 139
planning risk *see* taking risk
post-traumatic stress disorder (PTSD) 58–9
power of attorney 62
powers 49
precedents 49
predicting harm 96–7, 112–13
  achievements, challenges, prospects 125–6
  actuarial approaches 114, 115–18, 120–1,
    215–16
  base rates 124–5
  clinical approach 45, 113–14, 120–1, 215–16
  criterion-based judgements 18, 126–8, 216
  from experience 113–15
  false positives and false negatives 122–4, 124*t*
  mitigating factors 130, 131–2
  practice issues 128–30, 214–15
  risk and blame 112–13
  risk factors 113–15, 119–20
  statistical prediction in practice 120–2
predisposing factors *see* vulnerabilities
Prentice [1993] 53
prescriptive approaches to studying human
    judgement 21, 22, 214, **229**
Pritchard, C. *et al.* 117–18
probability 10, 13, 14, **229**
problem solving 38–9, **229**
  and collaborative assessment 38–9
procedural propriety 51
Professional Capabilities Framework 4–5, 225*f*
professional indemnity insurance 68
professional judgement 2, 21, **229**
  bias 37, 97–9
  and client perspectives 93
  context, role and framing judgements 94–6
  criterion-based judgements 18, 126–8, 216
  and decision policies 126–9
  discretion 93–4
  expectations of 50

professional judgement *cont.*
  heuristics 99–101
  initial judgements 104
  psycho-social rationality model 22–3, 23*f*
  and reflective learning 94
  and reflective practice 94, 108–9
  structured professional judgement 23, **231**
  using knowledge of application of
    interventions 107–8
  using knowledge of effectiveness of
    interventions 104–7
  using knowledge of risk 96–7
  using professional knowledge 101–4
professional knowledge 2
  defined 21
  to inform judgements 101–4
  and reflective practice 108–9
professional supervision, support and training
  7, 206–8
professionals, regulation of 49–50
proportionality 51, 80
protective factors 130, 142–3, **229**
psycho-social interventions 71
psycho-social rationality 22–3, 23*f*, 131, 214,
  229–30
PTSD (post-traumatic stress disorder) 58–9

*R (on the application of KM) (by his mother
  and litigation friend JM) v Cambridgeshire
  County Council* [2012] 50, 93, 190
*R v HM Coroner for Reading ex parte West
  Berkshire Housing Consortium Ltd* [1995] 58
R (Daly) v Home Secretary [2001] 51
*R (on the application of Axon) v Secretary
  of State for Health (Family Planning
  Association intervening)* [2006] 63
randomised controlled studies 105
rational decision making 15, 50–1, 52
rational, ethical arguments 174–6
Re B-S (Children) [2013] 172, 173–4
Re: C (adult: refusal of medical treatment)
  [1994] 63
Re JC: D v JC [2012] 54, 61
Re M (Care Proceedings: Judicial Review) [2003]
  171, 173
Re N (Child Abuse: Evidence) [1996] 173
Reason (2000) 14
reassessment 189–90
recognition primed decision model 92, 100, 214
recording decisions 191–2
Reder, P. 197
Reeves, A. *et al.* 131
reflection-in-action 108
reflection-on-action 108
reflective learning 94
reflective practice 209, 215, 219–20
  and continuing professional development 6–7
  and learning from experience 91–3
  and professional judgement 94, 108–9
  and professional knowledge 108–9

Regina Respondent v Adomako Appellant
  [1994] 53
registration 49–50
regulations 128
Reimer, T. 168
Reinhard, M.-A. *et al.* 31
Reith, M. 162
relationships and risk in engaging with clients
  35–7
research and development 105–7, 217–18
residential child care 2
resilience 30, 130
resource allocation 204–5
review 209, **230**
Righthand, S. *et al.* 125
rights 2, 49, 51, 53–5, 143
risk 13–14, 27, 140, **230**
  blame and predicting harm 112–13
  conceptualising risk 149–51, 168–9, 170–1
  direct care risks **227**
  everyday risk 9–10
  framing the risks 95
  health and safety at work 139, 139*t*
  health and safety risks **228**
  health and social well-being 138
  indirect care risks **228**
  organisational risks **229**
  paradigms for conceptualising risk 97
  predicting from experience 113–15
  and professional judgement 96–7
  social construction of 169, **230–1**
  social work role 14–15, 16
  and uncertainty 14, 130, 138, **231**
risk assessment *see* assessing risk
risk-benefit communication 14, **230**
risk clusters 22, 131, 134, **230**
risk communication 14, 64–6, 168–9, **230**
  likelihoods 169–71
risk factors 13, 14, 114, 119–20, **230**
  categories 119
  for child abuse 115, 116–17*t*, 119, 120*t*
  child homicide 117–18
  dynamic risk factors 114, 115, 119
  mitigating factors 130, 131–2
  and predicting from experience 113–15
  static risk factors 114–15, 119
  suicide 118, 118*t*, 119
risk management 13, 19, 20, 178, **230**
  care decision pathways 188–9
  care plan objectives 183–4
  care planning 181–3, 186–7
  client ownership of the decision 45–6
  contingency planning 184
  evaluating decision processes 200–2
  inter-agency protocols 205–6
  managing risk **228–9**
  monitoring 186–7
  policies and systems 202–4
  principles 199–200, 200*f*
  risk-steps 187–8

risk management *cont.*
  strengths perspective 187
  time to make decisions 67, 179–81, 216
risk planning (taking risk) **231**
risk-steps 187–8
risk-taking 13, 35, 216
  and child development 145–6, 147*t*
  fear factor 149
  justifying taking risks 144–5, 145*f*
  and rights 143
  voluntary risk-taking 149
risk-taking decisions 137–8
  in assessment 149–51
  balancing benefits and harms 147–9, 152–4
  balancing values of benefits and harms
    151–2
  blame 112–13, 114–15
  consent 61–2, 70
  decision trees 155–7
  engaging clients 40
  foreseeability of harm 59–60
  liability for 60–1
  likelihoods of benefits and harms 154–5
  potential benefits 146, 147–9
Robertson, C. 91
Russell, T. 168

S v Gloucestershire County Council [2002] 52
safeguarding decisions 18, 111–12
  and confidentiality 66
  fairness and openness 171
  practice issues 128–30, 214–15
  risk assessment tools 86–7
  risk, blame and predicting harm 112–13
  see also predicting harm
satisficing models of decision making 22, 181,
    182*f*, 214, **230**
Schön, D.A. 108, 209
school monitoring for child protection 188
SCIE (Social Care Institute for Excellence) 102
Seidl, F.W. 166
Sellnow, T.L. 27
Senge, P. 165
sensory impairment 3
service users *see* clients
services, eligibility for 18
sexual abuse by young people: assessment
    tool 85
Seymour, C. 172, 173, 192
Seymour, R. 172
Shakespeare, W. 159
Sheldon, B. 128, 130, 196
Sheppard, D. 197
Shlonsky, A. 125
Shulman, L. 71, 152
*Sidaway v Governors of Bethlem Royal Hospital
    and the Maudsley Hospital* [1985] 64
Sidebotham, P. *et al.* 131, 202–3
signal detection theory 124
Signs of Safety approach 75

Simmonds, J. 9
Simon, H. 100
situational determinants *see* trigger factors
situational hazards *see* trigger factors
SMART objectives 184
Social Care Institute for Excellence (SCIE) 102
social construction of risk 169, **230–1**
social ill-health/social dis-ease 115
social media 28
Social Services Inspectorate (1993) 87
social work
  clinical social work **226**
  decisions 17–18, 19*f*
  hospital social work 3
  interactionist model 71
  in organisational context 19–21
  origins of 101
  place of decision making in 1–3
  as a profession 56
  role 14–15, 16, 20*f*
Soulsby, J. 55
Specific Affect Coding System 104
spirituality in personal decision making 31
Srivastava, O.P. *et al.* 81
standards of care 56–7, 128
  and reasonable risk-taking 57–8
Stanley, N. 196
Stevenson, M. *et al.* 169, 170–1
Stoner, J. 166
strengths *see* mitigating factors
structure of this book 5–6, 23, 24*f*
structured professional judgement 23, **231**
  see also psycho-social rationality
subjective expected utility theory 22, 34, 152,
    214, **231**
suicide risk factors 118, 118*t*, 119
sunk cost bias **231**
sunk costs 189
supervision 7, 206–8
Swanson, J. 115

taking risk **231**
  see also risk-taking
Tarasoff v Regents of the University of California
    [1976] 66
Taylor, B.J. *et al.* 6, 11, 16, 27–8, 31–2, 41, 43,
    52, 54, 72, 73, 74, 94, 96, 97, 105, 107–8,
    116, 151, 169, 170–1, 194, 213
teams *see* groups and teams
telephone monitoring 187
terminology 8, 71, 130, **226–31**
theoretical sources and models 213–14
Thompson, C. 157
Thornton, D. 126
threshold judgement 86–7, 111, 127–8, **231**
  and creativity for safeguarding 129
  criterion-based judgements 111, 216
time to make decisions 179–80, 216
  under time pressure 67, 180–1
Tissier, G. 198

Toulmin, S. 174
tragedies 67, 196–7
trigger factors 131–3, **231**
Tweedie, N. 188

uncertainty 14, 130, 138, **231**

values 2, 13, 28–30
    and risk-taking decisions in assessment 149–51
vicarious liability 55
Volavka, J. 115
Von Kleist, H. 111
vulnerabilities 131–3, **231**
vulnerable adults 14–15

W and Others v Essex County Council and
    Another [2002] 65
W v Edgell [1990] 66

Walker v Northumberland County Council
    [1995] 208
Walters, H. 64
wants 27
whistle-blowing schemes 209
White, C. 55
White, R. et al. 51
Wilsher v Essex Area Health Authority [1986] 66
Wimber, J. 214
Wood, J. et al. 162
Wood, J.M. 170
Wynne-Harley, D. 149

X v Bedfordshire County Council [1994] 56

Young, W.P. 137

Z v UK [2002] 53